DATE DUE

DEMCO 38-296

Designing Public Access Systems

To Mark

Designing Public Access Systems

Jennifer Rowley
and
Frances Slack

Gower

…blication may be reproduced, stored in a
…y form or by any means, electronic, mechanical,
…e without the permission of the publisher.

Aldershot
Hampshire GU11 3HR
England

Gower
Old Post Road
Brookfield
Vermont 05036
USA

Jennifer Rowley and Frances Slack have asserted their right under the Copyright,
Designs and Patents Act 1988 to be identified as the authors of this work.

British Library Cataloguing in Publication Data

Slack, Frances
    Designing public access systems
    1. Online information services   2. User interfaces (Computer
    systems) – Design and construction
    I. Title   II. Rowley, J. E. (Jennifer E.), 1950–
    025´.04

ISBN 0 566 08070 2

Library of Congress Cataloging-in-Publication Data

Slack, Frances, 1954–
    Public access interfaces to database resources / Frances Slack and
    Jennifer Rowley.
        p.   cm.
    Includes bibliographical references and index.
    ISBN 0-566-08070-2
    1. User interfaces (Computer systems)   2. Human–computer
    interaction.   3. Database management.   I. Rowley, J.E.   II. Title.
    Qa76.9.U83S63   1998
    005.74—dc21   98–5387
                                                                                    CIP

Typeset by Raven Typesetters, Chester and printed in Great Britain
by MPG Books Ltd, Bodmin.

Contents

List of figures

Preface

The range of environments in which public use of database resources is becoming important is growing significantly. These include the wide variety of resources available over the Internet, from teleshopping, e-mail, multimedia and numerical, financial and text-based databases to electronic books and other value-added services. Also, the public are being invited to experiment with the ever increasing availability of access to organizations' databases in order to fulfil transactions or to gather information. Multimedia kiosks, automated teller machines (ATMs), public access catalogues in libraries and store guides are all examples of public access information systems. The quality of the interface will influence the effectiveness with which the public can gather information and conduct transactions. Thus interface design in this context is particularly important. It is also particularly challenging. Interfaces in these environments need to be able to cater for a wide variety of different types of users, who have differing experience of using information systems and their component parts, such as keyboards, and who will be offered no training in the use of the system other than that which is available through the use of the system. It is therefore important that these interfaces be easy to use and self-explanatory. Similarly, although all users may be involved in simple data entry and corresponding data output, such systems need to accommodate the environment in which the transaction is performed, which, unlike office-based systems, may be in the home, or in a busy thoroughfare.

This book seeks to review the practice and principles of human–computer interaction (HCI) and apply them in the context of public access interfaces. This approach should be of interest to a wide audience, from information managers to information specialists and systems designers, and to retailers and others who use the systems to provide information or to otherwise interact with their customer. This is a novel focus. Other books on HCI have a focus that largely assumes that users are accessing information systems in an office environment within a specific organization. This perspective will clearly become ever more significant as the use of networks and multimedia databases further erodes the boundaries between organizations.

This is a textbook for those students who are studying HCI and wish to focus their study on public access information systems. Such students may be studying full- or part-time undergraduate or postgraduate courses in areas such as information and library management, information systems, computer science, business studies, retailing and marketing.

Each chapter is structured to allow students to identify the learning outcomes from a specific chapter and to reflect on their learning. To this end, each chapter will commence with a statement of learning objectives, will contain reflective questions embedded in the text and will conclude with a summary.

Chapter 1 introduces some basic definitions and ideas concerning the nature of interface design and the context of public access information systems. Chapters 2, 3, 4 and 5 deal with aspects of the components of the systems: users, tasks, the interaction environment and interaction styles. Chapters 6, 7, 8 and 9 focus on the process of design and evaluation of interfaces. Design methodologies and guidelines are introduced and, finally, approaches to evaluation are reviewed.

The wide range of existing and the potential for future applications of public access information systems means that the quality of the interaction with such systems will become almost as important as the quality of interaction that we experience in face-to-face communication; this is likely to bring this topic to the attention of a wide audience.

Jennifer Rowley and
Frances Slack

Acknowledgements

The authors are grateful to the many people and organizations who have knowingly or otherwise made a contribution to the completion of the project that has resulted in the creation of this book. We have drawn widely from the field of literature and acknowledge our debt to the many authors whose ideas have inspired our thinking about public access to information systems. In particular we are grateful to all the publishers, information industry organizations and authors who have permitted us to use extracts from their works. These extracts and figures are individually acknowledged as they appear.

On a personal note, we wish our families to know that we value their various contributions in the process of the writing of this book. Peter and Dave, Rachel, Shula and Zeta – you have not been forgotten, even if it has felt like that at times!

We would like to dedicate this book to the memory of Mark Freeman, our one-time colleague and fellow conspirator in the wonderful world of IT. We shall miss his stimulating wit and his challenging intellectual debates.

JR
FS

Chapter 1

The nature of interface design in public access systems

By the end of this chapter, you will have explored the nature of public access interfaces and have a framework for reading the remainder of the book. Specifically you will:

- be familiar with the concept of public access interfaces;
- be aware of the contexts in which such interfaces are likely to be encountered;
- appreciate the nature of human–computer interaction as a discipline;
- understand the importance of good interface design;
- be acquainted with the concept of usability;
- have explored the concepts of an interface, dialogue and interaction;
- be aware of the different types of public access systems.

Public access interfaces

The public use of database resources is an important consideration in interface design and such use is growing significantly in a range of environments. Examples of public access information systems include:

- a wide variety of resources on the Internet, from e-mail to teleshopping;
- multimedia and numerical, financial and text-based databases;
- electronic books and other value-added services;
- organizations' databases such as multimedia kiosks, automated teller machines (ATMs), public access catalogues in libraries and store guides.

The quality of the interface will influence the effectiveness with which the public can gather information and conduct transactions. Thus interface design in this context is particularly challenging. Interfaces in these environments need to cater for a wide variety of users, who have differing experience of using information systems and who will have no training in using the system other than that which is available through the interface. It is therefore important that these interfaces be easy to use and self-explanatory. In addition, since users may need to carry out simple data entry and corresponding data output, public access systems need to be designed to take into account the environment in which the transaction is performed. This, unlike office-based systems, may be in the street, a shopping centre, in the home or in a busy public location.

In reviewing the practice and principles of human–computer interaction (HCI) and applying them in the context of public access interfaces, this book takes a novel approach. Other books on HCI largely assume that users are accessing information systems in an office environment within a specific organization. Our novel perspective will become more significant as the use of networks and multimedia databases further erodes the boundaries between organizations. Indeed it could be argued that office-based systems are also public access systems, since the range of different types of users is extensive. The unique features of interface design for public access systems are that:

- the user group is somewhat undifferentiated, except possibly in terms of those market segments with which the designer wishes to communicate;
- the task is generally focused on retrieval;
- the context or environment will often be leisure-based or in the home and may or may not be conducive to effective concentration.

Interface design in all information systems is central to the effective use of the system. The designer's objective is to create an interface which provides the full spectrum of potential users with the full range of potential tasks that the user may seek to perform with the system. Human–computer interaction is concerned with how specific groups of people use computer systems to perform specific tasks in a specific context. Figure 1.1 summarizes some of the features of the four dimensions of the system that need to be considered in design. Figure 1.2 characterizes some of these features in terms of three different types of systems and illustrates the difference between specialist systems and public access systems.

Interface design in public access information systems demands special attention. Both the nature of the user profile and the nature of the task are unique.

The user profile has two aspects which contribute to making interface design more demanding:

- Users have a wide range of different educational backgrounds and levels of experience with the system. They range from domain novices and computer novices all the way to subject experts and computer

---

People – individual characteristics
user groups
frequency of usage

Work – task features
time constraints
error

Environment – general environmental factors
organization
user support

Technology – wider range
recognition of the importance of input devices other than the keyboard

---

Figure 1.1   Factors to be considered in design

	Specialist systems	Office systems	Public access systems
User characteristics	Expert, professional users, e.g. doctors, engineers	Office staff and managers	General public Wide age range and backgrounds
Environment	Factory, office, laboratory	Office, sometimes home or travel environments	Library, railway station, airport, home
Task	Decision support, control of systems	Communication-based. Document and database creation and information retrieval	Mostly retrieval or simple customer orders
Technology	Appropriate to environment, e.g. sensors, bar code readers	Graphical user interfaces (GUI) and disk operating system (DOS) based interfaces. Mouse and keyboard	Multimedia, touch screens, audio, voice, special keyboards

Figure 1.2   User, environment, task and technology

experts. The degree of knowledgeability of the computer user and the domain experience affects the design of the user interface prompts, alerts and help facilities. Developers must also consider the needs of the system manager as user.

- There is a large proportion of naive and new users who need to be able to adapt quickly to different systems. Many users are also subject novices and their system use is constrained by their inability to appreciate what the system can be expected to contain.

The task is ill-defined and there is an element of uncertainty in both

- what the user is likely to retrieve and accept as output from the process, and
- the search strategies which will prove the most effective.

These two characteristics of public access information systems demand that the interface be particularly carefully designed.

Research and practice

It is not the intention here to evaluate specific interfaces, but rather to provide a basis for the creation and evaluation of good interface design. To achieve this we present a mixture of research results and the significant literature on the evaluation of interfaces which takes a pragmatic perspective, and has been offered by its authors as 'good advice'. Another very real challenge is that with rapidly changing interfaces much of the research that informs design and evaluation was contextualized in a specific design paradigm and has only a limited contribution to make to present practice. Research on graphical user interfaces and multimedia interfaces is limited. As Preece et al. (1994) acknowledge, 'current research cannot usually deliver the prescriptions that many designers seek'.

During the period of writing this book there has been a significant, but not yet complete, shift towards graphical user interfaces (GUI). There is an embedded assumption that this shift will lead to more user-friendly interfaces. Graphical user interfaces certainly offer much more flexibility for enhancing the quality of the user interface but their flexibility also offers greater potential for misuse and confusion. It is also important to remember that screen design is only one, albeit significant, element of interface design. Other input devices such as the keyboard may be equally important, and output devices such as printers and speech and sound should not be overlooked.

Bodker (1991) entitled her book *Through the Interface: a Human Activity Approach to User Interface Design*. She identifies the phrase 'Through the interface' as the user's preferred perspective. In other words, the user views the interface not as something on which they operate, but rather something that they operate through in relation to other objects or subjects. The user interface is part of the software and hardware that supports this; that is, the user seeks to focus on the task, and would like to be able to use the computer intuitively and painlessly.

The nature of human–computer interaction

Human–computer interaction is concerned with how people use computer systems to perform particular tasks, usually in a real-life setting. It recognizes that people use particular computer systems to perform particular tasks in a specific context. A further tension is inherent in the multidisciplinary nature of interface design. The discipline draws on research traditions that have very distinct roots. Booth (1989) suggests that there are ten major disciplines that contribute to research in HCI:

- software engineering
- computational linguistics
- artificial intelligence
- cognitive science
- sociology
- ergonomics
- organizational psychology
- mathematics
- cognitive psychology
- social psychology.

These disciplines contribute differently to the different areas of interaction and interface design. Theoretically the subject has used traditions founded primarily on psychology. This could be described as the cognitive approach, which seeks first to focus on the user, and to answer questions such as: How can users be categorized or characterized? What does the user regard as a user-friendly interface? What does the user wish to do with the system?

The more practical tradition could be described as the technical approach. This approach assumes that certain features of the interface will assist users. For example, fast response times, better graphics and pull-down menus would all seem to be desirable components of good interface design. The technical approach is driven by a striving for ever better interfaces.

Benefits of good user interface design

Earlier in this chapter we described why it is seen as necessary to examine interface design. But why is interface design important? An effective user interface improves the success that the user has in using the system, and makes the system a better tool. Shneiderman (1987) identifies the following benefits of good user interface design:

- increased user acceptance of system prototypes and the eventual system

- increased frequency of use of the system
- lower error rates
- reduced training time
- increased speed of performance.

Booth (1989) identifies some of the undesirable effects of systems that users find difficult to cope with:

- Computer systems often do not provide the information that is needed or produce information in a form which is undesirable as far as the user is concerned. Alternatively, systems may provide information that is not required.
- Computer systems can seem confusing to new users.
- Computer systems sometimes do not provide all of the functions the user requires, and more often provide functions that the user does not need.
- Computer systems force users to perform tasks in undesirable ways.
- Computer systems can cause unacceptable changes in the structure and practices of organizations, creating dissatisfaction and conflict.

In general, interface design has become more important in the last ten to fifteen years, as the number and range of users has expanded. Early users of computer systems were often programmers or designers and could thus be classified as expert users. However, in recent years there has been an attempt to encourage much more general use of computers. Shackel (1990) offers the following summary:

> The users are no longer mainly computer professionals, but are mostly discretionary users. As a result, the designers are no longer typical of or equivalent to users; but the designers may not realise just how unique and therefore unrepresentative they are.

HCI has, then, over recent years developed a range of tools, techniques, design practices and methodologies that will inform design and development teams of how users behave at an interface, and what they require from a system.

Interface design is concerned with the study and theory of the interaction between humans and computers. Without appropriate attention to interface design, systems that are functionally excellent may be effectively unusable. HCI examines how current input and output technologies affect interaction and how these technologies might be put to best use. In order to examine such issues it is important that HCI also studies modelling and the knowledge that the user brings to the system. HCI is also concerned with the design process and focuses on techniques for the production of a user-centred, rather than a systems-centred, design.

Good interface design has other implications for individuals and organizations. Efficient system use within organizations leads to better task completion and more effective communication. In products such as CD-ROM and access to the Internet, interfaces contribute to the customers' perception of the quality of the product and are likely to be one feature that is evaluated in the purchase decision.

Usability

Usability is central to human–computer interface design and evaluation. It is concerned with making systems easy to use so that users can work efficiently, effectively and comfortably. This is the International Standards Organization's definition:

> The usability of a product is the degree to which specific users can achieve specific goals within a particular environment; effectively, efficiently and comfortably, and in an acceptable manner. (Booth, 1989, p.110)

More specifically, the components of usability, which were identified by Bennett (1984) and later operationalized by Shackel (1990) so that they could be tested, can be expressed in terms of:

- learnability, or ease of learning – the time and effort required to reach a specified level of use performance;
- throughput or ease of use – the tasks accomplished by experienced users, the speed of task execution and the errors made;
- flexibility – the extent to which the system can accommodate changes to the tasks and environments beyond those first specified;
- attitude – the positive attitude engendered in users by the system.

Specifying usability requirements can:

- help the customers to select products by comparing effectiveness, efficiency and satisfaction in two products used in the same context;
- help design teams to recognize the breadth of design issues associated with usability;
- help the supplier and customer when specifying requirements for custom-built systems.

There is a tendency to interpret usability in the rather narrow context of software design and, further, to treat software in isolation from the context of its use. Here we acknowledge this context as a significant element of public access information systems, and recognize that usability testing must concern itself with the wider environment.

Guidelines, rules, standards and metrics

Guidelines, rules, standards and metrics all need to be considered in the design and evaluation of interfaces. They summarize some desirable features of interfaces and interactions that should contribute towards usability. Here we differentiate between guidelines, rules, standards and metrics.

Guidelines should embody principles concerning the design of the interaction, which should contribute to its usability. For example, Preece et al. (1994) identifies the following widely applicable principles:

1. Know the user population.
2. Reduce cognitive load.
3. Engineer for errors.
4. Maintain consistency and clarity.

In general, design guidelines should form the principles that underlie the more specific design rules. A **design rule** is a specific instruction which should be acknowledged in the design of an interface for a specific application. Examples of design rules might be:

- Use only four colours in the design of an icon.
- Always design in confirmation dialogue after the user has selected 'Exit'.

Guidelines and rules are drawn from research and practical experience. Often research does not offer the detailed prescriptions that designers require, and with the advent of new interface styles and applications research may not always be available to inform practice.

Standards establish prescribed ways of doing something, and seek to promote consistency across products of the same type. Standards of interface design promote consistency which supports:

- development of common terminology. For example, standard measures of usability support the process of comparing different interfaces;
- maintainability and evolvability. Standard implementation techniques should lead to common program structures and styles, which support the further development of the software;
- a common identity – a common standard for display style or screen layout ensures that all systems have the same look and feel;
- reduction in training. If standard interaction techniques are used, user knowledge of one system will support learning of another.

Two specific standards which are important are:

1. ISO 9241 (1993), which addresses the ergonomic requirements for work with visual display terminals, covering both hardware and software

issues. The standard addresses: workstation layout and postural requirements, human–computer dialogue, software aspects of display design, keyboard requirements and user guidance.
2. EC Council Directive, 29 May 1990 (Macaulay, 1995), addresses the safety and health requirements of work with display screen equipment.

In addition to European and international standards, a number of organizations create their own **house style guidelines**. There are two kinds of style guidelines: commercial style guides produced by hardware and software manufacturers, and corporate style guides produced by companies for their internal use.

Standards make more sense if it is possible to measure or evaluate how closely an interface matches a standard or set of guidelines; this is achieved by the use of a metric. A **metric** is a measure of performance which in the context of interface design can be applied to measure the usability of an interface. Metrics can be divided into two categories: numeric and psychometric. Numeric metrics can be one of the following:

1. Duration metrics, which measure how much time is spent doing a particular thing.
2. Count measures, which count how many times an event happens.
3. Proportion of task-completed metrics.
4. Quality of output metrics.

Psychometrics are more subjective, and relate to factors such as control, helpfulness, likeability, learnability and efficiency.

Interfaces, dialogues and interaction

Users of public access systems are unlikely to have the time or the inclination to master complicated retrieval systems or to use them sufficiently frequently to retain any acquired expertise. Products must be straightforward to use, forgiving of errors and as acceptable as other kinds of commonly used software packages. Ease of use and acceptability depend upon a variety of factors including retrieval capabilities, data integrity and data currency, as well as the interface. However, the interface is crucial.

What is meant by the terms interface and dialogue? We start by offering some definitions of the term 'user interface'. Powell (1991) offers a simple definition:

> The term user interface specifies how the program and the user communicate.

Large (1991) offers the following, more explicit, definition:

As a minimum the user interface ought to refer to the means by which the user interacts with the program and data (the dialogue transaction): command language, menus, or direct manipulation (icons, links, etc.). This in turn raises questions about the display features (screen layout, colour and response time) and the interactive devices (keyboard, mouse, etc.). User assistance (error messages, on-screen help, tutorials and printed documentation) should also be included in any discussion of user interface. Other factors such as retrieval techniques, record structures and data quality (accuracy and currency), important as they are for the user, are not considered part of the user interface per se.

The distinction that Large (1991) makes between the interface and retrieval techniques cannot always be drawn as rigidly as is appropriate in CD-ROM systems. Vickery and Vickery (1993), for example, explore intelligent interfaces in on-line search design. They envisage an intelligent interface that can support the searching of external on-line databases. This would include the following capabilities:

- to indicate requirements that must be met if maximum aid is to be offered to the inexperienced searcher;
- to spell out the knowledge that must be incorporated in an interface if such aid is to be given;
- to describe some of the solutions that have already been implemented in experimental and operational interfaces.

Essentially, the inclusion of intelligence in the interface affects the dialogue components of the interface. We shall return to this later.

Shaw (1991) defines the user interface as 'what the user sees, hears and touches in interacting with a computer system', that is, primarily the VDT (video display terminal) screen and various input devices.

In his definition, Large (1991) also alludes to the concept of the dialogue. He further defines dialogue as: 'the means by which dialogue can be transacted, so to speak, between the user and the database in order to retrieve the sought information.'

Some researchers use the term 'dialogue' interchangeably with the term 'interface'. Booth (1989) feels that a distinction should be made between the two terms and prefers to use the term 'dialogue' to mean the process of communication that occurs at the interface.

Dialogue, then, is the process of communication between two or more agents. When we communicate, we do not just swap words; we exchange information and this exchange is dependent upon the meanings that are attached to the words that are used.

Meaning, however, does not only depend upon the words in a dialogue, but also on the context in which they are communicated and the recipient's knowledge of language and of the role generally. Booth (1989) offers the following definition of dialogue: 'the exchange of symbols between two or more parties, as well as being the meanings that the participants in the communicative process assign to these symbols.'

Human dialogue design is richer than this definition might imply and involves active listening and responding. In other words, we search for information in another person's speech and try to map this information on to our present knowledge structures. Human–computer dialogue, however, does not appear to possess this richness and variety.

Barnard and Hammond (1983) make a useful distinction between style, structure and content of human–computer dialogue. The **style** of the dialogue is defined as 'the character and control of the information exchange'. Command languages and menu selection are examples of different types of dialogue style.

The **structure** of the dialogue refers to the 'formal description of dialogue elements in terms of their constituent structure together with their ordering within and between dialogue exchanges' (Barnard and Hammond, 1983). The structure, then, reflects the progress of the interaction and may depend upon the tasks to be completed. A simple example in a command language is:

(1)   Janefile   delete
          (object)   (operation)
(2)   Delete   Janefile
          (operation)   (object)

In the first instance the object is specified first and the operation next. In the second case, the order is reversed. Thus the structure of the dialogue is important. In menu-based systems, the sequence of choice of menu options can be significant, and this is one element of the structure of the dialogue.

The **content** of the dialogue refers to

> the semantics of the information exchanged – in terms of the user's general knowledge of the meanings of words and specific knowledge of the nature and consequences of computer representations and actions. (Barnard and Hammond, 1983)

The **context** of a particular message is important. Messages are usually delivered in context. For example, if you type 'delete myfile' into the computer, the system may respond with 'Are you sure that you want to delete this file?' and you might type 'Yes'. The last two statements cannot be understood without reference to the previous statements.

The concept of dialogue is appropriate in systems in which text was typed in and responses displayed on the screen. As richer forms of communication between a user and a computer have become more common, including voice communication, manipulation of objects and tools, and touching the screen, so the exchange has become less like a dialogue that can be expressed as a language. It has become more appropriate to view the exchanges that occur between users and computers more generally, and to describe them as interactions.

Types of public access information systems

In later chapters we shall consider the following areas:

- users and cognitive modelling of users;
- environments;
- tasks, in particular, retrieval tasks; and
- technology, with a focus on input and output devices and interaction styles.

This section briefly introduces some of the different types of public access interfaces. Figure 1.3 compares these interfaces.

	User characteristics	Environment	Tasks	Technology
Public access kiosks	General public, shoppers	Shopping mall, centre, street. Public library, airport	Collecting cash, Placing orders, tickets, etc.	Touch screen, must be robust
CD-ROM	Depends on database – can include children, general public, library users, professional users and others	Library, airport, home, office	Retrieve information, download information and integrate information into other documents	Often multimedia, GUI, mouse
Internet	Internet surfers - preponderance of academics, students and males	Study/workplace, home	e-mail communication, shopping, file transfer	Desktop and portable PCs, with keyboard, screen and mouse
OPACs (on-line public access catalogues)	Library users – profile depends on type of library	In library In office/at home In other public venues	Narrowly defined • identify book availability • searching for information	Sometimes large screen, touch screen, special purpose keyboard but also accessed through standard office equipment. Remote and local access may use different workstations

Figure 1.3   **Different types of public access information systems**

On-line public access catalogues

On-line public access catalogues (OPACs) are typically an integral part of a library management system. Most library management systems provide both an OPAC designed for users and a staff enquiry function which may support more sophisticated searching and allow, for instance, the consultation of borrower records and records of items on order. OPACs are specifically designed for use by library users, either in the library or over remote networks. The core information to which an OPAC provides access is the catalogue database for the library which the user is using. This contains basic bibliographic records which typically comprise the following contents that can usefully be searched:

- ISBN
- author name
- title
- classification number
- subject index terms and/or subject headings.

Records are typically relatively short and provide only a limited number of potential search keys but, on the other hand, they are rigidly structured.

The OPAC module usually comes with a default OPAC that the library can use as a starting-point, but most libraries will prefer to take the opportunity to tailor the OPAC to their specific library, using the facility for individual OPAC design. It is therefore likely that many libraries will generate their own unique OPAC interfaces. So, for example, the library can identify and design specific menus for staff and public use; dialogue and messages can be defined, as can any information and help texts. Also, some systems allow the library to define which fields are to be indexed for staff and public, and also allow keyword indexing to be specified on given fields.

An important feature of OPACs is their increasing use over networks, including Internet access by remote users. This expands the user base significantly and has implications for interface design.

CD-ROM databases

Optical disks have become increasingly important as a medium for the storage and dissemination of information during the early 1990s. There are a number of different types of optical disk, including read only optical disks, write once read many times (WORM) disks and erasable optical disks. Compact disk-read only memory (CD-ROM) are a direct adaptation of the audio compact disks for publishing and data processing applications. Each disk can store the equivalent of 200 000 pages of text.

CD-ROMs can be purchased by users and consulted at their own workstation in the home or office. However, the price of many disks prohibits extensive personal purchase, and many CD-ROMs are bought by libraries and organizations on behalf of end-users. In this context CD-ROMs represent a means of access to information which is an alternative to on-line access to external databases via networks.

Databases available on CD-ROM include:

- Bibliographic databases with or without abstracts, which offer access to the literature of a subject field or list a type of publication, such as patents.
- Catalogue and book trade databases. Catalogue databases comprise the records in the catalogue of a major library. Book trade databases may be used either to identify the location of specific documents or in the selection of documents during collection development.
- Source databases contain the total contents of a document, including, as appropriate, computer software, images or sound, and maps and charts as well as any text and numeric data.
- Quick reference databases are a type of source database. They offer the kinds of facts and figures that are characteristic of directories.
- Mixed disks can be fitted into any of the above categories because they contain a mixture of bibliographic, full-text and quick reference data.
- Multimedia databases, including database in the CD-I, CD-ROM XA, DVI and CDTV formats. These products offer motion-picture graphics and sound and often the opportunity to interact with the computer.

Although many earlier CD-ROM databases were bibliographic in nature, there is now a significant percentage of databases in the category of general interest, leisure and recreation/arts and humanities.

External on-line hosts

A number of on-line service suppliers, otherwise known as hosts, mount a range of databases on a large computer system and offer users access to these databases, usually at a price. Some hosts have an international market and encourage and support users from all over the world. Other hosts, whilst they may have some users in other countries, operate an essentially national service. There are now over 4600 databases available via over 500 such hosts and mounted on computers based at various locations throughout the world. A supermarket host is a host which is responsible for marketing a range of databases produced by other agencies. They convert the databases into their own uniform format, thus introducing some standardization in element names so that the basic commands and search techniques apply across all the databases that are offered by a given vendor. However, since the interfaces between the different hosts are not consistent, this standardization will lead, for instance, to one database having different element names depending on the host on which it is mounted. Most supermarket hosts offer access to a range of between 50 and 350 databases.

The databases available via the on-line hosts span a wide range of subject areas. Databases can be categorized into either reference or source databases.

There are two distinct categories of user of on-line databases:

- the end-user, or the person who actually wants to use the information. The end-user should have a good understanding of the information being sought and the subject area in which the search is being performed;
- the intermediary, usually an information professional, such as a librarian or information manager. The intermediary may perform the search on behalf of the user or may support the user in executing a search. The intermediary should be an experienced searcher and should be able to adopt efficient and effective search strategies.

Intermediaries were accepted in the early days of on-line hosts because the early search systems had a command-based interface which required some considerable effort in familiarization before a user could expect to be able to search effectively. In addition, there were the hazards of unreliable telecommunications links to navigate, and since only a relatively limited number of searches were performed on-line, the intermediary might be needed to make a decision concerning whether a specific search should be conducted on-line or manually. More recently, with the advent of CD-ROM and the range of full-text databases, the on-line hosts have needed to market their services more actively to the end-user.

Multimedia kiosks

Multimedia kiosks are workstations which are specifically designed for public access. They may be stand-alone or networked through to a larger computer system. The description 'multimedia' implies that they present information in a variety of different media. The database which contains this information may be stored on a remote database or a local optical disk. In a number of environments in which it is useful to offer public access to a database, a kiosk format with the workstation just displaying a screen to the user is robust and attractive. Some kiosks also have keypads and card readers, but the most common means of communication through a kiosk is via a touch screen. Multimedia kiosks are an attractive and interesting means of presenting information, and have been used in museums and art galleries, advertising, retailing, banking, education and training and the provision of information and advice. Customers can use the kiosks to:

- view images or videos of the products or artifacts;
- compare items;

- find detailed information including, for example, whether it is necessary to purchase associated items such as batteries, or where a painting may be found in an art gallery;
- determine whether a product is in stock;
- locate details of substitute items if a given product is not in stock;
- order a product.

Internet

The Internet is a collection of interlinked computer networks, or a network of networks. Currently it connects over one million different computers and the rate of increase in use and new subscribers is growing on a month-by-month basis. The Internet provides global connectivity via a mesh of networks. Historically, the Internet was essentially an academic network, but business use is growing, so that the Internet is no longer an élite network for communication between eminent research centres, but is also accessible to small colleges, small businesses and libraries throughout the world. In many of these environments it is used for public access. The Internet offers a gateway to a myriad of on-line databases, library catalogues and collections and software and document archives, in addition to frequently used store-and-forward services, such as UseNet newsgroups and e-mail (electronic mail).

With such a vast array of databases and services available via the Internet it has been important to design interfaces that help users search the information sources and services available on it. Retrieval is recognized to be a significant problem on the Internet, with databases in a wide variety of different formats and numerous different search-retrieval software packages mounted on the different computers and providing access via different interfaces to subsets of the databases. Various print-based similes have been used to describe the situation, one of which is that the current state of the Internet can be likened to a library in which everyone in the community has donated a book and tossed it into the middle of the library floor. Tools that are used for searching the Internet often operate in client/server mode. Server software, which allows the user to search the database in a more intuitive way, has been set up on many computers on the Internet. The user's local system runs the equivalent client software, which communicates with the server software and gives a homogeneous interface to the data. The user does not need to know where the data is stored or how to manage the server system's file store structure.

There are two types of tools available to support searching on the World Wide Web: browsers and search engines. Browsers support browsing on the WWW; this involves the successive retrieval of individual documents on the basis of some relationship existing between one document and another. This is achieved through hypertext systems, which offer the representation of links. The most widely used hypertext system is the Web. Browsing is supported through:

- an addressing system that allows the location of any object stored on a networked computer to be uniquely identified by a Uniform Resource Locator (URL)
- a mark-up language (HTML) that allows the authors of documents to identify particular locations within their document as the source of links, and to specify the location of the target of those links
- a transfer protocol (HTTP) that allows copies of target documents stored on remote servers to be retrieved and displayed
- a client program, or Web browser such as Netscape Navigator or Internet Explorer that provides the user with control over the retrieval process and over the links to be activated.

People and organizations create home pages to present their own information, or service. A collection of home pages, located on the same server is called a web site. Access to these pages is via the Uniform Resource Locator (URL) using a browser. Examples of browsers are Lynx, Mosaic and Netscape. These addresses link the user to the host computer and their individual files; these are then displayed on the user's personal workstation. With the appropriate software, users can read documents, view pictures, listen to sound and retrieve information.

Whilst browsers encourage movement through a network of linked documents, browsing is not an effective approach to the identification of specific information; this requires a search engine.

A search engine is a retrieval mechanism which performs the basic retrieval task, the acceptance of a query, a comparison of the query with each of the records in a database, and the production of a retrieval set as output. Although the primary application of such search engines is to provide access to the resources that are available on the WWW, and stored on many different servers, a related area of application that is likely to grow in the next few years is the use of search engines as retrieval mechanisms in intranet environments for retrieval of documents from one organization's collection. This application is also likely to drive the development of the functionality of search engines until that functionality replicates that which is available in document management systems.

The Internet, and specifically the World Wide Web, is an important public access system that encourages international access to a wide range of information-based and commercial services.

Summary

Public access systems are becoming increasingly important. The unique features of such systems are: the undifferentiated user group, the task focus on retrieval, and the environment in which the system may be used. The factors that need to be considered in interaction design can be categorized into the categories: users, tasks, environment and technology. Usability is a central concept in interface design. Usability makes sound commercial sense since it impacts on user productivity and the learning associated with a new or upgraded system. Human–computer interaction is becoming increasingly important in the following areas:

- software development process;
- consideration of legal requirements for software;
- evaluation of competing products;
- successful software marketing strategy.

References

Barnard, P. J. and Hammond, N. V. (1983), *Cognitive Contexts and Interactive Communication*, IBM Hursley Human Factors Laboratory Report.

Bennett, J. L. (1984), 'Managing to meet usability requirements', in *Visual Display Terminals: Usability Issues and Health Concerns* (eds J. L. Bennett, D. Case, J. Sandelin and M. Smith), Prentice-Hall, Englewood Cliffs, NJ.

Bodker, S. (1991), *Through the Interface: a Human Activity Approach to User Interface Design*, Lawrence Erlbaum, Hillsdale, NJ.

Booth, P. (1989), *An Introduction to Human–Computer Interaction*, Lawrence Erlbaum, Hove.

ISO 9241 (1993), *Ergonomics Requirements for Office Work with Visual Display Terminals (VDTs)*, International Organization for Standardization, Geneva.

Large, J. A. (1991), 'The user interface to CD-ROM databases', *Journal of Librarianship and Information Science*, **23** (4), 203–17.

Macaulay, L. (1995), *Human–Computer Interaction for Software Designers*, International Thomson Computer Press, London.

Powell, J. E. (1991), *Designing User Interfaces*, Microtrend, San Marcos, CA.

Preece, J. et al. (1994), *Human–Computer Interaction*, Addison-Wesley, Wokingham.

Shackel, B. (1990), 'Human factors and usability', in *Human Computer Interaction: Selected Readings* (eds J. Preece and L. Keller), Prentice-Hall, London.

Shaw, D. (1991), 'The human computer interface for information retrieval', in *Annual Review of Information Science and Technology 26* (ed. M. E. Williams), pp. 155–95.

Shneiderman, B. (1987), *Designing the User Interface: Strategies for Effective Human–Computer Interaction*, Addison-Wesley, Reading, MA.

Vickery, B. and Vickery, A. (1993), 'On-line search interface design', *Journal of Documentation*, **49** (2), 103–87.

Chapter 2

Users and their needs

In this chapter you will gain an understanding of the importance of users of public access systems, their needs in the human–computer interface and the development and use of mental models in user interaction. Specifically you will discover:

- the characteristics of users;
- the use of mental models in developing the cognitive framework for users;
- how models of human perception and adult learning are important in design and evaluation of an interface.

Human–computer interaction

The design of the human–computer interface is vital in public access information systems. The ease of use depends upon the existence of an intuitive, easy-to-learn interface which allows users to make effective use of the information the system contains. Users are very adaptable and will learn to use a poorly designed information system if it is essential for their needs. However, poor human–computer interface design leads to:

- failure to retrieve appropriate data;
- slower completion of the task;
- poor understanding of what the system can do;
- discouragement for customers or visitors to use the system.

In systems where there are many users it is important to have an interface which is easy to use. An interface which is not intuitive discourages users and, when they use the system, they may not retrieve the information they require. End-users of public access database systems are unlikely to have the time or the inclination to master complicated retrieval systems or to use them frequently enough to retain any acquired expertise. The nature of the user interface is therefore crucial. Interfaces must be straightforward to use, forgiving of errors and as acceptable as any other kinds of commonly used software packages.

This chapter will examine the types of users who may need the information contained within public access systems; the use of mental models to assist both the system designers and the end-users; and the models of human perception used in designing human–computer interaction. Models of adult learning will also be used to describe the styles of learning that users bring to their interaction with public access database systems.

Types of users

Public access database systems, by their very nature, appeal to users from a wide variety of backgrounds and computer experience. Systems which range from banking automated teller machines (ATMs) through multimedia kiosks to library on-line public access catalogues (OPACs) and CD-ROM systems are available to all members of the general public. It is appropriate, therefore, to define the types of users of public access information systems. These may be classified in the following categories:

- Novice
- Expert
- Occasional
- Frequent
- Child
- Older adult
- User with special needs.

However, it is acknowledged that users may fall into more than one of the categories, and that none of the categories is mutually exclusive. In fact, some users may feel that they do not fit any of the categories exactly, but fall somewhere in between. The categories can be seen as ranges of experience of public access information databases and are shown in Figure 2.1.

Novice

A novice user has never used a particular public access database system before, does not know the functions of the system and cannot deal with problems that may arise in using the system. A novice user needs to learn how to complete the task for which the public access system is being used in as short a time as possible, and with such motivation that they will return to use the system again.

Figure 2.1   Scales of user experience

The novice user requires simple and intuitive interfaces, such as menus, and adequate instructions in order to use the system. In many public access systems it is not possible to train the novice user prior to use so instructions need to be embedded in the user interface.

However, a novice in relation to one system may have experience of using other information technology. Thus a novice user of an OPAC may be an experienced user of a banking ATM. Similarly, whenever an organization changes its system interface, users become novices, although they may have a conceptual framework concerning system functions that they are able to draw on from previous systems.

Expert

An expert user uses a public access database system on such a regular basis that he or she is familiar with most functions and can negotiate problems which may arise while using the system. Such a user is normally familiar with the underlying structure of the system and understands the main functions that it has been designed to perform. This means that the expert user can complete the task quickly, and may be frustrated by the use of menus, as these tend to slow the task down. An expert user may prefer to use a command language interface if this is available.

It can be difficult to design a public access database system with ease of use for both novice and expert users. Where the novice user will perform simple tasks, the expert user may also attempt much more complex tasks, for example, a subject or combination search on a library OPAC or CD-ROM system. Ideally a system should have more than one interaction style available to cater for the needs of expert users. A number of OPACs and CD-ROM systems allow expert users to use short-cut keys rather than menus and also offer 'expert user modes' so that individuals can execute complex search tasks. Examples of these are TALIS, Libertas, CAIRS and SilverPlatter.

Occasional

An occasional user uses a public access database system, or a related group of systems, on an infrequent basis and has some familiarity with some of the main functions of the system. This type of user may be a novice in many aspects of the system, but knows one or two areas reasonably well. An occasional user prefers a menu interface – as a reminder – which allows the task to be completed easily and without too much reliance on the memory for short-cut keys or command lines.

Frequent

A frequent user uses a public access database system, or a related group of systems, with enough frequency to become familiar with most functions and to be able to deal with some of the difficulties that may arise. A frequent user will prefer to use short-cut keys or commands for the functions with which he or she is familiar, but will rely on the menu structure for functions which are used less frequently.

Older adult

A user in this category may also be a novice or occasional user (Hill, 1995). This section of the population is increasing, with approximately 40 per cent of British adult users aged over 50. With wider public accessibility to computer-based information systems, the needs of this group must be considered in the interface (Morris, 1994; Hartley, 1994). This group may be apprehensive about using the interface, based on previous experience of failure. The older user's conception of computer systems may be based on experience of earlier generations of computer systems which were distinctly less user-friendly than today's systems. Such a user may lack keyboard skills and mouse familiarity and may also lack the willingness or confidence to acquire these skills. Some older users may also be users with special needs and may require support for vision or hearing impairments, or lack of manual dexterity.

Older users prefer simple layouts with clear, well-contrasted text in the menu interface. It is particularly important that interfaces should be intuitive for this category of user, so as not to deter them from using the system again.

Child

A user in this category is quite likely to be a frequent user. However, some children may use public access database systems at an age when their reading skills are not yet fully proficient (Solomon, 1993). Touch screens or interfaces where icons can be manipulated are more appropriate for the younger end of this group and intuitive interfaces are essential (Robertson, 1994). A child may, however, have a better learning capacity and memory for tasks and will certainly be willing to 'experiment' with the system to explore its functions. On the other hand, a child or young teenager may bring only limited experience to a system. For example, a teenager using an ATM for the first time may experience a learning curve associated with understanding the banking procedures embedded in the use of an ATM which offers access to a range of banking services.

Special needs

A user with special needs may be vision- or hearing-impaired, or may have specific physical or learning disabilities. He or she may also be an expert user or a novice user. However, the main point is that the user interface must be capable of supporting the user's special needs.

For a user who is hearing-impaired, the interface must give clear visual cues; for the user who is visually impaired the interface must provide speech output, which is readily available, and other aural cues to guide the user. An example of a prototype rail travel enquiry system is VODIS (voice-operated database enquiry system), which was designed to be voice-operated and could also be used over the telephone (Preece et al., 1994). The dialogue had to be created in such a way that users were restricted to limited recognized single-word or phrase responses in order to avoid errors in information retrieval.

For severely disabled users it is too costly to provide specialist input and output devices on database systems designed for general public use. However, the interface should be designed to be intuitive with clear and un-ambiguous menus and commands.

Other users

Other types of users of public access information systems may be categorized by their role in developing and preparing the system for public use. These may be identified as:

- personnel responsible for the system, for example system programmers, designers, managers;
- personnel responsible for the data and services associated with the system, for example records managers, information officers, administrators;

- personnel who use the data in the system, but do not amend it, for example clerks, sales or advisory staff, information providers.

Review and apply:	Where would you place yourself as a user of:
	(a) public access systems in general?
	(b) the OPAC in your local library?
Answer:	This depends upon you as a user and the public access systems that you use in daily life. A student in a university is likely to be a frequent user of a range of public access systems – from the university library OPAC to the local bank ATM and including perhaps the Internet and the campus information system. An older person living and working in a smaller town may be an occasional user of a bank ATM and a novice user of other public access information systems.

The characteristics of users of public access database systems are identified by using tools as described in Chapter 9. It is important to use the same tools, techniques and methods for evaluation as those used to collect information to prepare the design of the system.

The interdisciplinary background

As was shown in Chapter 1, human–computer interaction is an interdisciplinary field (Booth, 1989) which makes use of aspects from disciplines such as:

- cognitive psychology
- computer science
- information science
- ergonomics and human factors
- artificial intelligence
- philosophy
- anthropology
- sociology
- design and engineering.

All of these are important in the design and evaluation of public access database systems.

Review and apply: Think about the public access database systems with which you are most familiar. How many of the aspects above can you identify in the interface of those systems? Which would you consider to be the most important to the end-user?

Answer: It should be possible to identify the contribution made by computer science, since without the developments in this field most public access database systems would not be possible. Design and engineering aspects can be identified in the hardware surrounding the system, particularly in a banking ATM where a secure facility is paramount. The design of the keypad and screen has been developed from research in ergonomics and human factors, making the system comfortable to use. Other aspects, less easy to see, include the contribution of information science to the way the information is stored in, searched for and retrieved from the data-base. Artificial intelligence, philosophy, anthropology and sociology, all studies of people, have contributed to the design of the software, and cognitive psychology plays an important role in the design and development of the human–computer interface for the user.

Mental models

For users to make effective use of public access database systems they must have a cognitive framework upon which to hang their understanding of the system. This cognitive framework is known as a mental model (Craik, 1943; Johnson-Laird, 1989), a user's simplified mental 'picture' of what the system does which assists the user through their interaction with aspects of the system. Research in the field of cognitive psychology into mental models in the area of human–computer interaction has shown that users need to have an appropriate mental picture or analogy of the system they are using (Briggs, 1990) so that they can make appropriate decisions and take appropriate actions at the user interface and accomplish their desired task. System designers also need to be able to define these mental models if they are to understand important features of the system.

In order to define mental models it is important to distinguish other types of models which are referred to in the literature. Norman (1983) described four possible models within any system. These are shown in Figure 2.2:

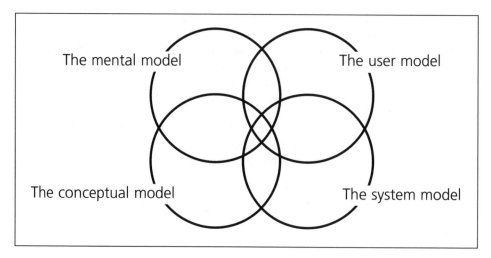

The mental model   The user model

The conceptual model   The system model

Figure 2.2   Models of the system

- The user's mental representation of the system – the mental model.
- The designer's conceptual framework for the description of the system – the user model.
- The image the system presents to its users – the system model.
- The psychologist's conceptual model of the user's mental model – the conceptual model.

It is evident from the literature that the general aim is to produce the conceptual model, where the mental model, the user model and the system model are all consistent. Chapter 6 gives a definition and explanation of the development of soft systems methodology (SSM) and its use in the development of conceptual models.

Definitions of mental models include:

- prior expectations of the system, both helping and hindering learning;
- mental structures from which to 'hang' information about the system;
- new concepts described in terms of familiar ones.

Booth (1989) states that mental models are cognitive in that the user holds a model both of the task they are performing and of the system they are using. It is commonly accepted that the mental model formed by the user guides behaviour at the interface. But 'we still do not know exactly how humans form and use their mental models' (Booth, 1989, p. 72). Prior expectations of how to use the public access system may be a help or a hindrance, depending upon how close the user's mental model comes to the conceptual framework, or system model, of the database itself.

There are a number of problems associated with mental models and these have been identified in the literature (Norman, 1983):

- Mental models are incomplete and are *'constructed from within'* (Cuff et al., 1992; p. 173) as the user works with the system.
- Mental models are unstable and details of the system can be forgotten.
- Mental models have no firm boundaries and the way to use different systems can be confused by the user.
- Mental models are unscientific and incorrect assumptions can be made about the system.
- Mental models can become superstitious beliefs, in that once a system is sufficiently understood to allow some use, then little or no effort is made to gain further knowledge or understanding.

According to Briggs (1990), some analogies may be useless and even harmful – for example, the model that the computer is a 'giant brain' and therefore both frightening and clever. 'Only after much experience do users form a more precise and representative model of the system with which they are dealing' (Briggs, 1990, p. 73). Such analogies may be contrasted with the characteristics of good design models: that is, simplicity, consistency, completeness and hierarchy. The discussion of cognitive task analysis in Chapter 7 shows how the user model is developed by the system designer.

However, mental models are important in that they are owned by the individual users. Every user will develop a mental model of the system which they use in order to build surrogates or metaphors which help them to understand complex concepts and add new knowledge to what already exists. The aim of interface designers is to attempt to bring the system designer's model and the user model into harmony with the user's mental model.

Review and apply:	What are the main characteristics of a user's mental model?
	Consider the public access database systems which you use. What analogies or metaphors have you used to help you understand the system? Note down any which you have found particularly useful.
	Compare your mental models with those of other users of the same systems. How do they differ from your mental model? In what ways are they the same?

The user's mental model of a printed encyclopaedia should not differ greatly from the system model of a multimedia encyclopaedia on CD-ROM. In order to find an entry in a printed encyclopaedia the user will search for the keyword required in the alphabetical list of entries. He/she will then expect to see some paragraphs of text defining, describing and explaining the entry. The entry may also have pictures or diagrams attached which help to clarify the text and may conclude with a list of other related entries and further reading. In the same way the user of a CD-ROM-based encyclopaedia will type the required keyword into the search interface screen and the system will retrieve an entry consisting of text, pictures and diagrams. In addition, the entry may contain sound-bites and video clips to illustrate the entry, and links to other related entries will be provided through the medium of hypertext. The use of a multimedia encyclopaedia equates quite well to the mental model acquired from using a printed encyclopaedia.

Users of CD-ROM-based dictionaries, however, will find that their mental model derived from a printed dictionary is very limited. A multimedia dictionary allows the user to carry out far more complex and extensive tasks than are possible in a printed dictionary. Hypertext facilities allow the user to jump from one definition to another; sound-bites provide guidance to pronunciation; etymology and word derivations are illustrated more fully than in a printed dictionary. The user will find that the existing mental model is incomplete and can only be developed by use of the electronic version of the dictionary.

Users of library catalogues have found that OPACs differ considerably from the mental models which they may bring from card or microfiche catalogues (Slack, 1991). Research has shown that subject searching, in particular, brings a number of conceptual difficulties which are not included in users' mental models of manual catalogues. These fall into four main categories (Slack, 1991):

- general OPAC instructions, including: unhelpful instructions and too many menu options;
- inputting search terms, including: the correct form of name, two-word search terms and identifying the appropriate keyword;
- refining search strategies, including: narrowing the search and handling voluminous subjects;
- subject description, including: identifying the type of document retrieved.

OPACs offer a number of options for subject searching – by title; by keyword; by keyword in title; by subject heading; and by keyword in subject heading. Each of the options is appropriate for a different type of subject search but users find the range of options confusing. In searching for a corporate name as a subject (for example, The Royal Institute of British Architects) users may find it difficult to frame the search in the first instance and then to refine the search when large numbers of references are retrieved. This is due to an incomplete mental model of the catalogue database and of the way in which the OPAC both holds the data and searches for the terms required. A naive user of an OPAC may find this off-putting in their first use of the system, but as they become more frequent users they should develop a better understanding of how the OPAC retrieves the required data.

Perceptual models

Perceptual models of users (Rowley, 1996) describe the way in which users receive, perceive and process information. Users receive information from external sources, interpret the information based upon previous experiences, identify a response to the received information and respond according to their decision. This basic 'human information processing model' (Preece et al., 1994, p.63) has a number of key features which need to be considered in the design of public access database systems and these are detailed below.

Perception

The user sees and interprets visual images from the public access database on the screen; these may be icons, pointers or cursors, or textual instructions and information.

In multimedia applications auditory messages are also used as part of the system, and the user hears and responds to this information or stimulus.

Attention

In order to receive information a user will filter the incoming stimuli and focus on what is perceived to be the most important information. This selective attention allows the user to switch between tasks and to regain attention after distraction by elements of the database system, or from external sources. For example, a user of a banking ATM may be distracted by activity in a busy street whereas a user of a library OPAC or CD-ROM may be distracted from their search by a retrieved item which may not be central to the search in progress, but may be useful for another purpose.

Information processing

As part of the system design and modelling process a number of stages for specific tasks within the database system are identified. The user's approaches to an information system are then matched with the information processing model and the system is designed accordingly. Elements of the information processing model may be related to the model of adult learning described below and are also discussed in detail in Chapter 7.

Memory

The use of human memory is important in learning how to use the public access database system, and also in recalling how to use it. The short-term memory and the long-term memory both play a part in this process and it is recognized that, as memory is variable in humans, it must be accommodated in the system. The short-term memory, or 'working memory' (Baddeley and Hitch, 1974), allows the user to deal with the tasks of a public access database on each separate occasion. The ability to recall how to complete specific tasks is lodged in the long-term memory, which holds information until it begins to decay or is interfered with.

Learning to use the technology

In order to use the public access database system successfully and effectively it is important for the user to learn to use the technology. A public access system which is not well designed, or presents a complex interface, or is not intuitive, will be difficult for the user to learn. Learning strategies which may be employed by the users include: learning through doing, active thinking, setting goals and creating plans, analogy, learning from errors. These aspects need to be incorporated into the interface design.

Review and apply:	For a user to have a successful encounter with a public access system, which aspects of the perceptual model are important?
Answer:	A successful interaction, which matches appropriate aspects of the perceptual model and allows effective use of the public access system, depends on:

- the user's previous experience with the system – memory, information processing;
- the user's previous experience of similar systems – memory, learning to use the technology;
- the user's familiarity with tasks that the system is designed to perform – perception, information processing;
- the user's previous experience with computer systems in general – learning to use the technology, memory;
- the user's willingness and ability to learn – attention, perception;
- the system's dialogues tailored to the specific requirements of the user – information processing, attention, perception.

Models of adult learning

The majority of users of public access database systems are adults, therefore the way in which adults learn must be considered by system designers and evaluators. The models of adult learning need to be incorporated into the design of a public access database system to ensure that user interactions are effective and successful. The significance of the context of learning and how it relates to public access systems becomes even more evident when the characteristics of adult learning are considered. Rogers (1986) includes characteristics such as:

- Learners bring a package of prior experience and values to the learning process. The learning process needs to relate to and build on this experience.
- Learners approach learning with a set of intentions and the meaning and significance of their learning will be coloured by these intentions.
- Learners have expectations in respect of the learning process, both in relation to how learning occurs and their own abilities. These need to be taken into account.
- Learners already possess set patterns of learning. New learning needs to build on their established patterns of learning.
- Learning is often episodic in nature and is usually associated with the accomplishment of a concrete task.

All these aspects of adult learning need to be taken into account in the design of a public access database system. Equally, given the nature of adult learning, when users sense the need to learn they will undertake learning on the basis of the task that confronts them, and the process will be shaped by their expectations with respect to the learning process and their already established patterns of learning. In a learning situation, such as using a public access database system for the first time, all these facets of the learning process need to be managed.

Kolb's (1984) learning cycle offers another useful perspective on adult learning: see Figure 2.3. Different users have different learning styles. Four learning styles can be matched to the four stages of the learning cycle: those of the activist, reflector, theorist and pragmatist. The identification of preferred learning styles can be useful in appreciating the way in which individuals learn, and the design of public access database interfaces should incorporate aspects which are appropriate to a range of learning styles. End-users will learn from both success and failure and need support from the interface in enhancing their ability to evaluate experience and not just to repeat it.

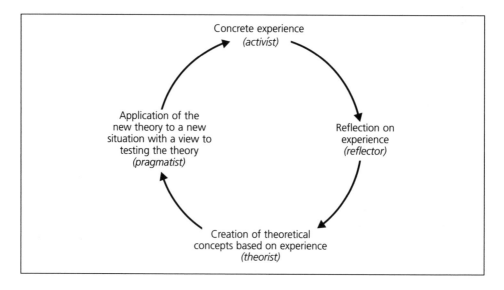

Figure 2.3   Kolb's learning cycle

Summary

The range of users who may interact with public access database systems is as wide as may be imagined by the use of the word 'public'. For this reason the design and evaluation of any public access database system must be done in the light of its users. The cognitive frameworks which such users bring to bear on their interaction, the use of mental models and the users' perceptual models are important aspects for the learning and recall of system functions. Adult learning models describe the characteristics of users and should inform the development of systems for public access.

References

Baddeley, A. D. and Hitch, G. (1974), 'Working memory', in *The Psychology of Learning and Motivation* (ed. G. H. Bower), Academic Press, London.

Booth, P. (1989), *An Introduction to Human–Computer Interaction*, Lawrence Erlbaum, Hove.

Briggs, P. (1990), 'The role of the user model in learning as an internally and externally directed activity', in *Mental Models and Human Computer Interaction*, 1 (eds D. Ackermann and M. J. Tauber), North-Holland, Amsterdam, pp. 195–208.

Craik, K. J. W. (1943), *The Nature of Explanation*, Cambridge University Press, Cambridge.

Cuff, E. C. et al. (1992), *Perspectives in Sociology*, 3rd edn, Routledge, London.

Hartley, J. (1994), 'Designing instructional text for older readers: a literature review', *British Journal of Educational Technology*, **25**(3), 172–88.

Hill, S. (1995), *A Practical Guide to the Human–Computer Interface*, DP Publications, London.

Johnson-Laird, P. N. (1989), 'Mental models', in *Foundations of Cognitive Science* (ed. M. I. Posner), MIT Press, Cambridge, MA, pp. 469–93.

Kolb, D. (1984), *Experiential Learning*, Prentice-Hall, Englewood Cliffs, NJ.

Morris, J. (1994), 'User interface design for older adults', in *Interacting with Computers*, **6**(4), 373–93.

Norman, D. A. (1983), 'Some observations on mental models', in *Mental Models* (eds D. Gentner and A. L. Stevens), Lawrence Erlbaum, Hillsdale, NJ, pp. 7–14.

Preece, J. et al. (1994), *Human–Computer Interaction*, Addison-Wesley, Wokingham.

Robertson, J. W. (1994), 'Usability and children's software: a user-centered design methodology', *Journal of Computing in Childhood Education*, **5**(3/4), 257–71.

Rogers, A. (1986), *Teaching Adults*, Open University Press, Buckingham.

Rowley, J. (1996), *The Basics of Information Systems*, Library Association Publishing, London.

Slack, F. E. (1991), 'OPACs: using enhanced transaction logs to achieve more effective online help for subject searching', PhD thesis, Manchester Polytechnic, Manchester (unpublished).

Solomon, P. (1993), 'Children's information retrieval behaviour: a case analysis of an OPAC', *Journal of the American Society for Information Science*, **44**(5), 245–64.

Chapter 3

The interaction environment

The objective of this chapter is to explore the environments in which human–computer interaction with public access databases takes place. These environments range from the external location of the access point to the internal facilities and technologies which allow the interaction to take place.

By the end of this chapter, you will be aware of:

- the external environments in which public access information systems can be found;
- the range of data and interface environments for public access;
- the types of input and output devices available;
- networking platforms and standards for public interaction.

Computer terminals which give access to public databases can be found in a wide range of environments from busy street corners to the privacy of the user's own home. The computer equipment for public access also varies depending upon the task and the nature of the information requirement. This chapter will outline the locations where public access databases can be found, the computer hardware used to access the databases, and the computer platforms and standards used to provide adequate interaction with public systems.

External environments

The origins of public access database systems can be traced to libraries, where on-line catalogues, bibliographic databases and local information have been available for more than a decade. These developments led to museums and art galleries providing collection information to the public by means of computer terminals. Since the advent of multimedia (image and sound) systems these have become more widespread and easier to use. An excellent example of this can be seen in The National Gallery in London, where the collection can be searched on a multimedia system, and selected screens of both text and chosen paintings can be printed (Cawkell, 1996). To guide the user to view the selected paintings, a map of The National Gallery can be printed which shows the locations of the chosen works. This facility is housed in a specially adapted room in the Gallery and has twelve workstations available to the public. Theme parks are now pursuing the latest developments of such systems by providing guides to attractions, maps of the site and other useful local information.

Banks and building societies probably offer the most ubiquitous public access systems through their automated teller machines (ATMs) situated outside local branches, at supermarkets and shopping centres, in railway stations, motorway services and airports. There are also a few automated banking halls established in branches which are no longer staffed by bank employees. These systems are robust, secure and easy to use. As well as providing information about bank services and personal accounts, they also fulfil the purpose of dispensing cash. In addition to ATMs, bus and railway stations and airports are now beginning to offer (still experimental) information databases allowing the user to find out train times, bus services and flight information. Tickets for holidays, flights, bus and train journeys can be booked on-line in travel agents, or even in some cases via the Internet. Theatre and cinema information and booking is also being developed for the user by means of the database systems which are currently used by booking office staff.

Within offices, workshops or industrial locations and professional practices, access to information on a daily basis takes place through public access database systems, either networked from a central computer or through CD-ROM technology on a stand-alone computer. In the home, in schools and colleges and in offices, users are also turning to the Internet for sources of electronic information not previously available.

Figure 3.1 shows the variety of locations in which public access database systems may be found; the users of the systems; the tasks in which the users may be engaged; the external environment in which the public access terminals may be installed; and the technology used to provide the systems. The people who may use the systems are either members of the public or employees of the organization in which the terminal is located. The tasks carried out on public access database systems range from bibliographic searches, through enquiries to locate objects for viewing or purchase, to searches for booking information for travel or entertainment, to enquiries for financial and other professional or occupational information. Environments may be indoor or outdoor, in specially designed locations or placed where users pass frequently. The technology used to provide public access database systems may be a networked terminal, or a stand-alone machine which provides access to databases held on CD-ROM, or by access to the Internet. Different locations within

Location	People	Task	Environment	Technology
Library	Clients	Bibliographic	Indoor	Networked, stand-alone
Museum	Visitors	Object	Indoor	Stand-alone
Art gallery	Visitors	Object	Indoor	Stand-alone
Theme park	Visitors	Object, information	Outdoor, indoor	Stand-alone, networked
Store	Clients	Object	Indoor	Networked
Shopping mall	Visitors, clients	Object, information	Indoor, outdoor	Networked, stand-alone
Travel agents	Clients, staff	Information	Indoor	Networked
Train/bus station	Clients, staff	Information	Indoor, outdoor	Networked
Airport	Clients, staff	Information	Indoor	Networked
Theatre, cinema	Clients, staff	Information	Indoor	Networked
Bank, building society	Clients	Financial, information	Indoor, outdoor	Networked
Office	Staff	Multiple tasks	Indoor	Networked, stand-alone
Industry, workshop	Staff	Object, information, multiple tasks	Indoor	Networked, stand-alone
Professional practice	Staff	Multiple tasks	Indoor	Networked, stand-alone
Home	Family	Multiple tasks	Indoor	Networked, stand-alone

Figure 3.1   **Characteristics of public access environments**

the same organization may provide different technologies, depending upon the services offered. For example, libraries offer networked access to their OPAC and some CD-ROM services, and stand-alone access to other, perhaps less frequently used, CD-ROM databases.

Review and apply:	Use Figure 3.1 to list briefly the characteristics of the public access databases which you use. Identify where these systems are located; are you client, visitor, staff or family? What tasks do you perform on the systems? Where are the terminals located, and are they networked or stand-alone?
	If you do not know the answer to any of the above questions, find out the relevant information from the providers of the services you use.

The purpose of each public access database system affects its location, its users, its tasks, its environment and its technology. In turn, the environment in which a system is located affects the way in which it is used. Users of a banking ATM located in a busy street will prefer to use the facility quickly, as there is often a queue waiting for the service. When OPACs were first introduced into libraries it was found that users would also queue to use the system (Rice, 1988), and that once seated at an OPAC, a user would browse at length through the screens. For that reason OPAC terminals were soon placed on counters where users had to stand to search the catalogue – thus reducing the amount of time that one user would spend on the search – and the number of OPAC terminals was increased to cater for the increased usage of the library catalogue.

Other conditions of the location include the height and position of public access systems. Wheelchair users and other users with special needs require terminals to be provided in appropriate and accessible locations. Banking ATMs are positioned at a variety of heights and access is provided by means of ramps to users with mobility difficulties. The public access terminals to the ordering system in large branches of Argos stores are mounted in specially designed modules, which also provide slots for users to pay directly by credit card. The height of these modules is such that users of short stature would find them awkward to access and wheelchair users would find them impossible. Presumably, the design is intentional to deter children from 'playing' with the touch screen – however, on one occasion we observed children, on tip-toe and at full stretch, succeeding in using the system!

One of the key environmental issues for ATMs is the security both of the facility itself and of the users. External security is supplied by solid engineering on the outside and alarm systems on the inside. Lighting around the ATM and clear walkways, not obscured by buildings or places where a thief could hide, enhance the security of users. Most ATMs are under surveillance by CCTV installed above the terminal; this acts as a deterrent to thieves as it not only discourages thefts from legitimate users of the ATM, but also video-records all users, legitimate and illegitimate, with a time-stamp which can be linked to the ATM transaction. Users of stolen bank cards can then be identified from the videotape.

As public access information systems become more widespread, more effective and more familiar, users may find that they will have to queue to use a terminal. For this reason external locations must be congenial and interfaces must be as intuitive and simple to use as possible, in order to promote ease and speed of use for all members of the public.

The information environment

Public access to database resources has increased and developed over the last twenty years, and especially over the last five years with the reduction in cost of the hardware and networks required to support such systems. The types of data which can now be retrieved in the public domain cover a wide range of sources and scenarios. What were once raw numerical and bibliographic data held on computer files have now been transformed into information with added value for users. However, each new type of information made available electronically brings with it complexities about the way in which it is presented and the way it can be retrieved. The issue of information retrieval and the searching task will be covered in Chapter 4. This section will look at the relationship between the information and the interface environment within which it is made available.

Library uses

The first public access database systems to be generally available, albeit to a limited clientele, were the university library OPACs, developed in the USA in the early 1970s from computer-generated microform catalogues (Hildreth, 1985). OPACs are now available in all academic libraries in the UK and in the majority of public libraries. The types of data sought on OPACs would be bibliographic details of library holdings, including:

- author, joint author, editor(s)
- title
- classification number
- corporate name
- conference name
- series title
- subject heading
- additional notes.

The types of library holdings cover:

- books and pamphlets
- theses, research reports and conference proceedings
- government and official publications
- periodicals and newspapers
- audio materials such as vinyl disks, CDs and cassettes
- visual materials such as paintings, photographs, videotapes
- computer and CD-ROM software
- specialist collections, which may include manuscripts and ephemera.

The information sought is normally whether an item is held by the library, where it is located, whether it is available for lending or for reference and whether it is on loan or on the shelf. The interface would allow these questions to be answered by allowing the user to type in the author or title of the item (a known-item search). If this information is not known by the user, then the interface should allow a search for the subject of the item to be made (a subject search). The result of the search is then displayed on computer screen (see Figure 3.2). OPACs are not normally attached to a printer, so many libraries provide a box of scrap paper alongside the OPAC terminals so that users can jot down the information they have found.

Libraries also offer CD-ROM resources which allow access to biblio-

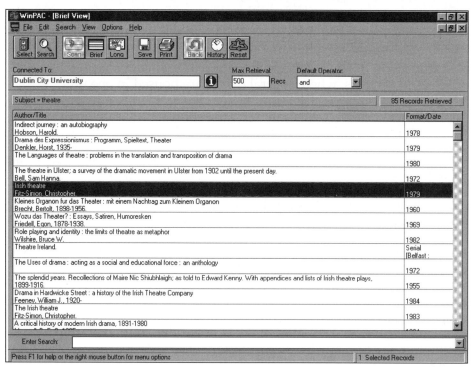

Source: Dynix Library Systems (UK) Ltd

Figure 3.2   Windows-based OPAC results screen

graphical and reference data once held only in printed format (Rowley, 1993). Access again is through a known-item search or a subject search. These resources include:

1. Bibliographic databases, which offer indexes to periodicals, access to the literature of a subject field or list a type of publication, such as patents.
2. Source databases, which contain the total contents of a document. Examples may be encyclopaedias, atlases and the full text of daily newspapers, learned journals and organizational reports.
3. Quick-reference databases which hold the types of facts and figures characteristic of dictionaries and directories.
4. Catalogue and book trade databases which may be used to identify the location and publication details of documents.
5. Mixed databases which contain a mixture of bibliographic, full-text and quick-reference data.
6. Multimedia databases which are available in CD-I, CD-ROM XA, DVI and CDTV formats.

The basic configuration of a CD-ROM system is a stand-alone computer, a CD-ROM drive, appropriate software and a printer. In order to make CD-ROMs more widely available within libraries, it is common to link the basic configuration into a network. The CD-ROM drives for multiple users and multiple disks are based around:

- daisy-chain drives, where several drives are linked together;
- stacked systems, where several drives are housed in one unit;
- jukebox systems, which work in a similar fashion to a record jukebox. Multi-drive jukeboxes allow more flexibility in that several users can search the same disk or one user can search a number of disks.

Retrieved information can be printed by the user, either through an attached printer, or directly on to a floppy disk or to their own e-mail or network address.

Access to on-line databases has been available in academic libraries since the late 1960s, but searches are normally carried out through the mediation of a reference librarian who has been trained in the various search facilities. In the 1990s these services have been developed for a wider clientele through the medium of CD-ROM and the Internet. Command language interfaces are being supplemented with menu-driven interfaces which attempt to support occasional users. Known-item and subject searches can both be carried out and the results can be printed locally or remotely. A number of hosts now offer an e-mail or fax service to deliver retrieved articles direct to the user's desktop.

Applications for museums and art galleries

The development of optical disk technology in CD-ROMs and laser-disks has allowed museums, art galleries and botanical gardens to exploit their collections by making them available to a wider public (Taylor et al., 1992). Multimedia and hypermedia systems are being used as practical applications, and Visser (1993) lists four categories:

- Documentary, providing library/encyclopaedic information primarily for professional users.
- General information covering a wide range of topics intended for the general public.
- Supporting information system, for instance for use at exhibitions, and so on, for providing limited information.
- Point of information stand-alone systems associated with a collection (Cawkell, 1996, p. 338).

The interface to a number of systems has been built around an Apple Macintosh platform using HyperCard. The Apple Macintosh platform is used extensively in the multimedia environment because it has a high-resolution screen, capable of giving excellent graphical reproduction and it also has a simple and innovative graphical user interface, developed in the mid-1980s from the Xerox Star (Preece et al., 1994; Cawkell, 1996). Hyper-Card provided a control medium for a database containing both text and images. The user is required to select 'buttons' on a card and click on them to execute a search or move on to the next screen. Examples taken from a HyperCard stack 'Celtic Museum', developed by Michael Newton (1991), show how a user can select an item to view from a gallery of artifacts. The pointing finger icon indicates that the user has selected the Austrian Belt Hook from the gallery in Figure 3.3 and the artifact is then displayed and explained in Figure 3.4.

The use of public access systems in museums, art galleries, botanical gardens and even some theme parks as sources of information about the attractions and exhibits is likely to continue. Hoffos (1992) describes 25 computerized museum and art gallery systems being used in the UK. There are a number of advantages (Valls, 1994) and some disadvantages (Cawkell, 1996) which include some issues related to public access.

Advantages:

- improved access to a collection with the minimum of risk;
- improved access to the content; visual as well as textual information available at the same time;
- reduction in dependence upon verbal descriptions;
- support for educational activities.

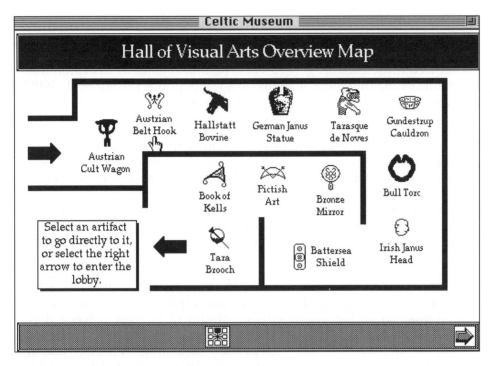

Figure 3.3 Celtic Museum Visual Arts Gallery

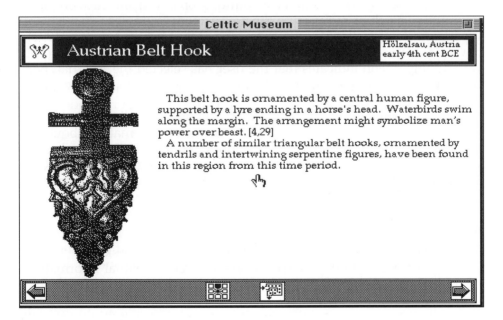

Figure 3.4 Celtic Museum artifact

Disadvantages:

- technology must be robust and compatible;
- copyright issues mean that some catalogues are not complete;
- image description for searching purposes needs some standardization.

Banking and financial services

For the past twenty years banks in the United Kingdom have been developing ATMs for the use of their customers. The first 'hole-in-the-wall' machines were operated by coded plastic cards which dispensed a pre-arranged sum of money, were retained by the machine and then returned to the user by post some days later. With the technological developments in the coding of debit and credit cards and the advances in telecommunications, today's ATMs seem positively friendly! Users of banks and building societies can interrogate their bank account, receive 'mini-statements' and check their balance, withdraw cash and order financial services from ATMs located outside local branches, inside supermarkets, in hospitals and on university campuses.

Internal security for the users is the requirement that all public access is carried out by means of a personal identification number (PIN). These are randomly generated in sealed envelopes by computer at the issuing financial service and posted directly to the user. Many systems now allow the user to change the PIN on their first transaction with a new card. This should act as a double blind against a user's PIN being accidentally or fraudulently discovered by a bank employee.

A typical configuration of an ATM consists of a secure card reader, a keypad, a screen with special keys set into the frame, an integral printer and a dispensing slot. Some ATMs have touch screens rather than special keys and some have a receiving slot so that deposits can be made. Communication between the ATM terminal and financial service provider's database is via a dedicated data network because speed is of the essence in ATM transactions. The interface is intuitive and is based around a question and answer dialogue, where the user presses the appropriate buttons in response to questions posed by the system. A typical dialogue is shown in Figure 3.5.

A typical transaction normally takes between one and two minutes if the ATM is located outdoors or in an open environment such as a shopping centre. However, ATMs have been installed in some unstaffed branches of banks and users are more likely to spend longer in an indoor location where they can find out about other financial services in more comfort.

Other uses for ATMs include currency exchange transactions where users can insert currency from one country and receive an appropriate amount of another currency. These are commonly found in airports,

ATM SCREEN	USER ACTION
Please insert your card	*User inserts cashcard into secure reader slot*
Please enter your personal number	*User types PIN using keypad*
Please select service required	*Available services are displayed on the terminal screen. User presses special key alongside the service required (the word* BALANCE*)*
Do you want your current balance displayed on screen or printed?	*User presses special key alongside the word* SCREEN
Your current balance is £243.66	*User presses* PROCEED *on the keypad*
You may withdraw up to £200 today Press PROCEED if you wish to withdraw cash.	
How much cash do you want to withdraw?	*User presses special key alongside:* £20
The bank is dealing with your request	*User waits*
Please take your cash promptly	*User takes cash from the dispenser slot*
Do you want another service?	*User presses special key alongside the word* NO
Please remove your card	*User takes cashcard as it emerges from the secure card reader slot*

Figure 3.5   A typical ATM dialogue

railway stations and passenger ferry terminals. We have also observed and used such a facility in a street location in a major continental European city. The interface for this type of ATM must be intuitive and accessible in more than one language.

Business uses

Public access information systems in the business world are developing on two main fronts: those of multimedia kiosks and the Internet. These are beginning to make a mark upon traditional business areas in a way that has not been seen since supermarkets replaced the corner shop. In retailing and in other business environments such as travel, entertainment, advertising, property marketing and building, the Internet and multimedia kiosks are being used to provide information and services directly to the customers.

   Multimedia kiosks are being tested by a number of retailers in the USA and the UK, and many more are believed to be testing kiosks behind closed doors. They can be viewed as a significant advance on in-store promotion and bring text-based information to life with animation, video,

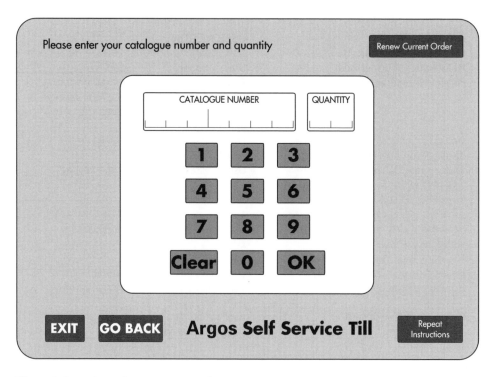

Figure 3.6   A catalogue store touch screen

stills, graphics, diagrams, audio and text. In making some decisions, customers require detailed information which the salesperson is not always able to provide. Kiosks are a means of providing a wealth of product information tailored to individual needs and presented in an interesting and user-friendly fashion (Rowley, 1995). The basic requirement is a multi-media terminal which has a computer with sufficient memory to support either a large hard disk or a CD-ROM drive. Some networking may also be necessary if customers can place orders through the kiosk. Interaction is normally via a touch screen interface on the high-resolution screen. The user touches buttons on the screen and selects specified transactions, as shown in Figure 3.6. Some kiosks also have card readers and keyboards.

Public access to business information also comes via the Internet, and in particular through the World Wide Web. Many businesses are using the Internet as an additional marketing communications and sales channel and http:\\ addresses can be seen on television and newspaper advertisements. A wide range of information is available for users to purchase online (books, CDs and tee-shirts seem to sell well), to visit sites where products can be viewed (many car manufacturers have a Web site) and for smaller businesses to serve a larger niche market. Flynn (1995) expects that

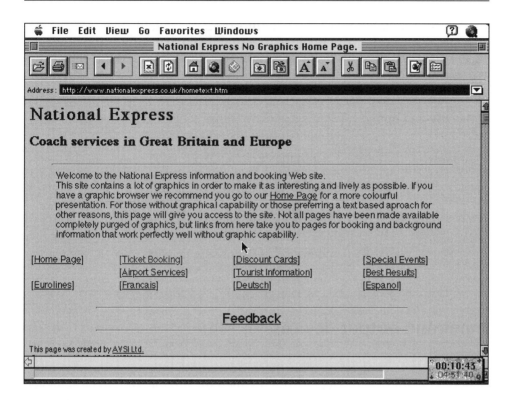

Figure 3.7   Internet text screen

15 per cent of all retail sales in the USA will be via the Internet by the year 2000.

In addition to advertising and marketing information, users can also access business directories, commercial databases, electronic yellow pages and other services. Some have free access and other services require paid registration before a user can investigate their services. Travel, tourist and entertainment information is freely available on the Internet. It is possible for a user to read local information about an area that he or she would like to visit and book both accommodation and travel tickets through the Internet (see Figure 3.7). Listings of shows or concerts in the area may also be available.

Internet access requires a stand-alone computer with a modem and appropriate communications software; this may be based in the workplace, in a public or academic library or at home. Once access is made, the interface depends upon the information provider. Most sites on the World Wide Web use a GUI and many have clear, well-designed sites. Some information providers have links straight into sites which they consider to be well designed and useful to their users. The main accessibility issue with the Internet is that there is so much information available that it is difficult to generalize about the many interfaces available. It is important, however, to ensure that sites used for business information are those which are maintained and updated on a regular basis.

Review and apply:	Why is it important that public access information systems are maintained and updated?
Answer:	For information to be of any value a user must be confident that it is accurate, timely, appropriate, valid, available and replicable. A well-maintained public access system reassures the user that the organization is spending time updating the information. A system which is frequently off-line or contains out-of-date information will not inspire confidence in the end-user.

Input and output devices

This section is concerned with the hardware of human–computer interaction. The physical devices through which the interaction can be achieved impose important restrictions on the nature of the interaction, and the development of new physical devices offers new opportunities for differing styles of interaction. However, the introduction of a new physical device alone will not solve all the problems of public access interfaces. The purpose of any developments in this area is to create input and output devices that maximize the advantages of human physical, cognitive and perceptual characteristics and so promote efficient, reliable and possibly even enjoyable interaction with the system.

In general, the number of interaction devices is continuing to expand and many of these devices are finding new niches with different types of tasks. There is some debate concerning the significance of interaction devices in the effective interface. Some regard the devices as central, while others would recognize that such devices do not present a panacea for the many problems associated with public access to information databases – many of these problems are indeed concept-based. The focus in this section will be on those input and output devices that are encountered in users' interface with public access information systems.

Input devices

Input devices are the means whereby both data and programs enter the system and are the devices used by the end-user in the interaction to input their responses in the dialogue. There are a number of different input devices and the most suitable depends upon the data to be entered into the system, the user and the environment.

Keyboard

The keyboard is the most common data entry device. The keyboard is based on the traditional typewriter QWERTY keyboard to which a few keys have been added to support some specific computer-based functions, such as ENTER and PGDN and cursor keys. This keyboard arrangement was designed in the late nineteenth century to slow typists down so that they did not jam the keys. Research into the ergonomics of keyboard design has led to a number of recommendations in this area (Booth, 1989) and significant changes in the design of keyboards in recent years, such as adjusting the curve and the slope to make input more comfortable. More efficient keyboard layouts, such as DVORAK (Preece et al., 1994, p. 215), have been designed but it is unlikely that they will be adopted since the QWERTY keyboard is so well established and the cost of replacing equipment and retraining staff would be prohibitive.

Keyboards are normally used in conjunction with a screen on which the data input is displayed. Keyboards are widely used in both data input and in searching databases where the user may key commands into the system. They offer a flexible method of data entry and can be used in most applications. They do, however, have some limitations. Keyboarding is a relatively slow method of bulk data entry. Also, more importantly for the design of interfaces for public access, not all users can be assumed to have proficient keyboard skills. Figure 3.8 lists some of the features that might be sought in well-designed keyboards.

Special keys

Some public access systems, in particular OPACs, have customized or made specialized use of the twelve function keys at the top of the normal keyboard. In early OPACs, such as Okapi (Walker, 1989), key tops were coloured to match instructions on the colour interface. Later developments in both OPACs' and CD-ROM databases' function keys were given consistent meanings (for example, F1 for Help) and users were instructed in the particular use of these keys.

Special keys and keypads can also be found on ATMs. As most of the end-user input to an ATM is numeric, it is sensible for a numeric keypad top to be made available. Special keys are installed alongside the ATM screen and these are used to select options displayed on the screen (see Figure 3.5).

General criteria
- Should be detachable from the screen
- Should be heavy enough to stay where it is put
- Should be thick enough to be stable and comfortable, but not too bulky
- The angle of the keyboard should be comfortable and preferably adjustable

Key characteristics
- Key pressure – the keyboard should be responsive to a comfortable amount of pressure
- Key travel – the keys should move sufficiently far so that it is clear when they have been depressed, but should not have a deep travel that slows keying speed
- Key tops – the size and shape should be sufficiently large with a concave shape
- Key spacing – should be sufficient so that the adjacent keys are not hit when keying
- Key activation – should be accompanied by a signal, such as an audible click or snap action

Keyboard layout
- The layout of the alphabetic and numeric keys should correspond to that of a conventional typewriter keyboard
- If users are involved in entering numbers an auxiliary numeric keyset can be useful
- The different function key blocks should be distinguished from other keys by either shape, colour or position
- Function keys are normally in a row along the top of the keyboard
- Cursor keys are best arranged in a cross or an inverted T shape
- The position and size of all the following keys should be considered: ESC, ENTER, BACKSPACE, CONTROL and SHIFT.

Figure 3.8   Keyboard features

Touch-sensitive screens

Touch-sensitive screens allow the user to select an item from a screen display by touching it with a finger. The touch breaks the network of horizontal and vertical infra-red beams and thus the touch can be detected. These screens have been used in OPACs and other public access terminals such as catalogue store ordering systems and tourist information terminals. They are attractive in these applications because they avoid the use of the keyboard or can replace a keyboard with numbers and letters displayed on the touch screen (see Figure 3.6). They are useful where the user needs to choose commands or select items and their use appears to be intuitive. Their chief disadvantages are:

- the range of options that can be satisfactorily displayed on the screen is limited by the size of users' fingers!;
- the screens tend to get covered in finger marks and need regular cleaning in order to retain their readability;
- extensive use of touch screens can be very tiring.

EuroTunnel has a booking service and information system available at a motorway service station on the M25 which permits use even when the shop in which it is installed is closed, because its touch screen is bonded to the shop window (Cawkell, 1996).

Speech input

At present speech input has a very limited use in public access systems, although clear advantages can be noted for users with impairments. This is an area where there has been a history of research but progress continues to be slow. Booth (1989) offers the following advantages:

- Speech is a natural form of communication, so the training of new users is easier.
- Speech input does not require physical contact with the system, so a user can carry out other actions and move around freely.
- Speech input offers opportunities for users with motor impairment or visual impairment to use new technology.

Preece et al. (1994) identify some disadvantages:

- Speech input has been used only in specialized areas and tasks.
- Speech recognizers have limitations in distinguishing between similar sounding words and phrases.
- Speech recognizers are subject to interference, although this can be somewhat improved by using a telephone-style headset.
- The natural form of human language can be difficult for a computer to interpret.

Drawing, positioning and pointing devices

A drawing or pointing device is generally used to select a menu option displayed on a public access terminal screen. There continues to be an expansion in the range of drawing, positioning and pointing devices but not many are used at present in public access situations. Virtual reality equipment such as datagloves and helmets are not commonly found in locations where users are seeking public information (Preece et al., 1994). The touch-sensitive screen (see above) can also be regarded as a pointing device, but in public access it is mainly used for data input.

Cursor keys

A cursor is a shape that indicates where the text will be entered on the screen. Cursor keys are usually just four keys on the keyboard which will respectively move the cursor up, down, to the right and to the left. The main limitation of cursor keys is that it is difficult to move the cursor across the screen rapidly and other more effective methods for rapid movement of the cursor are therefore useful.

Mouse

A mouse is a small device with a ball underneath and buttons on the top which moves the cursor or pointer across the screen. Once the pointer has been appropriately positioned, an item or option may be selected by clicking on the mouse button. The mouse is normally moved on a flat surface beside the screen or keyboard. Most mice have one, two or three buttons, with two buttons being the most common. Operations may be performed by clicking on the button once, or by double clicking.

The mouse is a relatively accurate pointing device and can be used to move the pointer quickly across the screen. The main disadvantage is the desk space that the device requires, although this can be improved by using a mouse mat.

Tracker ball and track pad

Tracker balls are very similar in operation to a mouse. The device may rest on the desktop, be attached to the side of the computer or, as in some laptop computers, be placed within the keyboard. The ball can be rotated with the thumb and as the ball moves left, so the pointer on the screen moves left, and vice versa. The buttons for a tracker ball are positioned on either side of the ball. Tracker balls are, like mice, quick and accurate in positioning the cursor, but, unlike mice, do not require desk space.

A tracker ball was used to provide access to the interactive guide to Liverpool University's Ness Botanical Gardens (Taylor et al., 1992). Although the system was used by a number of older users, the tracker ball appeared to present no difficulties in use.

Track pads, which are often found on laptop computers, are operated in a similar way to a tracker ball and are used to position the cursor on the screen. A smooth pad of touch-sensitive material responds to the user's finger and moves the cursor about. Selections are made by pressing the appropriate buttons placed alongside the track pad.

Bar-code reader and lightpen

The bar-code reader and the lightpen are based upon similar technology. The lightpen is used mainly as a direct manipulation device and the bar-code reader is used to read data from bar codes directly into a system.

All the previously mentioned devices have been indirect pointing devices, that is, they are not used to point directly at the screen, but have a pointer on the screen which they manipulate. Lightpens can be direct pointing devices as items are selected by pointing directly at the screen. They do not require the same degree of hand–eye coordination that mice and tracker balls demand. The user can control what is on the screen very directly and therefore lightpens are useful for drawing as well as pointing and positioning. A major disadvantage to using a lightpen for pointing is that such use for any period of time can be very tiring.

Portable bar-code readers are now available to the public in self-service situations, for example to self-issue books in a library, where the bar code on both the library card and on the book label need to be read. Supermarkets are experimenting with public bar-code readers so that shoppers can scan the bar codes on their purchases as they move around the store, and so save time at the checkout.

Other devices

Joysticks are widely used for games and flight simulators and the like, but have a very restricted field of use in public access. The joystick works in a very similar way to the mouse or the tracker ball. If pressure is applied to the stick towards the left, then the pointer on the screen moves left, and so on.

A graphics tablet works in a similar way to a lightpen, except that the movement is made by an electronic pen on to a specifically prepared flat tablet in front of the screen. As the stylus is moved about the tablet, a corresponding pointer moves about the screen.

Criteria for input devices

Research into input devices has demonstrated that the best devices for any particular task will depend on the nature and characteristics of the task in question. Reid (1985) summarizes Newman and Sproull's (1979) recommendations as shown in Figure 3.9. These activities relate to public access information systems, although drawing is not a common activity in this context.

Review and apply:	What are the advantages and disadvantages of using a standard keyboard as a method of data input?
Answer:	The advantages are that a standard keyboard is familiar to most users, therefore intuitive; it is flexible in its use; response and feedback on the interface are almost instantaneous. The disadvantages include the fact that some users are not proficient in keyboard use; the use of special keys or key combinations may not be clear.

Activity	Best device
Picking	Mouse and joystick, followed by tracker ball and lightpen
Positioning	Mouse and joystick, followed by tracker ball and lightpen
Numeric input	Numeric keypad followed by alphanumeric keypad (QWERTY keyboard)
Text input	Alphanumeric keypad (QWERTY keyboard)
Drawing	Graphics tablet followed by mouse followed by lightpen

Figure 3.9   Matching input devices to activity

Output devices

Output is what emerges from the public access information system for the user to read or act upon and to guide the user in the search process. The visual display unit (VDU) screen and printer are the two main means of output in the public access context. However, voice output from synthesizers is used in a growing number of applications where visual output is not appropriate, such as in systems for visually impaired people.

VDU screens

Screens support dialogue with the computer and are the chief means used by the computer to output data and messages. They offer fast and virtually cost-free output of information. The screen displays everything that is entered at the keyboard as well as messages and data from the information system.

The trend in VDU screens in public access systems is towards colour and most public access software uses colour. Monochrome screens are adequate for text and number entry and are found in banking applications such as ATMs. Colour screens come into their own in graphics and multi-media applications, but as the price of colour screens continues to drop they are becoming widespread in all types of applications. Modern screens offer a high-resolution, stable image. This is important both for the display of graphics and for the ergonomic comfort of the operator. Some of the characteristics that should be considered when evaluating a VDU screen are listed below:

- The character image should appear sharp and well defined.
- The displayed character image should be stable and not flicker.
- Background screen luminance should be acceptable and adjustable.
- Contrast between character and background should be adequate.

- Graphics display should have adequately high resolution.
- Monochrome or colour display should be appropriate for the task.

Multimedia screens

In order to display multimedia databases, especially those which have detailed graphics and video content, it is important to have a monitor or screen with appropriate resolution, scanning rate and colour capabilities. Cawkell (1996) lists the essential requirements for a screen which will display multimedia applications:

- A good-quality colour monitor, that is, one produced by a recognized manufacturer.
- 640 × 840 pixel (IBM VGA resolution) – this is the minimum standard.
- Scanning rate ranges of 30–57 KHz horizontal and 40–75 Hz vertical – this ensures a stable image.
- RGB analog or RGB TTL to run NTSC or PAL composite video signals – in order to process and run video clips smoothly.

Personal computers with multimedia capabilities are now generally available and the cost of high specification monitors is decreasing. However, it must be remembered that in a public access context all equipment must be as robust and tamper-proof as possible.

Speech and sound output

Speech and sound output is much easier to accomplish than speech input and a variety of public access systems make use of both speech and sound. Many public access systems use simple sounds, such as beeps, to indicate that an incorrect command or an error has occurred; for example, an OPAC will make a beep if an invalid option has been selected or if the final item of the display has been reached. Others use synthesized or recorded speech to guide the user through the interface or to enhance the information presented on the screen. The ordering system in Argos stores uses spoken instructions to complement the textual information on the screen.

In multimedia information systems, sound and speech are integral components of the presentation. The majority of computer systems now come with a sound card already installed. For high-quality sound output, especially music, the system must be capable of running a CD player through good speakers.

The position of public access information systems with sound output must be carefully considered, as an installation in a library, for instance, may be annoying if it is within earshot of quiet study areas. The use of headphones, or the option to turn the sound off, should be considered.

Printers

Printers and their output are a further important interface device although, since the printout once created is remote from the information system, it is easy to ignore the significance of printers in the design of the interface in public access information databases. There tends to be an assumption, particularly in relation to public access applications, that once appropriate records have been retrieved the printed form in which they are presented to the user is immaterial. Without pursuing the pros and cons of this debate further, it is appropriate to review the range and type of printers and to indicate some of the characteristics that should be considered in their selection. The quality of printout depends not only upon the printer that is used, but also upon the facilities available in the public access system software for formatting printout.

Printers can be categorized in accordance with the amount printed by one command: line printers print a line at a time; serial printers print a character at a time; and page printers print a page at a time. Output from a search session may be printed directly during the enquiry or saved to a file from which it may then be printed. Hence a wide range of types of printers may be used for printing output. Serial printers include daisy-wheel printers, dot-matrix printers, inkjet and bubblejet printers. Laser printers are page printers. Many applications are now almost entirely based on inkjet or bubblejet printers and laser printers.

The key characteristics that should be evaluated in the selection of a printer are as follows:

- speed
- quality of output
- range of type fonts available
- graphics capabilities
- whether colour is available
- noise levels
- option to produce multiple copies
- cost of purchase
- cost of operation
- compactness
- reliability
- support for special forms and paper sizes.

There are some applications, such as ATMs, multimedia kiosks and supermarket bar-code readers, which contain small integral printers to issue receipts, printed information or 'mini-statements'. These are normally inkjet or dot-matrix printers and have been developed from the technology of point-of-sales equipment.

Platforms and standards

In order for databases to be provided to the public in a variety of locations and on a range of different computer installations, agreed standards must be met by the database providers. A 'platform' may be defined as the configuration of the computer hardware and software which conforms to a minimum specification to support the database for public access. In other words, if a public access database requires a windows interface, then the platform for that service should have hardware and software to at least the minimum level capable of running and displaying a windows interface.

There are a number of different standards within the computer industry which allow database providers to ensure that public access systems can support the interfaces which have been designed and installed for users. The standards can be categorized as open systems, client–server architecture and Z39.50.

Open systems

This term is used most frequently to describe true interoperability where computer components, both hardware and software, can be mixed and matched to fit the requirements of the database system and its users. In particular, this means that providers of public access databases can upgrade and expand the capabilities of their system in a modular way, without the need to replace all the existing system. Open systems are designed around industry-wide standards, used by vendors and manufacturers of computer hardware and software, network environments and communications protocols. These 'vendor-independent' standards allow the systems to be designed with the needs of the users of the database in mind (Ward, 1994).

Client–server architecture

Client–server systems represent the most flexible of open systems. This computer 'architecture' separates the functions of a public access database between the 'client' who accesses the data and the 'server' which stores, indexes and manages the data. In this way it is possible for different 'clients' and different 'servers' to work together easily. For example, from a library terminal a user may be able to access networked CD-ROMs, the library OPAC and the Internet; an ATM (Barclays, for instance) can be configured to allow users of other bank debit and credit cards to withdraw cash using their own card in the Barclays machine. The use of such a system is apparently seamless to the end-user.

Z39.50

The Z39.50 standard was developed in the USA by the National Information Standards Association (NISO) to retrieve bibliographic and abstract data from servers independent of the system used. It allows users to search a variety of different sources by using a single interface, is maintained by the Library of Congress and is 'vendor-independent'. The standard dictates protocols to both the client and the server so that each can recognize the instructions and responses generated by the other. As Watson states, 'in theory any client then implementing the standard can search and retrieve from any server that has implemented the standard' (1996, p. 72).

Systems operating under the Z39.50 standard will be able to set up client software to access all the information resources in the library or information service. Users can then choose their preferred operating system – DOS, Windows, UNIX – and search from their own desktop not only the library systems, but also the Internet, BIDS, other OPACs and other information providers. The Z39.50 standard should also allow users to see whether references retrieved from other subject databases are available in their local collection – a 'seamless integration of library holdings information with subject databases' (Watson, 1996, p. 72).

Summary

The physical and technological environments of public access database systems affect the interface to the resources. The locations in which public access systems may be found are important factors in issues such as the security of the users and congeniality of the systems' use. The types of data to be found require different interfaces through which this information is provided; these, in turn, require a variety of technologies for data input and output for public access. The development of these technologies, and particularly some of the common platforms and standards for information transfer, will lead to a greater awareness of the importance of design and evaluation in the public access context.

References

Booth, P. (1989), *An Introduction to Human–Computer Interaction*, Lawrence Erlbaum, Hove.

Cawkell, A. (1996), *The Multimedia Handbook*, Routledge, London.

Flynn, L. (1995), 'The pieces of Internet business', *New York Times*, 5 February, D10.

Hildreth, C. R. (1985), 'Online public access catalogs', in *Annual Review of Information Science and Technology 20* (ed. M. E. Williams), Knowledge Industry Publications, pp. 233–85.

Hoffos, S. (1992), 'Multimedia and the interactive display', *Library and Research Report 87*, The British Library Publications Unit, Boston Spa.

Newman, W. M. and Sproull, R. F. (1979), *Principles of Interactive Computer Graphics*, 2nd edn, McGraw-Hill, New York.

Newton, M. (1991), *Celtic Museum*, HyperCard stack, 40522 Eady Lane, Boulevard, CA 91905.

Preece, J. et al. (1994), *Human–Computer Interaction*, Addison-Wesley, Wokingham.

Reid, P. (1985), 'Work station design, activities and display techniques', in *Fundamentals of Human–Computer Interaction* (ed. A. F. Monk), Academic Press, London.

Rice, J. (1988), 'Serendipity and holism: the beauty of OPACs', *Library Journal*, 138–41.

Rowley, J. E. (1993), *Computers for Libraries*, 3rd edn, Library Association Publishing, London.

Rowley, J. E. (1995), 'Multimedia kiosks in retailing', *International Journal of Retail and Distribution Management*, **23** (5), 32–40.

Taylor, M. J., Mortimer, A. M., Addison, M. A. R. and Turner, M. C. R. (1992), ' "Ness-plants": an interactive multi-media information system for botanic gardens', in *Information Retrieval: New Systems and Current Research* (ed. R. Leon), Taylor Graham, London, pp. 119–36.

Valls, C. (1994), 'Multimedia in museums: an overview of its developments', *Program*, **28** (3), 263–74.

Visser, F. E. H. (1993), 'The European museums network: an interactive multi-media application for the museum visitor', in *Proceedings of the 1993 Electronic Imaging and Visual Arts Conference (EVA 93)* (ed. J. Hemsley), Brameur and Vasari Enterprises, Aldershot, pp. 204–17.

Walker, S. (1989), 'The Okapi online catalogue research projects', in *The Online Catalogue: Developments and Directions* (ed. C. R. Hildreth), Library Association Publishing, London, pp. 84–106.

Ward, M. (1994), 'Z39.50: benefits to searchers', *Online Information 94: Proceedings*, Learned Information, Oxford, pp. 33–5.

Watson, M. (1996), 'Improving user access to CD-ROM databases: technical issues', in *The End-user Revolution: CD-ROM, Internet and the Changing Role of the Information Professional* (ed. R. Biddiscombe), Library Association Publishing, London, pp. 64–78.

Chapter 4

The searching task

The objective of this chapter is to introduce the reader to the searching and requesting tasks related to public access information systems. You will be able to identify:

- the types of searching facilities available to users;
- the theory behind the development of cognitive models;
- the searching strategies employed by users;
- the contrast between searching and browsing strategies;
- how these tools and strategies are used in various public access applications.

A special category of task

Users of public access database systems are normally searching for information to answer a query. Where can I find this book? Does the store sell cushion covers? Is there a flight to Rome tomorrow? Are there any seats available for the show next week? and so on. The queries may be specific or, more probably, somewhat vague: If there is not a flight to Rome tomorrow, when is the next one? Are there any seats available on it? How much does it cost? Is there a cheaper flight from another airport? The interface must match the likely dialogue from the end-user with the likely responses from the database, in such a way that the requirements of the user are met.

When designing or evaluating an interface for a public access information system, it is important to consider closely the task of searching for information. This task is unlike the operations involved in word processing or using a spreadsheet, for example. Even requesting specific information from a public access system is different from the searching task, although this may equate to known-item searching, which is described later in the chapter. A user may have a query but not a specific goal – the goal is to book the theatre ticket, to write the essay, to buy cushion covers. Searching a public access system is one step on the way towards that goal, but is not the goal in itself, as Markey (1984) states: 'It is rather a momentary task performed during an otherwise busy day full of unrelated events and actions' (p. 64). This chapter will explore the facilities available to users in their search for the answer to their queries, the theoretical approach to information retrieval, the cognitive models and search strategies identified through research, and the way these aspects relate to the practical applications of public access information systems.

Much of the research cited in this chapter is related to information retrieval in OPACs since this was one of the first areas in which public access systems were designed. The searching task at an OPAC is of particular concern and complexity because it is often the first time an end-user has access to a very large data set covering a wide range of subjects (often the 'universe of knowledge'). Research into on-line systems has mainly focused on trained intermediaries, although some work in public access has been carried out. Both on-line systems and CD-ROMs are products which provide access to a single subject, or related subject, area and so do not present end-users with the same information retrieval problems as a library catalogue. Multimedia kiosks tend to avoid complex searching by taking the user through a series of straightforward instructions and provide no facilities for searching the catalogue for terms – this will be discussed later in the chapter. Searching on the Internet makes high use of universal resource locator (URL) addresses and so can be seen to be at an early stage of development. Public access use of OPACs is the arena in which most work has been done and developments in the newer public access information systems have come out of OPAC research.

Searching facilities

The search facilities within any public access information system are based upon the structure of the data stored in the database. Indexing languages are those used as part of the data structure and are the 'terms and codes that might be used as access points in an index' (Rowley, 1993, p. 117). A searching language is employed by a user to enter the requirements of the query brought to the public access information system. The searching language cannot be controlled by the system designer, but the indexing language should allow the creation of links between the data and the users' needs. There are three main categories of indexing languages:

- **Controlled vocabulary** or assigned-term systems. Terms are assigned by an indexer to the subjects within the database using a controlled vocabulary where synonyms are cross-referenced and a hierarchical structure from broad terms to narrow terms is developed. Alphabetical indexing languages are stored as thesauri and subject heading lists. Classification schemes (such as the Dewey decimal classification) are also controlled vocabulary, and the terms used are represented by a code or notation. A controlled vocabulary is claimed to be more consistent in representing a subject area, but a user may find it difficult to phrase a query using the appropriate terms (Rowley, 1993; Shneiderman, 1992).

- **Natural language** or derived-term systems. These are not really a distinct language in their own right but are the 'natural' or ordinary language of the documents being indexed. Derived-term systems are created from all descriptors from the documents, including author, title and citations, and emphasis was traditionally put on the terms taken from the title and abstract. However, with the increased availability of full-text systems, the basis of the natural language index is derived from the document. The system may exclude very common terms and may also use a thesaurus to support the selection of terms. Most public access information systems allow searching on both controlled vocabulary and natural language (Rowley, 1993).

- **Free term** or free indexing language. This is a type of indexing where there are no constraints on the terms that can be used in the process – any appropriate terms can be assigned to the document by a human indexer, based upon their own knowledge and experience of the subject. However, in computerized systems where index terms are assigned automatically, a free indexing language is, for all practical purposes, the same as natural language indexing in that the computer must assign terms based upon the text of the documents (Svenonius, 1986; Rowley, 1993).

Boolean searching

Boolean search logic is used in most public access systems to specify combinations of terms to match the query. The operators AND, OR and NOT allow terms to be linked to synonyms and related terms in controlled vocabulary and with spelling variants and quasi-synonyms in natural language searches. Figure 4.1 shows how the operators may be used.

Searching using Boolean operators was originally developed for use by expert searchers of large subject-based databases where precision in search statements was required. 'The methods may not be as precise as experienced searchers would like, but they are usable by the public' (Bills and Helgerson, 1988, p. 79). However, Ensor (1992) found that users of the

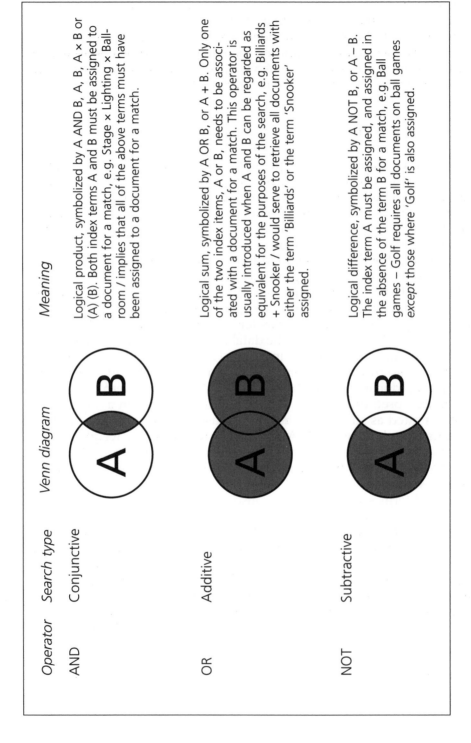

Operator	Search type	Venn diagram	Meaning
AND	Conjunctive		Logical product, symbolized by A AND B, A, B, A × B or (A) (B). Both index terms A and B must be assigned to a document for a match, e.g. Stage × Lighting × Ball-room / implies that all of the above terms must have been assigned to a document for a match.
OR	Additive		Logical sum, symbolized by A OR B, or A + B. Only one of the two index items, A or B, needs to be associated with a document for a match. This operator is usually introduced when A and B can be regarded as equivalent for the purposes of the search, e.g. Billiards + Snooker / would serve to retrieve all documents with either the term 'Billiards' or the term 'Snooker' assigned.
NOT	Subtractive		Logical difference, symbolized by A NOT B, or A¯– B. The index term A must be assigned, and assigned in the absence of the term B for a match, e.g. Ball games – Golf requires all documents on ball games *except those where 'Golf' is also assigned.*

Figure 4.1   Boolean logic operators

OPAC at Indiana State University were unfamiliar with Boolean operators and so perceived them to be difficult to learn.

A number of OPACs have provided the facility of implicit logic to support user searches, without requiring them to use an explicit Boolean operator. This is normally found as an AND operator where a two-word search term is automatically AND-ed by the system (Slack, 1991).

Relevancy ranking

In most search statements it is possible to designate certain concepts as being more significant than their neighbours. This can be achieved through the use of weighted-term logic or relevancy ranking. Weighted-term logic may be introduced either as a search logic in its own right, or as a means of reducing or ranking (relevancy ranking) the search output from a search whose basic logic is Boolean.

In an application where weighted-term logic is the primary search logic, each search term in a search profile is allocated a weight. These weights can be allocated by the searcher, but more commonly are allocated automatically. Automatic allocation of weights is usually based on the inverse frequency algorithm which weights terms in accordance with the inverse frequency of their occurrence in the database. Thus common words are not seen to be particularly valuable in uniquely identifying documents. If the weights are assigned by the searcher they are associated with a relevance ranking on a document which is found containing that term as a search term. Search profiles combine terms and their weights in a simple sum, and items rated as suitable for retrieval must have weights which exceed a specified theshold weight. Alternatively no threshold weight may be used, and then users will simply be presented with records in ranked order, and can make their own choice as to how far down the list they choose to scan.

Weighted-term search logic may also be used to supplement Boolean logic. Here weighted-term logic is a means of limiting or ranking the output from a search that has been conducted with the use of a search profile which was framed in terms of Boolean logic operators. In the search, and prior to display or printing, references or records are ranked according to the weighting that they achieve, and records with sufficiently high rankings will be deemed most relevant, and be selected for display or printing. In this application, relevancy ranking is most often achieved through an analysis of the number of occurrences of search terms or hits in the document.

Keywords

Keywords form the basis of natural language indexes and are common in public access information systems because they are straightforward and relatively cheap to create. They can be taken from the title, abstract and full text of the document and are normally matched against a stop-list of useless or redundant words. The stop-list would contain terms such as: and, the, them, his, her, its, other, and so on. Any term not found in the stop-list would then be designated a keyword and added to the index.

Criticisms of this facility are mostly concerned with the absence of terminology control. Irrelevant retrievals (known as 'false drops') are inevitable as the mere appearance of a term in a document does not mean that it is discussed at length. An example of this may be a search for the term 'polish' which would retrieve items related to the cleaning process, but may also retrieve items related to the country of Poland. Keyword search facilities often allow an implicit AND (see above) to permit keywords which would normally be linked in a phrase (for example, *drug abuse*) to be retrieved from the same document.

Ensor's study (1992) of OPAC users at Indiana State University in the early 1990s revealed a lack of knowledge about keyword searching. We have observed a similar lack of understanding among undergraduate students in the mid-1990s; these students now have regular access to OPACs, CD-ROMs and the Internet but they are still unsure of how to use a keyword search to the best advantage. Is this a problem with users, or with the public access systems?

Phrase searching and proximity operators

Often a subject is best described by a phrase of two, three or more words (see *drug abuse* above). Subjects such as Commonwealth Games and Artificial Intelligence need two words to describe them. If the system allows, an implicit AND operator (as described above) would search for the two words together, for example:

Commonwealth AND Games.

This would retrieve records containing the phrase along with other records where both words appear but not next to each other. This method allows only crude phrase searching.

Another option is to store the terms as phrases indicated, for example, by the insertion of a hyphen, thus Human-Computer-Interaction. This option is primarily used for controlled vocabulary since the phrases must be marked at input, and end-users must enter the search term in exactly the form in which it was originally entered.

Proximity operators can be used with natural language and free term indexes as well as controlled vocabulary. They allow the user to state whether the terms should be searched for:

- where the terms appear next to each other (for example, Artificial Intelligence);
- where the terms appear in the same field or paragraph (for example, User, Interface, Design);
- where the terms are within a specified distance of each other, with the maximum number of words to come between them (for example, the Proposal for the Research project).

Indicating terms in proximity or adjacent to other terms assists the user to carry out a more precise search (Rowley, 1993; Vickery and Vickery, 1993).

Truncation and string searching

Truncation allows terms to be searched for by their word stems, indicated by a special character such as $ or *. The system will then search for a string of characters, regardless of whether that string is a complete word. For example, if a search is entered for the term Theat$ this would retrieve records containing the words Theatre, Theater, Theatres, Theaters and Theatrical. The use of truncation eliminates the need to specify each word variant and thus simplifies search strategies. This is particularly useful in natural language and free term indexes where word variations are uncontrolled.

The most basic truncation is right-hand truncation where characters to the right of the character string are ignored. Left-hand truncation can be useful in circumstances where a variety of prefixes might occur, such as in chemical databases. For example, $ethane might retrieve records of methane, chloroethane and bromoethane.

Truncation, or masking as it is known in this context, is sometimes available in the middle of words. This is a useful facility to handle alternative spellings, so that Organisation and Organization would both be retrieved by the search term Organi%ation.

String searching and truncation are useful methods to narrow down an extensive retrieved set of records, but they would be very slow techniques to use on a large bibliographic or full-text database. String searching and truncation are widely available on on-line systems where users tend to be trained intermediaries. On OPACs, however, these facilities are less common and even when they are available they are seldom used. Yee (1991) reports on research findings that between 6 per cent and 10 per cent of users take advantage of truncation in a search.

Subject headings

Where a controlled indexing language has been used to provide index terms, a thesaurus or list of subject headings will often be available within the public access system. The thesaurus displays the controlled vocabulary used and shows the relationship between terms. It is therefore a useful facility for narrowing or broadening searches. A subject heading list is normally displayed in alphabetical order and helps the user to use the correct phrase for the search. Library of Congress Subject Headings (LCSH) are most commonly found in OPACs, although in the UK the subject approach is often derived from the classification scheme (O'Brien, 1994). Some locally generated subject indexes have been provided on OPACs with varying degrees of success.

It is useful if the thesaurus or subject heading list can be displayed in a window to assist users as they attempt to create a search strategy. This facility is available on most CD-ROMs and on a number of OPACs (Bills and Helgerson, 1988).

Hypertext-type functions

A number of systems boast 'hypertext-type' searching; these are mainly CD-ROM and Internet applications. True hypertext searching relies upon

	OPAC	CD-ROM	On-line host	Multimedia kiosk	Internet
Controlled vocabulary	✔	✔	✔	✔	✔
Natural language	✔	✔	✔	✔	✔
Free terms	✔	✔			✔
Boolean logic	✔	✔	✔		✔
Keywords	✔	✔	✔	✔	✔
Phrase searching	✔	✔	✔	✔	✔
Proximity operators		✔	✔		✔
Truncation	✔	✔	✔		✔
String searching	✔	✔	✔		✔
Subject headings	✔	✔	✔		✔
Hypertext links	✔	✔	✔		✔

Figure 4.2   Searching facilities within applications

an indexer establishing conceptual links between documents. This is very labour-intensive. An alternative is to rely upon the text of the document and use the occurrence of words as the basis for hypertext links. Thus, if the same word appears in two documents, the user may move from one document to another without explicitly returning to the index. It has been a criticism of hypermedia that users find it difficult to navigate through the links. Crawford (1992) states that 'naive users may find hyperlinks totally befuddling'. It is important that users are able to backtrack through their search, so that they do not get lost in the hyperlinks.

Searching facilities within applications are presented in Figure 4.2.

Known-item searching: author and title

Known-item searching is performed by users when they know what they are looking for and usually possess some characteristic of the information such as author, editor or title. In academic OPACs it is common to find students performing known-item searches with a course reading list in order to discover the location of recommended texts. Searches on an OPAC or other bibliographic database would be carried out under the Author field, the Title field or under a special Author/Title field which allows users to enter an appropriate combination of characters from the author and title headings of the item.

Users perceive known-item searching as being without particular difficulty, and if the query produces a response of no items retrieved, the user thinks that the library does not hold that item (Drabenstott, 1991). It was found in research studies, however, that users do make errors in entering known-item searches and that some systems require known-item terms to be entered in a fixed way. Frequent errors reported include:

- incorrect order of name elements, for example Roald Dahl instead of Dahl, Roald;
- incorrect surname, for example Laurence, D. H. instead of Lawrence, D. H;
- inclusion of the initial article in a title, for example *The Jazz Anthology* instead of *Jazz Anthology*;
- incorrect spelling of a search term, for example *Jurrasic Park* instead of *Jurassic Park*.

A reported 10 per cent failure rate of known-item searches on academic library OPACs (Dwyer et al., 1991) does indicate a 90 per cent success rate. It must be ensured, however, that all public access information systems are as free from inconsistencies and provide as complete and as good-quality data as possible.

Range searching and limiting

Range searching is particularly useful when selecting records on the basis of numeric or data fields. Selection of records according to a price field or publication date field can be carried out through range operators. Common range operators are:

EQ	equal to	LT	less than
NE	not equal to	NL	not less than
GT	greater than	WL	within the limits
NG	not greater than	OL	outside the limits.

These operators are found more commonly on on-line hosts and CD-ROMs, but date ranges can be set on many OPACs (Rowley, 1993).

Search history and management

These facilities include the opportunity to review the search strategy adopted and to save, permanently or temporarily, a search profile for subsequent use. With the development of more networked library and bibliographic database services and the implementation of the Z39.50 standard (see Chapter 3), such management facilities will be used more by end-users for controlling and managing their own searches (Rowley, 1993; Danilowicz, 1994; Watson, 1996).

Record display

Once a successful search has been performed, it is necessary to display the records. OPACs first display one-line records and then allow the user to display the full record. On-line search services and CD-ROMs offer a variety of facilities for displaying the records. These include:

- on the screen
- off-line printing
- downloading to disk.

Default formats are the norm but user-defined formats are becoming more common. In addition to specifying the format, users need to be able to specify which records are displayed. OPACs tend to let users select records and display them one at a time. CD-ROM and on-line systems have facilities which allow the set of records for display to be indicated.

Review and apply:	What search facilities might you use to find the following subject terms on an OPAC?
	● Logistics
	● Drug Abuse
	● The Ecology of Sand Dunes
	● John Fitzgerald Kennedy
	● The Royal Institute of British Architects
Answer:	*Logistics* could be entered as a keyword. A phrase search for *Drug Abuse* may make use of the implicit AND if it is available. Use of Boolean operators in the search for *Ecology of Sand Dunes* would ensure that a broad topic (Ecology) is narrowed to one specific area. A known-item search under the Author heading should retrieve material about *John Fitzgerald Kennedy* because biographical subjects are often held under the Author heading. The search for *The Royal Institute of British Architects* is probably the most difficult. You may start by checking the Subject Headings list; AND-ing the terms would be very slow, as all of them are widely used words. In a number of OPACs the best approach is to truncate the term *Architect$* and carry out a keyword search. Try these terms for yourself next time you use an OPAC.

Information retrieval theory

This section serves to outline in brief the theoretical background to information retrieval in order to illuminate how the subject has developed and contributed to the public access information systems which we encounter today. There is a vast literature and tradition behind the subject of information retrieval and contributions come from the fields of computer science, mathematics, information science and cognitive psychology. Ellis's book (1996) introduces the principal approaches to information retrieval and offers a state-of-the-art review. It is essential reading for anyone who wishes to pursue the subject further.

Ellis (1996) identifies two main paradigms in information retrieval research:

● the objectivist approach, associated with the Cranfield tests;
● the subjectivist approach, based upon cognitive research.

These two approaches will be described briefly below. For further reading in this area, a number of useful and interesting texts are listed in the references at the end of the chapter.

Recall and precision

The tests carried out on the Uniterm system in 1953 were the beginning of information retrieval research (Thorne, 1955). In the UK these tests were performed at the Cranfield College of Aeronautics and so became known as the Cranfield tests, which continued through the 1950s and early 1960s (Cleverdon, 1967). A collection of source documents was established and queries were performed to identify relevant documents in the collection. Extensive testing led to the development of retrieval performance criteria for **recall**:

$$\text{Recall} = \frac{\text{Relevant documents retrieved}}{\text{Total of relevant documents in collection}}$$

and **precision**:

$$\text{Precision} = \frac{\text{Relevant documents retrieved}}{\text{Total of documents retrieved}}$$

This, in turn, led to the testing of statistical and probabilistic retrieval techniques (Ellis, 1996); to the SMART retrieval system; to document clustering research; and, since the early 1990s the Text Retrieval Conference (TREC) collection and linguistic approaches (Robertson and Beaulieu, 1997).

Recall and precision have been used as performance criteria (Su, 1994) since the late 1950s, but since the late 1970s a change of emphasis and progress in the technology for information retrieval has led researchers to an interest in cognitive modelling.

Cognitive modelling

By taking a subjectivist approach to information retrieval research, the

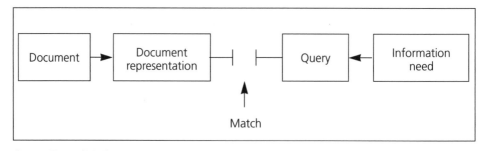

Source: Bates (1989)

Figure 4.3   The classic information retrieval model

nature of the user's needs were modelled. In the late 1970s technology allowed more sophisticated information retrieval systems to be developed and researchers began to model the way that a user carried out a search. These cognitive user models were then used to improve and enhance information retrieval system design (Ellis, 1996). A retrieval program known as THOMAS was designed around a network of associations which appeared to work well for a small collection of documents but had difficulties in coping with a large document collection. However, the research provided valuable insights into the searching behaviour of users (Oddy, 1977).

Another early cognitive model of the user can be found in Belkin's (1980) work around the concept of an 'anomalous state of knowledge' (ASK). This model identifies a user's deficiency or anomaly in their state of knowledge and describes their interaction with an information retrieval system. Although this concept was criticized, it did show that users sometimes find it difficult to formulate a query and that the interaction between a user and an information retrieval system should be examined from different angles.

Although the development of public access information systems has been informed by the objectivist research in information retrieval, it is the work on cognitive models which is important in designing and evaluating such systems for end-users.

Charting techniques for analysing users' searches

Transaction logging provides a way of unobtrusively observing a user's actions and creates a record of how the user has performed a search on the public access information system (Jones et al., 1997). The success or failure of a user's search strategy can be examined in more detail and their task can be analysed in a structured way. The data collected from this method can be fed back into the design and evaluation process. In order to generate useful information from transaction log data, the actions taken and the process of the searches must be charted. These charts allow searches and strategies to be compared and can be used to evaluate the steps taken by the end-user and the success or failure of a search. A public access information system can then be tested for ease of use both during the design stage and after implementation.

Tasks carried out in a public access information system tend to be heuristic, with the user progressing towards a (perhaps hazily defined) goal, but in some cases not reaching it. The need to discover useful search strategies and common error patterns, both mechanical and conceptual, is paramount when investigating end-user searching. It is for this type of end-user search that search path maps (SPMs) were developed and evaluated (Slack, 1991, 1996). By charting the searches it could be seen how

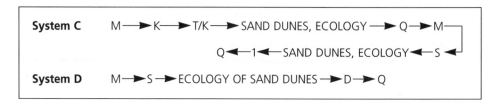

M = Main menu; K = Keyword; T/K = Title keyword; S = Subject; D = Display records; Q = Return to main menu. Arabic numbers indicate line numbers on index or brief record screens.

Figure 4.4   Search path maps for the subject term ECOLOGY OF SAND DUNES

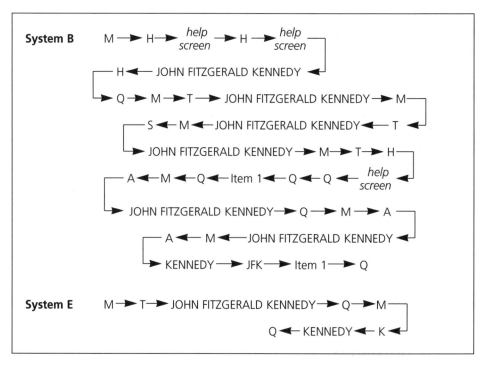

M = Main menu; H = Help; T = Title; S = Subject; A = Author; K = Keyword; Q = Return to main menu. Arabic numbers indicate line numbers on index or brief record screens.

Figure 4.5   Search path maps for the subject term JOHN FITZGERALD KENNEDY

users moved around the OPAC. Search strategies could be compared across the searches and across the systems investigated.

Figure 4.4 shows that it was necessary to select the most appropriate terms for this search. ECOLOGY is too broad a term to produce a satisfactory response and so the terms SAND and DUNES must be combined to search effectively. In the data collected a large number of users tried the search using the term ECOLOGY and the keyword search option. This was a conceptual problem, showing that users have difficulty in selecting an appropriate keyword for a complex subject search.

The user of System C was confused by the two options available for subject searching. One option (S) permitted a controlled vocabulary search of subject headings; the other (T/K) allowed a search by a single keyword taken from either the title or the subject heading. In many of the cases collected, users attempted subject searches first by one option and then by the other. System D permitted subject access by natural language input and used term weighting to produce a listing of the records most relevant to the search terms. This is important when complex searches are being constructed.

Searches for personal names as subject terms are more difficult than searches for topical subject terms, because of the way that the name index is constructed in many OPACs. It can be seen in the search path maps (Figure 4.5) how users found it necessary to browse forwards and backwards in order to identify a suitable document for the term JOHN FITZGERALD KENNEDY. In the data collected, many users tried more than one option to locate records for personal names as subject terms. A surprising number of cases collected showed that JOHN was used as an initial search term – this resulted in a system response listing names such as John, Augustus; John, King of England; John the Baptist. Other users entered 'JOHN FITZGERALD KENNEDY' as a phrase search. Another search strategy was to enter KENNEDY and JOHN as an implicit AND search. Searches were also conducted under the title option, with some success.

The charting technique of search path maps allowed users' searches to be compared across a number of OPACs. The search strategies (or lack of them) were easily identified and the analysis allowed the searches to be quantified in terms of success, use of on-line help, mechanical errors (such as spelling) and conceptual problems encountered by users.

Search strategies

There has been considerable research over the last ten to fifteen years to explore how users search on information databases and what strategies they employ. Every searcher aims to

- retrieve sufficient relevant records;

and to avoid:

- retrieving irrelevant records;
- retrieving too many records;
- retrieving too few records.

Interaction with the interface allows users to modify and iterate their searches in order to retrieve relevant information to answer their query. Shenouda (1990) has identified the principal types of modification and reformulation which may be made during a search:

- Adding a term or facet
- Deleting a term or facet
- Use of different Boolean operators
- Breaking down search statement structure
- Re-use of search strategy
- Correcting an error
- Limitation of search results (by date, language, field, source, and so on)
- Expanding
- Changing output format.

Fidel (1990) studied expert searchers on an on-line database and categorized them into 'operationalist' and 'conceptualist' searchers. She identified that operationalist searchers preferred to use keywords in their query formulation whereas conceptualist searchers preferred subject descriptors and would more readily use the system's thesaurus. Her conclusions indicated that to a certain extent searching style affects searching behaviour and that some searching characteristics are inherent to the user, while other searching characteristics are acquired as the user gains experience. Designers of public access information systems must, therefore, be cognizant of the strategies and styles of searching employed by the potential users of their system.

As public access information systems and the facilities which they offer have developed, researchers have categorized end-user search strategies in different ways. This section will focus on some of the more common strategies presented in the literature.

Query expansion

Query expansion in an OPAC has been developed over a number of years as part of the Okapi research now based at City University, London (Walker and Hancock-Beaulieu, 1991). In the initial work a method of automatically expanding a user's query (AQE) was tested; this was followed up with the implementation of an interactive system of query expansion (IQE) where users could add appropriate terms, displayed by the system, to their search. A third project (ENQUIRE) offered users a windows interface where thesaurus terms were presented and could be added to query terms or rejected, as the user responded to the system (Beaulieu, 1997).

The initial AQE system was designed to be hidden from the user. The system presented the user with an option to 'Type M to see more books similar to the ones you have chosen' and, once this option was selected, the query expansion was performed automatically to enhance the user's original query and provide a new set of retrieved records. Results from the AQE showed that it was used by approximately one-third of users, both frequent users and occasional or even first-time users.

The second, IQE, system was designed to give the user an interactive control over their search and was presented in a GUI. This allowed the IQE to be presented to the user in another window where selection of relevant items could be made. Surprisingly, the results showed that use of the IQE facility was very limited and that about half of the users found it difficult to choose relevant terms from those offered.

The third approach attempted to provide a facility where the user's control over the query was better balanced against the system's functions. In the ENQUIRE interface the query was mapped to the database thesaurus and the user could expand the search by selecting terms from that window. In a separate window, query terms, thesaurus terms and new terms could be added or deleted by the user throughout the search in order to modify the results. Findings from the experiments revealed a more positive response by users, compared to the IQE system.

Beaulieu (1997) summarized the findings under three headings:

1. **Automatic versus interactive query expansion.**   In some information retrieval situations it is useful to offer a combination of both forms of query expansion. IQE can be effective in data-rich environments, and users must be presented with suitable expansion terms in a clear format.
2. **Explicit versus implicit use of the thesaurus.**   When modifying a query, thesaurus terms chosen explicitly by the user are particularly useful. However, implicit use of the thesaurus is also beneficial in query expansion.
3. **Document versus query space.**   Interaction on the ENQUIRE system is linked between viewing retrieved records and formulating the query. This allows the user to focus on the query and to make relevance judgements based upon both the documents retrieved and the thesaurus terms offered.

The Okapi experiments are ongoing and continue to lead research into the understanding of cognitive processes in information retrieval.

Chaining or citation growing

Citation growing uses a small set of records or just one record as a source for suitable search terms and the user then performs searches under these terms. Also known as chaining (Ellis, 1989), citation growing can take two forms:

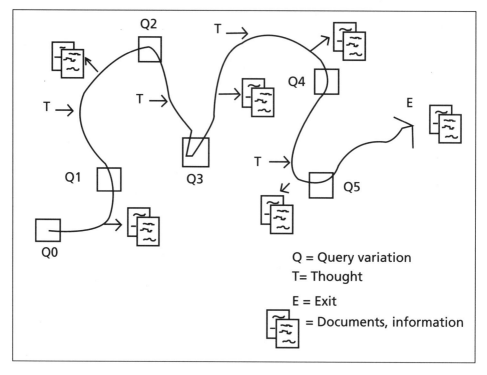

Source: Bates (1989)

Figure 4.6   **A berrypicking, evolving search**

1. Backward chaining allows the user to follow up references, citations and other useful notes from a relevant item. This method is traditionally used by academic researchers in all disciplines and is useful for collecting information quickly.
2. Forward chaining requires access to a citation index in order to find out who cited a relevant paper. This is a rather specialized method, but citation indexes are now available both on-line and on CD-ROM. We would expect forward chaining to be used more widely in the future.

An example of backward chaining would be a user searching for articles on the development of multimedia systems. Starting from a recent textbook on the subject, the user would then identify useful articles from the list of references. Forward chaining, on the other hand, would allow a user to take a seminal paper (for example, Carroll and Mack, 1985) and find out who had cited the author(s) in more recent writings, using a citation index.

Berrypicking

Bates (1989) uses an analogy of picking blueberries in the forest to describe a strategy for information seeking in on-line systems or OPACs. In the same way that berries are scattered on bushes and must be picked one at a time, so information is gathered by incrementally altering the search until the information needs are fulfilled.

The classic model of information retrieval (see Figure 4.3) is compared by Bates (1989) (Figure 4.6) to her proposed model in several ways:

- typical search queries are not static, but rather evolve;
- searchers commonly gather information in bits and pieces instead of in one grand best retrieved set;
- searchers use a wide variety of search techniques which extend beyond those commonly associated with bibliographical databases;
- searchers use a wide variety of sources other than bibliographical databases.

Solomon's study (1993) of the use of an OPAC by children identified search strategies which are similar to Bates's berrypicking model. Over a quarter of the children studied used reactive and exploratory strategies to search for information.

This model might be of value in today's networked information environment where users may search an OPAC, CD-ROMs, on-line databases and the Internet, from their desktop. Such users may be a student carrying out an academic assignment, or a doctor searching for the latest information on a drug treatment. The implementation of Z39.50 (Watson, 1996) will offer facilities which would support a berrypicking approach to information retrieval.

Hypertext

Hypertext requires search strategies with a very different approach, although some aspects of the berrypicking model (see above) may be useful in this context. Hypertext moves away from linear text and supports association between related concepts throughout a document. The essential components of a hypertext database are the items of information which are to be linked, and the links between those items. Hypermedia systems that integrate text, data, images and sound into a single database also have these two components. Shneiderman (1992, p. 412) lists a number of features which are important in developing hypertext searching techniques and these are summarized in Figure 4.7.

In order to develop a search strategy in a hypertext environment, a user must identify the methods of navigation through the system. Once an item

Content	Interaction
<ul><li>Nodes (text, graphics, video, sound)</li><li>Links (typed versus single type)</li><li>Formatting, margins, fonts, spacing</li><li>Screen resolution, size and colour</li><li>Window size and management</li></ul>	<ul><li>Selection mechanism (touch, mouse, keys)</li><li>Response time and display rate</li><li>Video and animation control panels</li><li>Invocation of external programs and databases</li></ul>
Navigation	**Recording**
<ul><li>Structure of graphics</li><li>Multiple tables of contents</li><li>Graphic versus tabular overviews</li><li>Indexing versus keyword search</li><li>Position and size indicators</li></ul>	<ul><li>Path history and bookmarks</li><li>Annotation</li><li>Exportation</li><li>Save status and search results</li></ul>

Figure 4.7   User interface features in a hypertext system

has been located by a keyword search, for instance, the user can then move to other items, records or documents by using the hyperlinks provided in the system. Research by Instone et al. (1992) showed that users of a hypertext encyclopaedia navigated initially by using the nodes and the hierarchical structure of the information, but later became less reliant on the hierarchy. Users should also be able to backtrack, to click on tables of contents or to see graphical representations of the database structure. A search for aspects of the Mayan civilization on a CD-ROM encyclopaedia could use the following hypertext links:

Central America: → Mexico: → Belize: → Guatemala: → Pre-Colombian history: → Post-Colombian history: → Astronomy: → Calendars: → Mathematics: → Religion: → Language: → Tourism: and so on.

Clear navigational links and nodes should be present within any hypermedia system so that users can identify the location of their search and not become lost in hyperspace.

Browsing as a search strategy

'Browsing is an important and integral part of the information-seeking activities' (Beheshti, 1992, p. 221). It is performed when the user has a less precise view of the information or documents that may be available and is not sure whether the requirements of the query can be met or precisely how they may be met. Browsing may be either general or purposive. Purposive browsing occurs when a user has a fairly specific requirement, whereas general browsing may be used as an opportunity to refine the user's perception of the query.

One user might retrieve a document as a result of a known-item search whereas another user might retrieve that same document as a result of general browsing. The public access information system must be able to support both types of user in their searches. One of the most significant challenges in the design of a public access information system is the need to be able to cater for different users with different requirements (Rowley, 1992). Browsing a museum or art gallery information system is a useful technique and can allow a user to see, for example, images of the museum's collection of Japanese artifacts or the art gallery's portrait collection.

Many users make subject requests in a general way, and with an OPAC it is possible for them to broaden or narrow the search as they require. Browsing offers a flexible approach to subject searching and many users prefer this method of searching – even when they have retrieved what appears to be a direct hit, users will still browse through the references around their original search term. Bates (1986) indicated that users prefer to browse for subject headings and variant terms and she suggested that an end-user thesaurus may be one method of assisting user navigation. The Council on Library Resources survey also noted the use of browsing, and 50 per cent of the survey's respondents 'answered that they had browsed randomly under a word they knew' (Markey, 1985, p. 39). Rice (1988) showed how browsing can produce what he called 'holism' (an appreciation of what the catalogue, as a whole, contains) and 'serendipity' (the unexpected discovery of a useful item) for users of OPACs. Other writers, however, have pointed out that it is difficult for the end-user to know what the catalogue contains, and are often not aware that potentially relevant material may have been missed in their search (Bates, 1986). Equally a number of information systems are limited to very specific areas, and users may find that their searches do not retrieve material which is outside the scope of the system.

Through the use of keywords and browsing strategies, what may appear to be a known-item search can develop into a subject search, with the user employing the known item as a lead into other authors or titles on the same or a related subject. This has been demonstrated by Hancock-Beaulieu (1989) in her work at City University, London, where users were not only intercepted at the catalogue, but were also followed to the shelves in order to achieve a clear picture of how their whole search proceeded. It has been shown that browsing the material by using class numbers, as if it were on the library shelf, is an effective search strategy (Beheshti, 1992). The cognitive user model for browsing in an OPAC or on-line information system therefore requires a spatial awareness on the part of the user. Perhaps the next development of a GUI OPAC will include simulated books and bookshelves.

> **Review and apply:**   Which search strategy matches your approach to searching for information?

Searching tasks within applications

This chapter has considered information seeking in public access systems mainly in the context of OPACs and other bibliographic databases. In OPACs, bibliographic CD-ROMs and on-line bibliographic databases the searching tasks carried out are related to known-item searching, subject searching and browsing. It is important that both the design and the evaluation of the user interface identifies methods of supporting these searching tasks and the strategies by which they are carried out (Bates, 1991).

CD-ROMs are available with a wide range of interface styles; in some cases the same database is available from different CD-ROM publishers with different interfaces and facilities. This can pose a problem to libraries providing access and training for these services. However, it does not appear to be too much of a problem for the end-users themselves. Ford et al. (1994) studied a group of searchers on a CD-ROM service and noted that there were correlations between users' cognitive styles and their searching strategies and that training should be matched to the preferred learning styles of the users.

End-user searches on on-line bibliographical databases were traditionally carried out by trained intermediaries and were normally used for subject searching and some known-item searching; the high cost of telecommunications ruled out any thought of browsing the databases. In a study of trained searchers, Saracevic and Kantor (1991) found that there was a wide difference in search strategies between the trained searchers and that systems designers must be aware of this, in order to maximize the effectiveness of the searching task. This is especially true because it appears that end-users with only minimal training will have even more disparate search strategies. As the cost of telecommunications falls and the number of end-users searching on-line databases grows, the design of public access systems must be made more efficient and effective for all types of user.

We will now consider the types of searching tasks used in other public access information systems. Multimedia kiosks and ATMs are used primarily for known-item searching. ATMs can be used for little more than interrogating the user's own bank account, except on those ATMs which are linked to a system which will give the user information about the bank's services. In the type of multimedia kiosk to be found in locations such as catalogue stores, the user can search for a known item. It is not normally possible, at present, to browse through the catalogue in a systematic way.

Types of hypertext-based public access products include (Furner and Willett, 1995):

- point-of-information (POI) systems (such as library tours or guides);
- OPACs with hypertext features;
- on-line databases with hypertext features;
- CD-ROM databases with hypertext features;
- wide area network retrieval systems with hypertext features, of which the World Wide Web is the best known;
- text retrieval packages with hypertext features.

The searching tasks performed on hypermedia systems are more related to browsing and exploratory searches. Known items may be looked for as a starting-point but then the user can develop the capabilities in hypertext to explore strands and layers of information (Grice and Ridgway, 1993).

Subject searching and browsing (or surfing, as it is known) on the Internet are the principal tasks on this huge network of networks. Different information retrieval engines on the World Wide Web provide access to information through many of the search facilities mentioned earlier in this chapter, such as Boolean operators and inverted indexes (Ellman and Tait, 1996). The Internet presents a significant challenge to information retrieval research and particularly to user modelling because both the information held on the Internet and the users who seek the information cover a very wide range of provision and experience.

Summary

The special category of task that is searching for information has required the development of appropriate searching facilities to be made available on public access information systems. Research into the theoretical perspectives of information retrieval is ongoing and will continue to contribute to the wide variety of both search strategies used and public access information systems encountered. Further research can lead not only to the enhancement of searching facilities on text-based information systems but also, and perhaps more importantly, to the development of graphical, image-based and multimedia public access information systems.

References

Bates, M. J. (1986), 'Subject access in online catalogs: a design model', *Journal of the American Society for Information Science*, **37** (6), 357–76.

Bates, M. J. (1989), 'The design of browsing and berrypicking techniques for the online search interface', *Online Review*, **13** (5), 407–24.

Bates, M. J. (1991), 'OPAC use and users: breaking out of the assumptions', in *Think Tank on the Present and Future of the Online Catalog: Proceedings* (RASD occasional papers: 9), ALA Midwinter Meeting, Chicago, 11–12 January (ed. N. van Pulis), RASD/ALA, pp. 49–58.

Beaulieu, M. (1997), 'Experiments on interfaces to support query expansion', *Journal of Documentation*, **53** (1), 8–19.

Beheshti, J. (1992), 'Browsing through public access catalogs', *Information Technology and Libraries*, **11** (3), 220–28.

Belkin, N. J. (1980), 'Anomalous states of knowledge as the basis for information retrieval', *Canadian Journal of Information Science*, **5**, 133–43.

Bills, L. G. and Helgerson, L. W. (1988), 'User interfaces for CD-ROM PACs', *Library Hi-tech*, **6** (2), 73–115.

Carroll, J. M. and Mack, R. L. (1985), 'Metaphor, computing systems, and active learning', *International Journal of Man–Machine Studies*, **22**, 39–57.

Cleverdon, C. W. (1967), 'The Cranfield tests of index language devices', *Aslib Proceedings*, **19**, 173–94.

Crawford, W. (1992), 'Starting over: current issues in online catalog user interface design', *Information Technology and Libraries*, **11** (1), 62–76.

Danilowicz, C. (1994), 'Modelling of user preferences and needs in Boolean retrieval systems', *Information Processing and Management*, **30** (3), 363–78.

Drabenstott, K. M. (1991), 'Online catalog user needs and behavior', in *Think Tank on the Present and Future of the Online Catalog: Proceedings* (RASD occasional papers: 9), ALA Midwinter Meeting, Chicago, 11–12 January (ed. N. van Pulis), RASD/ALA, pp. 59–83.

Dwyer, C. M., Gossen, E. A. and Martin, L. M. (1991), 'Known-item search failure in an OPAC', *Reference Quarterly*, **31** (2), 228–36.

Ellis, D. (1989), 'A behavioural approach to information retrieval system design', *Journal of Documentation*, **45** (3), 171–212.

Ellis, D. (1996), *Progress and Problems in Information Retrieval*, 2nd edn, Library Association Publishing, London.

Ellman, J. and Tait, J. (1996), 'INTERNET challenges for information retrieval', in *Proceedings of the 18th BCS IRSG Annual Colloquium on Information Retrieval Research*, 26–27 March, Manchester (ed. F. C. Johnson), British Computer Society Information Retrieval Specialist Group, Manchester, pp. 1–12.

Ensor, P. (1992), 'User practices in keyword and Boolean searching on an online public access catalog', *Information Technology and Libraries*, **11** (3), 210–19.

Fidel, R. (1990), 'Online searching styles', in *ASIS '90: Proceedings of the 53rd ASIS Annual Meeting*, Toronto, 4–8 November (ed. D. Henderson), Learned Information, Medford, NJ, pp. 98–103.

Ford, N., Wood, F. and Walsh, C. (1994), 'Cognitive styles and searching', *Online and CD-ROM Review*, **18** (2), 79–86.

Furner, J. and Willett, P. (1995), 'A survey of hypertext-based public-access point-of-information systems in UK libraries', *Journal of Information Science*, **21** (4), 243–55.

Grice, R. A. and Ridgway, L. S. (1993), 'Usability and hypermedia: toward a set of usability criteria and measures', *Technical Communications*, **40** (3), 429–37.

Hancock-Beaulieu, M. (1989), 'Online catalogues: a case for the user', in *The Online Catalogue: Developments and Directions* (ed. C. R. Hildreth), Library Association, London, pp. 25–46.

Instone, K., Leventhal, L. M., Teasley, B. M., Farhat, J. and Rohlman, D. S. (1992), 'What do I want? And how do I get there? Performance and navigation in information retrieval tasks with hypertext documents', in *East–West International Conference on Human–Computer Interaction*, St Petersburg, pp. 85–95.

Jones, S., Gatford, M., Do, T. and Walker, S. (1997), 'Transaction logging', *Journal of Documentation*, **53** (1), 35–50.

Markey, K. (1984), 'Offline and online user assistance for online catalog searchers', *Online*, **8** (3), 54–66.

Markey, K. (1985), 'Subject searching experiences and needs of online catalog users: implications for library classification', *Library Resources and Technical Services*, **29** (1), 34–51.

O'Brien, A. (1994), 'Online catalogs: enhancements and developments', in *Annual Review of Information Science and Technology*, *29* (ed. M. E. Williams), Learned Information, Medford, NJ, pp. 219–42.

Oddy, R. N. (1977), 'Information retrieval through man–machine dialogue', *Journal of Documentation*, **33**, 1–14.

Rice, J. (1988), 'Serendipity and holism: the beauty of OPACs', *Library Journal*, 138–41.

Robertson, S. E. and Beaulieu, M. (1997), 'Research and evaluation in information retrieval', *Journal of Documentation*, **53** (1), 51–7.

Rowley, J. E. (1992), *Organizing Knowledge*, 2nd edn, Ashgate, Aldershot.

Rowley, J. E. (1993), *Computers for Libraries*, 3rd edn, Library Association Publishing, London.

Saracevic, T. and Kantor, P. (1991), 'Online searching: still an imprecise art', *Library Journal*, 1 October, 47–51.

Shenouda, W. (1990), 'Online bibliographic searching: how end-users modify their search strategies', in *ASIS '90: Proceedings of the 53rd ASIS Annual Meeting*, Toronto, 4–8 November (ed. D. Henderson), Learned Information, Medford, NJ, pp. 117–28.

Shneiderman, B. (1992), *Designing the User Interface: Strategies for Effective Human–Computer Interaction*, 2nd edn, Addison-Wesley, Reading, MA.

Slack, F. E. (1991), 'OPACs: using enhanced transaction logs to achieve more effective online help facilities for subject searching', PhD thesis, Manchester Polytechnic, Manchester (unpublished).

Slack, F. E. (1996), 'End user searches and search path maps: a discussion', *Library Review*, **45** (2), 41–51.

Solomon, P. (1993), 'Children's information retrieval behavior: a case analysis of an OPAC', *Journal of the American Society for Information Science*, **44** (5), 245–64.

Su, L. T. (1994), 'The relevance of recall and precision in user evaluation', *Journal of the American Society for Information Science*, **45** (3), 207–17.

Svenonius, E. (1986), 'Unanswered questions in the design of controlled vocabularies', *Journal of the American Society for Information Science*, **37** (5), 331–40.

Thorne, R. G. (1955), 'The efficiency of subject catalogues and the cost of information searches', *Journal of Documentation*, **11**, 130–48.

Vickery, B. and Vickery, A. (1993), 'Online search interface design', *Journal of Documentation*, **49** (2), 103–87.

Walker, S. and Hancock-Beaulieu, M. (1991), *Okapi at City: an Evaluation Facility for Interactive IR* (British Library Research Report: 6056), British Library, London.

Watson, M. (1996), 'Improving user access to CD-ROM databases: technical issues', in *The End-user Revolution: CD-ROM, Internet and the Changing Role of the Information Professional* (ed. R. Biddiscombe), Library Association Publishing, London, pp. 64–78.

Yee, M. M. (1991), 'System design and cataloging meet the user: user interfaces to online public access catalogs', *Journal of the American Society for Information Science*, **42** (2), 78–98.

Chapter 5

Interaction styles

Interaction style is a generic term which includes all the ways in which users communicate or interact with computer systems.

By the end of this chapter, you will:

- be acquainted with the main interaction styles;
- understand some of the important aspects of design for each of these styles;
- appreciate how these styles can be used together, in particular in the graphical user interface (GUI) environment.

This chapter introduces the following interaction styles: command languages, menus, function keys, question and answer, form filling, GUIs and direct manipulation, natural languages and voice-based dialogues.

The following topics are also considered:

- displaying and entering data in interface design;
- effective messaging;
- colour in interface design.

In many public access systems graphical user interfaces (GUIs), and sometimes multimedia interfaces, are the norm. Kiosks often use simple multimedia interfaces which incorporate graphics and sound, although they may not offer direct manipulation, frequently because a mouse may not be sufficiently robust to survive in a public access environment. Increasing numbers of OPACs and CD-ROM interfaces are GUIs, and access to the Internet is increasingly through GUIs. Accordingly, this chapter has a significant focus on GUIs. Nevertheless, other interaction styles which were historically important are still evident in some systems, and form elements in GUIs.

Interfaces and interactions

Central to HCI design has been the style of the interaction, with the screen as the central output device, although users may input their responses through a variety of input devices, including a mouse, a touch screen and the keyboard. Furthermore, the categories of interaction style are not exclusive or mutually dependent. Advanced voice systems will offer a form of natural language interface, and icons are a different way of presenting menus. The designer must consider which combination of interface styles to use, and how to apply the components of that style in the design of an effective interface. These must be considered in the context of the user and the task that the user wishes to perform with the system. In public access applications, it is particularly important that the actions required of the user are self-evident, and that the user is able very quickly to locate any relevant instructions. Some systems, such as OPACs, need to accommodate both expert and/or frequent users and novice and/or occasional users. This is especially so where familiarity leads to more sophisticated system use. Interaction styles such as command languages, which require memory, may be appropriate. In many other cases priority needs to be accorded to interaction styles that are self-explanatory.

Command languages and form-filling interfaces were the basis for early interaction with computer systems. Command languages were appropriate for expert users, who often were accustomed to working with complex programming languages. Form-filling interaction was designed for clerical workers, to allow them to enter data in a way that appeared to be very similar to the manual task of form filling. Gradually, as the range of types of users and the tasks that they seek to complete has expanded, more supportive interaction styles have become necessary. Initially, this led to the development of menus and question and answer sequences. Subsequently, the recognition that users may seek to use systems for a variety of different purposes and have varying degrees of experience has led to systems that incorporate a wide range of interaction styles, such as those based on GUIs. Public access systems range from those where interface design can be relatively simple because the tasks to be completed are straightforward, to those where the user is seeking to search large full-text databases, where the searching task is complex and, for optimum performance, requires the user to perform a sequence of complex actions.

A number of the figures in this chapter offer a compilation of guidelines for good practice in relation to design that employs a specific interaction style or component. As with all HCI guidelines, these are based on a mixture of theory and practical experience. In common with all guidelines, they need to be applied with reference to the users, the task and the environment of a specific application. The guidelines offered in the figures should be viewed as generic, illustrating some of the issues that need to be addressed in an interface using the specific interaction style.

Command languages

Command languages are one of the oldest and most widely used inter-action styles. In dialogues based on commands the user enters instructions in the form of commands. The computer recognizes these commands and takes appropriate action. For example, if the user types in PRINT 1-2, the computer responds with a prompt to indicate that the command has been carried out or a message stating why the command cannot be executed. The command language for a given system is a feature of the software under which the system runs. There are command languages associated with operating systems, and with applications software. Most early sys-tems were based on command languages, and in the context of public access systems they were widely used in early OPACs and for over twenty years were virtually the only way of searching the databases mounted by the on-line hosts. It is perhaps ironic that in these systems the user instructed the computer, whereas in many more recent public access systems the computer instructs the user, via a prompt, such as Enter user name or PIN number!

The command language must include commands for all the functions that the user might choose to perform, and therefore, since different sys-tems perform different functions, it is inevitable that command languages will differ between systems. Some attempts have been made to adopt standard command languages for systems that perform similar functions, and one result of this is the Common Command Language used by some of the on-line hosts. However, standardization is difficult and an inherent feature of command-based dialogues is the need for users to become famil-iar with the command language used. An intermediate option which is widely used, and is suitable for users with some familiarity with the system, is the use of commands in menus, so that the menus prompt users in their use of commands. This is not, however, effective for novice users because they cannot be expected to know what the commands displayed on the menus mean.

Command languages are potentially the most powerful interface, but this brings the penalty of difficulty of learning. The user must learn both the actual commands and also their syntax, including the order in which commands must be written. The placing and choice of separators such as spaces, commas, semicolons and colons is often crucial to whether a sys-tem will accept and execute a command. For example, to display the author-inverted file around the author J Keen on DIALOG, the searcher needs to know that the correct syntax of the search statement is:

EXPAND AU=KEEN,J

The main advantages of command languages are the economy of screen space, the direct addressing of objects and functions by name, and the flexibility of system function which a combination of commands can provide.

All command languages have a word set, described as a **lexicon**, and rules that state how words may be combined, which is a **grammar**.

The lexicon needs words to identify objects and operations. Objects will be devices, such as files upon which the commands of the language operate. Objects will be described by nouns and operations by verbs. Both word sets need to be as meaningful as possible. Usually abbreviations will be available for commands. The norm is three-letter truncations, such as DIR for Directory and DIS for Display. Care needs to be exercised to ensure that each abbreviation is unique so that, for example, DIS is not used as an abbreviation for both Display and Disconnect.

The language syntax may be in the form of simple one-word keywords, or keywords where a qualifying argument or condition is added. The most sophisticated languages are grammar-based. Here a set of rules is introduced to formulate a set of phrases that can be divided by combinations of command words. The rules dictate which word types may occur in sequence within a command word string. Some grammatical command languages have the complexity of programming languages. They are powerful and flexible, but impose a considerable learning burden on the user.

Guidelines for designing a command language are shown in Figure 5.1.

Although menu-based interfaces and Internet-based GUIs are offered by many of the on-line hosts, command languages are still used extensively. These command languages have become increasingly complex as the range of facilities offered by the hosts has expanded. Some while ago, Negus (1979) identified the fourteen basic functions for which commands must be present in any on-line command language. These command functions are listed in Figure 5.2. They form the basis of the EURONET

- Create an explicit model of objects and actions
- Choose meaningful, specific and distinctive command names
- Provide a consistent language usage structure
- Be consistent with command words and abbreviations
- Minimize the use of punctuation and delimiters
- Entry should be flexible and forgiving. Double spaces between words should be ignored and mis-spellings corrected if possible
- Use natural and familiar command words and syntactic sequences, e.g. COPY from File A to File B
- Unnecessary complexity should be eliminated, and, in the first instance, this will be achieved by limiting the number of commands in the language
- It should be possible to edit the command string
- Offer frequent users the opportunity to create macros

Figure 5.1   Guidelines for command language design

CONNECT	to provide for logging on
BASE	to identify the database to be searched
FIND	to input a search term
DISPLAY	to display a list of alphabetically linked terms
RELATE	to display logically related terms
SHOW	to print references on screen
PRINT	to print references on-line
FORMAT	to specify the format to be displayed
DELETE	to delete search terms or print requests
SAVE	to save a search formulation for later use on the same or another database on the same system
OWN	to use a system's own command language when the standardized command language does not cater for a specific function
STOP	to end the session and log-off
MORE	to request the system to display more information, for instance, to continue the alphabetical display of terms
HELP	to obtain guidance when in difficulty

Figure 5.2   The command functions in the Common Command Language

Common Command Language which has been adopted by some hosts as an alternative to their own command language, in recognition of the benefits to users of some standardization in the command language.

Review and apply:	Why, despite the cognitive overheads associated with command languages, are command languages still used in public access systems?
Answer:	Command languages are useful in two contexts:
	• Command-based interactions. Command languages offer power and precision in search specification, in applications such as in searching full-text databases.
	• Commands in menus. Embedding the commands in menus acts as a reminder of the potential commands that can be selected.

Menus

Menus are an alternative to commands that avoid the problem of learning commands. Menus present the user with a number of alternatives or, otherwise, a menu on the screen, and ask them to select one option in order to change the state of the interface. The menu options are usually displayed as commands, which are particularly appropriate for more experienced users, or as short explanatory pieces of text. Pictures, or icons, may also be used to represent the menu options. The appropriate option is selected by keying in a code (often a number or letter) for that option, or by pointing to the required option with a mouse or other pointing device. Menus are generally recognized to be a sound approach for the occasional or novice user. Additional help is rarely necessary, and little data entry is required of the user. In creating the menus the system designer has restricted the total set of options, and thus the novice user has less potential for mistakes. Equally users not familiar with the terminology of the interface can be assisted since the menus restrict the choice set. If menus are appropriately structured, and the items selected carefully, menus can be quick and easy to use, often requiring only one or two key presses or mouse clicks to complete a selection. Also, since any input must be one of the options offered, menu-based systems are easy to program.

Menus can be frustrating and confining to more experienced users, if they are constrained to work through them in a linear sequence. However, clicking on a menu option can be much faster than having to type a command or file name, especially if the user cannot recall the precise form of the file name (Shneiderman, 1986). Menu-based interfaces must be closely defined with the user in mind. This involves careful consideration of menu structure, key presses required and menu bypass techniques. For example, expert users should have the option of accessing a specific screen or making a selection without necessarily passing through all previous menu selections.

The first rule of good menu design is to include only those options that are necessary, and therefore the designer's first task is to identify which options must be included in a menu. Where there are many possible options and displaying them all might be difficult, then menus are sometimes organized hierarchically in tree-like structures. In other words, a menu might not only contain options, but also routes to other menus. Figure 5.3 shows two menus that follow one from another. Where there are a number of menus each with a different set of options, a user needs to know where to look for the desired option. This can be facilitated by organizing the options within a specific menu. Alternatives for ordering options include: alphabetical, categorical, frequency of use, or order of use. For example, the pull-down file menu on the windows interface is ordered according to the sequence in which a user might be expected to perform the operations (Figure 5.4).

The sequencing of menus also needs to be considered. There are two basic options:

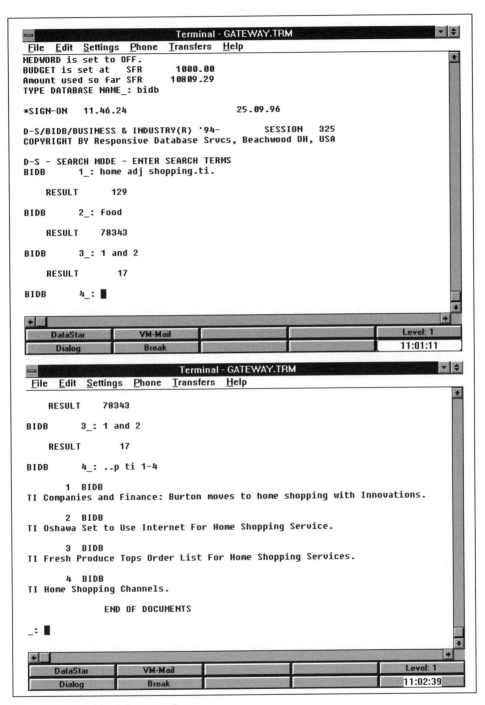

Source: Knight-Ridder Information Inc.

Figure 5.3   Two menus that follow one from another

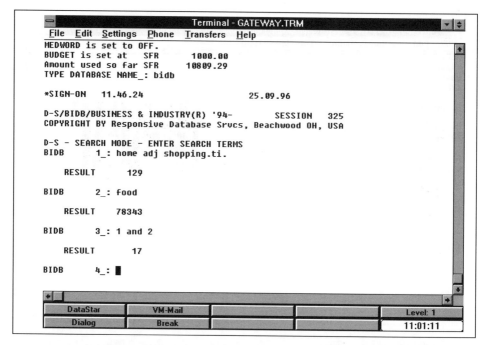

Figure 5.4   **A pull-down file menu**

- A linear sequence of menus is appropriate where the interface is designed to guide the user through a sequence of actions, as in Wizards in Windows applications or in some multimedia kiosks where the user is taken through a sequence such as item selection, ordering and payment.
- A tree structure of menus, where there is a wider variety of possible routes that specific users may choose to take through the tree.

Although menus can be very useful in retrieval, they do have some limitations. These include:

- Menus are not suitable for inputting data such as numbers or text, although they may provide an access route to forms where such operations can take place.
- A lot of information is presented in the menu, and this information takes time to read.
- Only a limited number of options may be presented on one menu and in order to offer a large number of options it is necessary to design a hierarchy of menus.
- Once a hierarchy of menus and submenus is included, it is important to give the user the menus to keep track of where they are, and to be able to trace a path through the hierarchy.

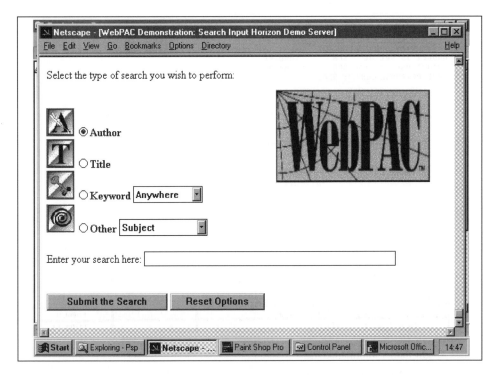

Source: Dynix Library Services (UK) Ltd

Figure 5.5   Menu from an Internet application

A disadvantage of early menu-based systems was that significant parts of the screen were occupied by menus, thus restricting the space available for the work area. This is still the case with many of the menus displayed on Internet applications (see Figure 5.5).

Today's interfaces use a number of different types of menus, often in combination. Commonly encountered menu types include:

- **Single option menus**, often used to request a confirmation of a response offered by a user.
- **Pop-up menus** pop up or appear, often in the centre of the screen, and request a response or a selection.
- **Pull-down menus** are often attached to a main menu across the top of the screen. When a user clicks on a menu option on the main menu bar, a further menu appears showing a number of options.
- **Step-down menus** or submenus are a series of menus. So, for example, a user may click on an option on the main menu bar at the top of the screen to display a pull-down menu. Options on this menu that will lead to the display of further menus may be indicated, for example, with three dots: PRINT... . Clicking on these options leads to a further

1. Select an appropriate menu type
2. Group logically related options together either as menu blocks or in separate menu screens
3. Order menu options by the usual criteria, such as operational sequence, frequency of use, importance
4. Use consistent grammar, layout and terminology
5. Make options brief, and begin with a keyword
6. Indicate the reply expected and associate it with the option
7. Title the menu according to its function
8. Give the user feedback about menu levels, and errors
9. Provide escape routes and bypasses, so that users can pass from one option to another without going up and down the hierarchy; in particular, users must be able to jump to previous and main menus
10. Avoid lengthy and convoluted menu structures in which the user can get lost or have difficulty in identifying where the required command is located. As the depth of a menu hierarchy increases, users have more difficulty with navigation
11. Avoid lengthy menus with too many options – the optimal number of items in a menu is in the range 4 to 8. A long menu is difficult to scan, but can be made easier to scan by positioning menu options according to their frequency of use, so that normally the user does not scan the complete menu. Also, scanning can be facilitated by grouping options into categories
12. Separate potentially contradictory options such as 'Save' and 'Delete'
13. Scrolling can on occasions be used to display a long list of options, such as an extract from an index file
14. An active menu or command is one that can be selected based on the current context of the system. Menus that are active usually appear in dark type on a white background, whilst inactive menus or commands are greyed out. Only active menus are selectable. This signals that the command is appropriate in a given context. Using active/inactive menus and commands helps the user to focus on what is appropriate and reduces the available choices
15. Avoid overlapping options and ambiguous option labels. The choice of a name for an option on a menu label can be difficult. The designer has to resolve the conflicting demands of clarity and brevity. The longer the description, the easier it is for the novice to follow, but the less easy it is to scan and the more space it occupies on the screen. Most designers opt for one-, two- or three-word descriptions

Figure 5.6   Guidelines for menu design

menu. This is known as a step-down menu. These menus can be particularly helpful when there is a series of actions to perform, since they can remind the user of the sequence in which these actions must be completed.

- **Main menu bars** appear at the top or bottom of the screen and remain on the screen while the user performs other functions and displays other menus. They may have pull-down menus attached as indicated above or may simply display some common menu options such as Help, Save and Exit.

Figure 5.6 offers some guidelines for menu design.

Use	To meet these needs	With these cautions
Permanent menus	Standard set of commands for use throughout systems modules System-wide navigation is easier Enable movement from one module to the next	Careful selection and labelling is required Placement on the screen must be prominent May require more than icons Requires thorough analysis of all commands the user needs to access
Single menu	Confirmation to an action is needed Response is binary (Y/N) All responses can be anticipated in advance	Requires well-stated prompt or question Requires list of possible responses Too many single menus together become tedious
Multiple choice menus	User needs only to select one item from a list Reduces demands on memory by enabling user to recognize, not recall, a response Reduces need for type-in, thus reducing errors	Requires that list of items from which to select is accurate and complete Choices should be at same level If list is too long, user cannot view and compare all options May require scrolling May require other option if desired item is not in list
Pop-up menus	Immediate user recognition or response is needed Task is well understood Messaging	Consistent position required to enhance recognition Contents are limited User should be able to scan and react quickly Must be limited set of options for response
Pull-down menus	Organizing hierarchically related parent/child commands Displaying subselections in logical fashion Reduces number of commands scanned at any one level	Organization must be logical Terms selected are critical to recognition and appropriate selection

Figure 5.7   General guidelines for the use of menu types

Review and apply: Use the guidelines in Figure 5.7 to compare the menus on two interfaces that are easily available to you.

Answer: The answer will depend upon the interfaces examined. Comments might relate to:

- menu type
- menu title
- menu terms or commands
- user feedback in respect of errors
- clarity and absence of movement between menus
- absence of ambiguity and length of menus
- use of scrolling
- active/inactive menu options.

Function keys

A set of function keys is a hardware equivalent of a menu with options allocated to special keys on the keyboard. Function keys might cover options such as copy, insert, delete, help, display record, and call menu.

Hard-coded function keys have an operation permanently allocated to a particular key, and are located accordingly. With soft coded keys the command call is allocated to the function key by the application program. Most keyboards have ten to twelve function keys; accordingly, the number of options that can be covered by these keys is extremely limited. Specially designed function keys have been extensively used in OPACs, with, for example, keys for 'Author' search and 'Next' screen.

Question and answer

The user of a question and answer dialogue is guided through the interaction by questions or prompts on the screen. The user responds to these by entering data through the keyboard. Often questions may require only a simple 'yes' or 'no' response, but on other occasions the user may be required to supply some data, such as a code, a password, their name or other textual data. Usually, however, one-word responses are expected. On receiving the user's response, the system will evaluate it and act accordingly. This may involve the display of data, additional questions or the execution of a task such as saving a file. The prompt information can easily be tailored to the requirements of the user, and this dialogue style

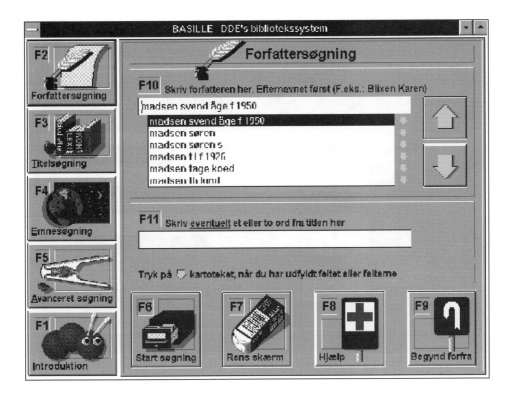

Source: Dansk Data Elektronik A/S

Figure 5.8   On-screen questionnaire

may therefore suit novice and casual users. The main drawback of this dialogue mode is that since an input data item must be validated at each step before continuing with the dialogue, the interaction can be slow. Rudimentary question and answer dialogues operated in command line systems where the system displayed some text, which the user then responded to by entering additional text. A variant on question and answer dialogue is widely used in a simple form in GUIs where a question might be posed in a dialogue box and the user is expected to respond by clicking the 'Yes' or 'No' button. On-screen questionnaires, as shown in Figure 5.8, may also be used; here users are asked to click on one of a number of options, using radio buttons.

Form filling

In a form-filling interaction the user works with a screen-based image of a form. The screen form will have labels, and space into which data are to be

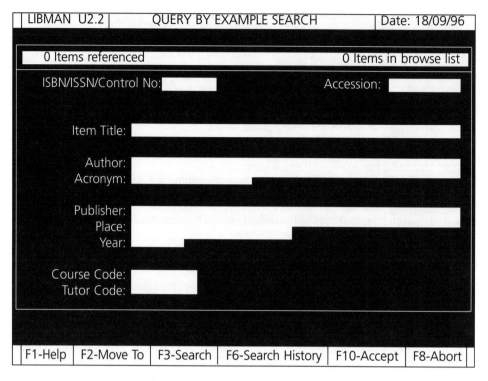

| LIBMAN U2.2 | QUERY BY EXAMPLE SEARCH | Date: 18/09/96 |

Source: Amtek Computer Systems Ltd

Figure 5.9   Query by example interface

entered. It should be possible to move a cursor to any appropriate position on the form for the entering of data. Labels will normally be protected from amendment or overwriting and some users may be able to amend only certain fields; other fields are protected. Form filling is a useful dialogue for inputting records and blocks of data. In searching it is used in query by example interfaces (see Figure 5.9). The screen form may be a duplicate of a paper form from which data are subscribed. All data input should be validated and errors reported to the user. Form filling, because it may involve large amounts of data entry, can take a lot of user's time and can be a source of frustration and errors. It is therefore important that the guidelines for form filling outlined in Figure 5.10, expanded from those of Smith and Mosier (1984), be noted.

In form-filling dialogues the user has little control over the dialogue, but the approach has the advantage that the user rarely needs to remember commands or their syntax.

In conventional form filling the user moves through the boxes, entering data in each in turn. In some applications, however, this process is assisted by coupling form filling with a question and answer dialogue.

1. Use a meaningful form title
2. Group and sequence field in a logical order
3. Seek a visually appealing layout
4. Use familiar field labels, and maintain consistency in terms and abbreviation use
5. Include visible space and boundaries for data entry fields
6. Attend to convenient cursor movement
7. Offer error correction for individual characters and entire fields
8. Offer error messages for unacceptable values
9. Mark optional fields clearly
10. Be consistent with data entry formats. For example, all date formats on all screens should be consistent with one another
11. Keep actions required by the user to a minimum. The designer needs to walk through each possible transaction
12. Facilitate user control of data entry when appropriate. Although consistency between screens should be the default option, the user should have the opportunity to modify the default when appropriate
13. Eliminate redundant data entry. The user should not be required to enter any given piece of data more than once
14. Provide useful, readable instructions and prompts
15. Manage operator overload by minimizing the amount of data, such as required formats, that the user must remember

Figure 5.10   Guidelines for form-filling design

Here the computer creates the form as it records responses to a question and answer dialogue. For example, in a kitchen design system, components may be gradually added to the CAD display and position on the plan of the kitchen. As this process evolves, the system creates an order form showing all the items that have been added to the plan. This form is then displayed on the screen so that the customer can check the order before it is actioned.

Graphical user interfaces and direct manipulation

The idea of direct manipulation is that the user's actions should directly affect what happens on the screen, in the sense that there is a feeling of physically manipulating objects on the screen. Typically, direct manipulation systems have icons representing objects which can be moved around the screen and manipulated by controlling a cursor with a mouse. For example, a file is moved by clicking on an icon representing the file and dragging it to a new location.

A graphical user interface or GUI is not the same as a direct manipulation interface; strictly it means an interface that uses bitmapped displays rather than character displays. Often the two terms are used interchangeably, although it is possible to have a GUI which does not use direct manipulation, and some of the more straightforward public access interfaces that are based primarily on touch screens are GUIs without direct manipulation.

Direct manipulation interfaces, led by Apple Macintosh, have become very widespread. Shneiderman (1982) identifies the following positive features of direct manipulation systems:

- Novices can learn basic functionality quickly (so that they can get started easily and learn more functionality as they work).
- Experienced users can work extremely rapidly to carry out a wide range of tasks.
- Users can see immediately if their actions are moving towards their goals and take corrective action if necessary.
- Users experience less anxiety because the system is comprehensible and actions are reversible.
- Users gain confidence and mastery because they initiate an action and can predict system responses.

Studies of direct manipulation interfaces have confirmed the advantages for at least some users and some tasks (for example, Margano and Shneiderman, 1987; Temple, Barker and Sloane Inc., 1990). GUIs are regarded as particularly useful when the user population is expected to contain a high proportion of novices or, alternatively, where the user population contains a mixture of novices and more experienced users.

The GUI is also tightly constrained. The user has only a limited number of objects on which a specified set of actions can be performed. When compared with natural languages interfaces, where users may make a wide range of errors ranging from spelling and grammatical errors to errors in the actual tasks to be completed, the interface designer is in a much stronger position to predict and cater for any errors that the user might make.

Some concepts in direct manipulation

In an attempt to analyse the nature of the interaction in direct manipulation a number of concepts have been proposed that might inform design. We first introduce two types of directness: semantic directness and articulatory directness:

Semantic directness concerns the relation between what the user wants to express and the meaning of the expressions available at the interface. In a search system, this concept would be concerned with how close the match is between the user's search formulation and the way that it can be expressed in the interface.

Articulatory directness concerns the relation between the meaning of expressions and their physical form. Thus, moving a slide down a slide bar should scroll down a document, and not across or up a document!

Four other concepts that are important in direct manipulation interface design are:

Affordances (Norman, 1992, p. 19), which is a 'technical term that refers to the properties of objects – what sorts of operations and manipulations can be done to a particular object'. So, for example, a word-processed file can be saved, deleted or opened, but not sorted. Systems objects ideally have a match between their perceived affordance and actual affordance.

Constraints limit the number of possibilities of what can be done with an object. For example, it is not culturally acceptable to draw a waste paper bin on its side.

Mappings are concerned with the match between the spatial and conceptual relations between parts of the system. Mapping should appear intuitive and natural to users.

Feedback is defined by Norman (1988, p. 27) as 'sending back to the user information about what action has actually been done and what result has been accomplished'.

Two other general guidelines for GUI design are:

- The look and feel of the interface must be consistent, so that on the basis of the user's experience with one screen or dialogue box, they should have some sense of how to interact with the next screen or control.
- Keyboard support must be available for all the functions that can be performed with a mouse.

Review and apply:	Is direct manipulation a relevant concept in the context of touch screen interfaces?
Answer:	In one sense touch screens offer the ultimate in direct manipulation, because the user touches the object on which they wish to perform an operation. However, few touch screen interfaces offer the opportunity to move objects on the screen, and the characteristic drag and drop of direct manipulation interfaces is rarely a feature of touch screen interfaces.

Components of GUIs

Interface design in windows and other GUI-based environments is determined by the standard components of the GUI. These components are used to design the software in its native state and in the design of any interfaces in applications based on the software. The standard GUI components are: windows, dialogue boxes, menus and commands, buttons and check boxes, icons and toolbars.

Windows

A window is a rectangular area on the screen in which an application or document can be viewed. Most windows can be opened, closed, moved and sized. Several windows can be opened simultaneously and most windows can be reduced to an icon, or enlarged to fill the entire desktop. Typically the view of their contents can be changed using scrolling or editing. Most windowing systems provide standard windows with a border area for controlling the window itself, and a content area to allow the user to interact with the contents. The content area typically handles both input and output between user and application program. Most windows have a title bar at the top or bottom. Sometimes windows are displayed within other windows.

There are two types of windows: tiled and overlapping. Tiled windows are where the screen is divided up in a regular manner into subscreens with no overlap. Overlapping windows can be nested on top of one another. Windows have a number of uses and allow screen areas to be separated for error messages, control menus, working area and help.

Tasks in windowing systems

Although there are variations between systems, most windowing systems incorporate facilities for managing input, changing window focus, managing single windows and managing multiple windows:

Managing input. Input to windowing systems is usually through the keyboard and mouse. Mice have one, two or three buttons, and there are typically five actions that can be carried out with any mouse button: point, click, press, drag and double click. The variety and convenience of tasks that can be carried out with a mouse can be extended by use of modifier keys, such as SHIFT and CTRL. Consistency of the operations required to carry out activities is important to avoid user confusion with respect to mouse actions.

Changing window focus. There must be some system for the user to direct input to any desired window, and to change the focus.

Managing single windows includes:

- moving – windows can usually be moved by selecting the title bar area and dragging;
- scrolling – to show information that cannot be displayed in one window. Typically scroll arrows are clicked on to scroll the windows in either direction;
- sizing – using maximize buttons and sizing controls, which the user can drag with the mouse, and thereby shrink or expand the window in the direction of drag.

Managing multiple windows. It is necessary to support users in operating with a number of open windows. This is achieved through iconification, which shrinks the windows down to a window icon, tiling of windows and overlapping of windows. Overlapping is the most popular and is very flexible, although it can lead to clutter and disorganization. There are various options relating to how windows should be sized and placed when they are opened.

Guidelines on window design are offered in Figure 5.11.

Dialogue boxes

Dialogue boxes are a type of on-screen control that the system displays to provide contextual information. They take the form of a special window that appears temporarily to request information. Many dialogue boxes contain options that the user selects to tell the software to execute a command. A dialogue box requests information from the user. For example, the user may need to select certain options, type some text or specify settings. Dialogue boxes may ask the user to:

- make a related set of choices;
- type in some information;
- choose from a set of options;
- acknowledge a piece of information before proceeding.

Menus

Most GUIs have a main menu bar at the top or bottom of the screen. Pull-down menus are normally attached to this bar. In addition pop-up menus may appear at a click for the selection of a button or option, anywhere on the screen. Some menus are not complete in themselves, but lead to

- Every window should have a name on its title bar
- Numeric labels added to window titles can help to track the order in which windows were opened
- Users need to know how to open, close, move, recess and scroll through windows and to have control over these activities
- Windows should appear in a consistent format. For example, one standard is to begin the display of the first window in the upper left area of the screen, and then to open the next window slightly down and to the right of the first, with the next window appearing staggered further down and to the right
- Develop and adhere to a set of guidelines concerning when to use windows and how they should be used
- Develop and adhere to a set of guidelines concerning what windows should look like, including features such as where the tile text is placed, the typeface, style and size of text used for the title, and colour use on the title and scroll bars and window frames
- Consider restricting the number of windows that need to be displayed at any one time to complete a task
- Windows should have default positions where they appear on the screen when first opened. However, the default position may determine the type of window and the relationship between the new window and existing windows

Figure 5.11   Guidelines on window design

subsequent interaction via a dialogue box. Menus may be displayed as a list of options, where the user clicks on an option, or with accompanying radio buttons or check boxes.

Cursors

Windowing systems usually have at least a text cursor and a mouse cursor. The mouse cursor shows where the current position of the pointer is; the cursor may adopt different shapes to indicate the current status of the system. Windows that handle text usually also have a text cursor which indicates where text input will be inserted.

Controls

Controls are objects that appear on a screen display in a GUI. They include sliders, buttons, check boxes, labels and text boxes. Windowing systems provide standard controls for operations such as moving, resizing and scrolling. Control panels typically consist of a collection of controls and displays that show the user the state of some object of interest and allow various parameters to be altered. It is important to choose appropriate controls for the task and to maintain consistency in the behaviour and placement of controls. Below we describe some specific controls.

Buttons and check boxes

Buttons and check boxes are similar in that the user clicks on them to select an option or to choose a command.

There are two types of button, command buttons and option buttons. Command buttons allow the user to choose a command, such as Save or Help. Command buttons appear as images of keys. Command buttons displayed with ..., such as Set-up, will display a further dialogue box when clicked. Option or radio buttons are usually shown as small circles. When clicked and selected the circle is filled with a smaller filled-in circle.

Review and apply:	What is the difference between: • a window and a dialogue box? • a check box and a radio button?
Answer:	Check boxes are shown as small boxes. When selected, the box is filled with an X and clicking on the box turns the option on or off. Often a series of check boxes may be shown in the dialogue box to allow the user to set a number of options or settings.

Icons

Icons are graphical representations of system objects, applications tools, utilities and commands. Icons are increasingly being used at the interface, because it is assumed that they can make a system easier to learn and use. An icon can be chosen by double clicking on it. For example, the Main window in Windows shows the main applications that are included in Windows, such as File Manager, Control Panel, Print Manager, Clipboard Viewer, MS-DOS Prompt, Windows Set-up, PIF Editor and Read Me. Group icons represent other groups of icons.

A user when faced with a new icon will attempt to interpret it using their previous experience (Carroll and Thomas, 1982). Another way of expressing this is to say that the GUI must be based upon an effective metaphor. Two interesting examples of the use of metaphors in public access systems are the use of flags to differentiate between different languages in a multilingual interface and the use of bitmaps of Visa and MasterCard logos on buttons that identify how a user might pay. However, not all users interpret an icon in the same way, and a person's knowledge and background play a significant role in how they perceive the metaphor that is presented. The metaphor selected must, then, take account of the users who will work with the system, their backgrounds and training, their level of expertise in the domain and the tasks that they need to accomplish. Once an appropriate metaphor has been selected, designers must select or design icons that:

- fit the metaphor;
- represent the task appropriately; and
- make sense to the user.

It is not always easy to find an appropriate icon to represent a command or action, and this is a particular challenge with abstract concepts. In addition it can be difficult to create icons that differentiate between similar concepts in a meaningful way.

Meaningfulness of icons is determined by the context in which the icon is being used, the task that is being performed, the form of representation and the nature of the underlying concept that the icon is seeking to represent.

There are three representational forms used in icons:

- concrete objects, such as files, floppy disks, country flags, books and scissors;
- abstract symbols, such as arrows, circles, dots and lines; and
- a combination of the two above.

In general the icons that are the most meaningful are those that use a combined form of representation, provided the users are familiar with the conventions depicted by the abstract symbols (Rogers, 1989).

Concrete objects such as files and folders are the easiest underlying concepts for which to create an icon; icons can be drawn so that they have a physical resemblance to the actual object. For more abstract concepts, such as warning signs, it is more difficult to design icons that have such a mapping, and representation is by indirect analogy, which means that in most cases the icons have to be learnt by the user. Indeed, as McGraw (1992) observes, Xerox, when labelling their copiers, are now beginning to recognize that an icon accompanied by a brief label is more helpful than a graphic representation alone. Textual labels or commands are becoming increasingly common, either as permanent labels or as word balloons that appear when the cursor is moved over an icon. Combining text with icons reduces the likelihood of the meaning of icons being confused. However, it is important to remember that such words fix the application in one language and sacrifice the multilingual potential of icons.

Colour is widely used in icon design; Mohan and Byrne (1995) remind us, however, that although most users prefer colour icons, icons that depend on colour can cause difficulty for those who are colour-blind, or when used on monochrome screens. Also colours convey different meanings in different countries. Colours may be used to establish hierarchies and apparent dimension in and among icons.

Guidelines for icon design are offered in Figure 5.12.

- Aim for simplicity. The simpler the icon, the easier it is to recognize
- Present a common frame, shape and size for all icons and, in general, aim for consistency in the graphic elements of icons within a system
- Use the same types of iconic graphics throughout a system, e.g. abstract or literal (pictorial)
- Consistency, so that the same icon is used in different but linked applications
- Choose a common background colour, which is the same colour as the GUI, unless contrast is especially necessary. Grey is becoming the *de facto* standard
- Choose colours that will map on to grey scales
- Work with no more than 16 colours
- Choose a dominant colour; the best colours are greens, dark blues and similar dominant colours

Figure 5.12   Guidelines for icon design

A further issue associated with the use of icons is how they are selected and placed on the screen. There are three issues: size, grouping and placement.

- **Size.** Does size have any meaning? Is a larger icon used for more frequently selected commands? How large does an icon need to be to be 'legible'? To what extent should icon size be determined by the screen space available?
- **Grouping.** Which icons should be placed next to each other? This depends on the most common task completion sequence.
- **Placement.** Where on the screen should icons be placed? This depends on the function of the icons. An important consideration is consistency. If icons appear on a series of screens they should remain in the same place on all screens. If one icon is used more frequently than another, that icon should be in the most visible, easily accessible location in the grouping.

Toolbars

Icons are assembled into toolbars, usually positioned horizontally across the top of the window. Some toolbars can be moved to a vertical position on the left or right of the window. Another alternative is the floating toolbar; these can be reduced from long horizontal boxes to smaller rectangles that the user can move freely about the window. Toolbar guidelines are included in Figure 5.13.

- Only the most frequently used menu options should be put on toolbar icons
- Only button-press or toggle-switch operation should be placed on toolbars
- Toolbars should not exceed the length of a typical window
- Icon order is important, and icons that appear on more than one toolbar should always appear in the same position
- Commonly used icons should be grouped on the left-hand side of the toolbar
- Functional groups (for example, copy, cut and paste) should be displayed together
- The colour of the toolbar should blend with the rest of the window. Grey is a good colour, because it neutralizes the toolbar backgrounds and blends with icons with a grey background

Figure 5.13   Guidelines on toolbar design

Natural language dialogues

Natural language dialogues allow the user to communicate in their native language, such as English, usually through a keyboard. The system needs to be able both to interpret inputs in natural language from the user, and to act upon them. In addition, it should preferably be able to generate natural language statements in response to user input. In order to achieve such a dialogue the system must include both language (at least English, preferably multilingual) understanding and generation capabilities. In addition, for the novice user such interfaces need to be able to accommodate spelling variants and mistakes, and keying errors. In general, natural language interfaces cannot yet be designed so that they can interpret every request correctly, but they can be used effectively in more structured environments where the set of all terminology, usage, phraseology and common requests is known or limited. Natural language interfaces have been used in various information retrieval applications, where searching is based on the entry of keywords or a natural language phrase. The system then has algorithms for breaking down that phrase into component search terms, performing a search, and providing feedback to the user on the set of retrieved documents.

The use of natural language in public access information systems depends primarily upon natural language understanding rather than natural language generation. Natural language generation is more difficult than the former, as the computer must be able to decide when to say something, as well as what to say and how to construct the selected ideas into phrases or words that the user understands. However, there are still a number of difficulties in generating interfaces with natural language understanding. These include:

- **Ambiguity.** Humans can afford to be ambiguous because they use different forms of communication such as actions, body language and pronoun antecedent relationships to assist in communication.

- **Context.** Words have multiple meanings depending upon their position in the sentence or the context of the communication.
- **Imprecision.** There are a number of words that are used in natural language, such as 'average', 'lots', 'few' and 'many', which are imprecise, and difficult for the system to translate into a specific number or range of numbers.

Natural language interfaces are generally regarded as being helpful to naive users in that they can approach the system with no knowledge of the system, the contents of the database or the retrieval strategies that the system will employ. More experienced users may find natural language interfaces frustrating in that they may wish to specify the range of retrieval facilities that are used in a search. For example, they may wish to specify whether truncation is used. The use of a command language may lend greater precision.

Experience with the use of natural language interfaces has shown that users have a number of difficulties with which the system must deal. These are:

- Users may have difficulty in framing their hypothesis or question as a query statement, even with a natural language interface.
- Users can have difficulty in choosing which words to select in framing their query statement.
- The operators AND and OR, whether they are used implicitly or explicitly, confuse users. They may believe that a query using AND will return more data, not less.
- Users too often use misspellings and incorrect syntax. Incorrect keying is also more likely, the longer the text to be keyed.
- Expert users use more complex phrases and clauses.

Designers of natural language interfaces need to be aware of all the potential problems listed above and need to seek strategies to minimize them. These include:

- Knowledge acquisition sessions with users which identify the vocabulary, abbreviations and syntax that users normally use.
- Planning for prompts, alerts and error messages that guide users as they work with the system.
- Considering techniques that support the reformulation and refinement of the query. The system compares query content and keyword attributes with what is stored in a database. It presents close matches for clarification and feedback. When the query is correct, it is executed. This approach improves the likelihood that the results meet the search goal.

Searching text databases is a significant application for natural language approaches. Considerable work has been conducted on aspects of best match searching, or nearest neighbour searching, or ranked output searching which uses statistical information concerning the frequency of occurrence of terms in records as the primary input to the retrieval algorithms. A best match search is based on the matching of a set of query words extracted from the natural language question statement against the set of words associated with each document in the database. A measure of similarity between the query and each document is calculated, and then the documents are sorted in order of decreasing similarity to the query. A typical measure of similarity is the number of terms in common between the query and a given document. The output from the system is a ranked list in which those documents having most terms in common with the query are at the top; these documents should have the highest probability of being relevant (Rowley, 1992; Salton and McGill, 1983).

Another approach in text retrieval that allows users to make use of natural language is where knowledge-based techniques have led to the creation of intelligent front ends. Such front ends typically support natural language search question formulation and modification (for example, Fox, 1987). A review of some of these approaches is available in Ashford and Willett (1989).

Voice-based dialogues

All the dialogues considered so far are concerned with screen-based communication, with the aid of keyboards, mice, touch screens and similar devices. There are many circumstances in which a voice-based dialogue would be most convenient for the user. Such dialogues would be attractive to the occasional user inputting only 'yes' and 'no' and other one-word answers and also to the user inputting large quantities of textual data. Voice-based dialogues might be voice-to-voice (that is, computer and person talk to each other), screen-to-voice (that is, computer talks, person operates keyboard).

With voice-to-voice dialogues communication may be remote from a workstation, through a telephone receiver and telecommunications link. All these modes may have their applications, and the dialogue modes outlined above (for example, menu, command, form filling) might be employed in a voice-based dialogue. Although there are some applications of such systems, they are limited by current technology for public access use and further development is to be expected.

Voice in the form of recorded instructions is used to direct the user through the sequence of tasks or menus being prompted by the screen display in some public access kiosks. This is especially relevant to users with special needs.

Review and apply:	Why is it important that voice instructions on public access kiosks can be disabled?
Answer:	Voice instructions can be irritating to both the user and other passing customers or members of the public. Some users may find them an unnecessary distraction from reading instructions and prompts offered on the screen. Accordingly, the option of turning off the voice output is valuable.

Combining user interface design styles

A system must be designed to:

- encompass all the tasks that need to be accomplished with the system;
- be used by different types of users;
- suit the environment;
- be appropriate for the technology.

Some public access systems, such as CD-ROM and on-line information retrieval from external hosts, via the Internet, may in some applications be effectively 'stand-alone' in that the only tasks to be performed by users are retrieval-oriented tasks. Other information retrieval systems, most notably OPACs, may be part of a larger system. A consistent interface design approach must be adopted across all the components of the system. A library management system, for example, needs to support the routine operations associated with the issue and return of books, as well as data inputting in relation to catalogue and borrower records, and information retrieval in the OPAC. GUIs are now commonplace. These incorporate a number of the interface styles that were previously viewed as alternatives, such as commands and menus.

In summary, Figure 5.14 reviews some of the advantages and disadvantages of different interface design styles or components.

Displaying and entering information

Displaying and entering information on the screen is the basic component of the most commonly encountered interface component, the screen. We have just reviewed the options for interface styles. Most of these styles involve the display or entry of data or both. This section briefly reviews some of the key issues for displaying and entering data on the screen, such as screen density and design and ease of data entry.

Style/component	Advantages	Disadvantages
Menus	Easy to learn. Easy to use. Easy to program. Suitable for novice users in access to system options	Slow to use in large systems. Limited choice per menu. Can be irritating to experienced users
Icons	Very easy to learn. Easy to use. Language-independent. Relatively easy to program. Suitable for novice users in system access and command interfaces	Not economic in use of screen space. Needs some text back-up
Question and answer	Easy to use. Easy to learn. Easy to program	Unsophisticated. Slow to use
Form filling	Quick to use. Easy to use. Easy to learn. Suitable for all user types, data entry, display and retrieval interfaces	Form only suitable for data entry. Unsophisticated
Command languages	Quick to use. Sophisticated. Suitable for expert users with complicated requirements	Difficult to learn. Difficult for novices to use. Difficult to program
Natural language	Natural communication. No learning required. Suitable for novice users in a restricted problem domain	Difficult to program. Needs knowledge base. Verbose input. Can be ambiguous

Figure 5.14   Interface design styles/components

It is important to recognize that when a user views a screen they are handling a number of tasks that make it more difficult for them to deal with attention, comprehension and memory. Users undertake the following tasks all at the same time:

- Recalling relevant material from long-term memory
- Forming and clarifying follow-up questions about misunderstandings
- Deciding what is important on the screen
- Recognizing words on the screen and retrieving their meanings
- Parsing the phrases in which the words appear
- Organizing ideas presented on the screen
- Integrating ideas with prior knowledge
- Determining what to do next.

In order to help them to cope with all these tasks simultaneously, people use a number of techniques. The structure of the display can help to prompt selection attention and indicate what the user should view next.

Hierarchical organization also makes it easier for the user to discover which are the more important parts of the screen.

Typography can be used to attract attention in most interface styles. Typical typographical devices include italic type, boldface type, colour, arrows and boxes. Legibility and readability are the two key variables that must be considered in selecting type.

Legibility is the ease with which one letter can be distinguished from another in a particular typeface (International Typeface Corporation, 1988). Designers do not have much control over legibility and can do no more than choose a type font that is legible. Readability is the degree of ease with which the viewer can read the text on a screen (International Typeface Corporation, 1988). Although it begins with the legibility of the type, it goes beyond this and addresses the user's ability to extract information from the text. The ease with which this can be achieved depends on:

- type size and style;
- amount of type on a line;
- grouping of type on a screen;
- manipulation of the space between letters and between lines.

Screen density is a measure of the amount of information displayed on a single frame or screen. Density can refer to both overall density and local density. Overall density is the total amount of screen display, measured, say, by how many pixels are used. Local density is a measure of the closeness of the packing of the items within the displays.

It is well established that high information density causes overload (Stewart, 1979), and that performance, measured in terms of the number of errors and the amount of time required to locate a target, deteriorates with increasing display density (Treisman, 1982; Callahan et al., 1988). Maximum desired density is generally regarded to be in the range 25 per cent to 31 per cent, although there is some debate about how such density can be measured.

It is generally recognized that space should be left between items on a display. The purpose of these open spaces is to:

- provide structure (Cakir et al., 1980);
- navigate the screen (Jones, 1978); or
- emphasize and maintain the logical sequencing or structure (Stewart, 1979).

Unfortunately there are no definite guidelines for optimal local density. Different researchers have measured different elements including line spacing, character separation, group separation and background dots.

Formatted screens, which display data in sections, can be created by grouping items. Groups help to organize information and grouping similar items in a display format improves their readability and highlights relationships between different groups (Bailey, 1985; Cakir et al., 1980; Galitz, 1980).

If several items are to be displayed on a screen in groups, this provides some structure to the screen but does not altogether eliminate layout complexity. The display format of a screen should minimize layout complexity and maximize visual predictability. The following general guidelines are useful:

- Use tabular formats of alphanumeric data. Tables provide a structured format that reduces density and makes the information in the table columns and rows easier to scan and process.
- Use vertically aligned lists with left justification to increase scanning speed.
- Align numeric data on the decimal point.

To return to the issue of space, white space or planned space on a screen can be important in helping users to focus attention. There are three primary reasons for using white space:

- to set off important items to enhance recall;
- to set off chunks of information from the remainder;
- to aid in the interpretation of complex tables, figures or graphics.

Effective messaging

The major type of system-to-user communication is data display in response to requests from the user. This includes the display of tabular data, graphics and other data. In addition to this display of data, the system may also need to communicate directions, alerts or error messages.

Directions to the user may be active or passive. A passive direction means that the action is inferred and that the user does not need to do anything specific. Passive directions are implied by the use of active and inactive windows, and active and inactive commands. Active directions require action by the user, and often appear in the form of screen prompts. Prompts tell users what to do next.

Alert and error messages offer guidance. (For their design, see Figure 5.15.) Typically they are used to indicate that the user has:

- requested an inappropriate action, given the current system context;
- selected a command that cannot be processed correctly owing to system problems;
- selected an action that may have far-reaching effects, such as overwriting existing files or losing data compiled to date;
- seemingly forgotten an important step in a sequence.

- Prompts must appear in a position that makes them instantly recognizable, such as in the centre of the screen
- Visual format and placement should be consistent
- Prompts should be specific in indicating what the problem is and what the user should do next
- Prompts should adhere to consistent and accurate use of terminology, grammatical form and abbreviations
- It should be easy for the user to respond to the prompt, probably via a response button. Such buttons should be carefully selected so that the user can predict what will happen next if they select one of the buttons
- Prompts must use terminology that the user understands, and should adopt a positive tone (that is, avoid condemnations)

Figure 5.15   Tips for alert and error message design

These messages require some type of response. Systems also offer messaging in the form of on-line help. We consider this issue more fully in the chapter on help systems (Chapter 8).

Colour in dialogue design

Colour screen displays are becoming the norm, and software developers make extensive use of colour in screen displays. Applications developers often have the opportunity to set colours in an appropriate manner for their specific application. A basic use of colour is in the background and the text on the screen. Many applications also make extensive use of colour in status bars, menus, icons and other areas of the screen. Colour can be an effective mechanism for communicating alerts, drawing attention and defining relationships. In a number of database displays colour is used to draw attention to specific parts of records. In general colour can be used to:

- draw attention to warnings;
- improve legibility and reduce eyestrain;
- highlight different parts of the screen display, such as status bars and menus;
- group elements in menus or status bars together, so that, for instance, an instruction is associated with the number of its function key.

Nevertheless, colour must be used with care and with an understanding of how potential users see colour differences and obtain information from them. Shneiderman (1986) states that colour can improve performance in the following kinds of tasks:

- a recall task, in which the user must retrieve something from memory;

- a search and locate task, in which the user must scan the screen to locate specific information;
- a retention task; and
- a decision judgement task.

Colour used inappropriately can be distracting, confusing or objectionable, and may lead to **colour pollution**, in which garish or clashing colours result in an interface which is difficult to read and uncomfortable to look at.

Colour offers considerable scope for enhancing screen design, but does demand that the designer exercise some design talents. When designing screen interfaces that make use of colour, designers should bear in mind that it may also be necessary for the interfaces to display effectively on a monochrome monitor. Although increasingly office monitors are colour, there remains older hardware in most organizations that includes monochrome monitors, and, if the system is likely to be accessed through a notebook computer, many of these still have monochrome monitors. Introducing colour at the final design stage also encourages its more effective functional use. Designers should consider the use of colour after they have selected a screen grid, determined the interface style and laid out the elements of the interface.

Colour has three qualities:

- wavelength, which determines the basic colour;
- saturation, or the amount of white mixed with a colour;
- brightness, or hue, the measure of colour luminance.

Issues in determining the effectiveness of colour in cognitive tasks can be grouped under:

Segmentation. Dividing a display into separate regions is very helpful in detection and search tasks. In particular, areas that need to be seen as belonging together should have the same colour.

Amount of colour. Too many colours in a display will increase search times, so colour should always be used conservatively.

Task demands. Colour is most powerful for search tasks and of less use in tasks requiring categorization and memorization of objects.

Experience of user. Colour, compared with monochrome, is of more benefit in search tasks for inexperienced users, rather than experienced users.

In addition, there are some generally accepted pragmatic guidelines which are recognized by many designers. These are summarized in Figure 5.16.

It is also important to note that colours have different qualities of subjective brightness and that colour affects shape resolution. Good pairings of screen backgrounds and foregrounds are suggested in Figure 5.17.

- Design the interface first, and then use colour to make already understandable displays even more effective
- Limit the number of colours in one display to a maximum of five or six (although some would prefer not to exceed three or four colours in a display – Shneiderman, 1986)
- Display unhighlighted information in low saturation, low hue or pale colours
- To show status, use: red = danger/stop; green = normal/proceed; and yellow = caution
- To draw attention, white, yellow and red are the most effective
- To order data, follow the spectrum
- To separate data, choose colours from different parts of the spectrum
- To group data, choose colours which are close neighbours in the spectrum
- Select colours in pairs for foreground and background colours. Background colour is the primary colour used for the display screen itself. Foreground colour is the primary colour used for the display of information against the background. Colours should be selected to give high contrast. Figure 5.17 shows some of the colours which form good pairings. The human eye is not equally efficient at extracting data from all colour pairings (Pace, 1984)
- Use colours consistently across all screens in the interface
- Choose colours carefully so that regardless of slight variations in hues that may exist between different monitors it is possible to interpret the meaning of the colour and differentiate one colour from another
- Take into account how the system will be used. Some colour combinations are less acceptable to users involved in use of the system for long periods of time
- Colour may mean that the designer needs to use a larger font, which takes up more screen space, to achieve the necessary contrast between background and foreground colours
- Remember that the use of colour involves more design time, and requires thorough testing to ensure that colours are meaningful to users.

Figure 5.16   **Guidelines on the use of colour**

Background	Foreground (text)
White	Bright true blue
Off-white	Black
Off-white	Navy blue
Light grey	Black
Black	White
Blue	White

Figure 5.17   **Good pairings of screen backgrounds and foregrounds**

Summary

A wide range of interaction styles is available in public access information systems. The main elements of these styles reflect the appropriate designs required for the variety of user interfaces. Data display, system messaging and the use of colour will continue to be developed and the importance of GUI design in public access systems has led to a number of research projects. As the availability of public access systems increases, the number of users grows and the range of information presented to the public is enhanced, the importance of the user interface and user interaction styles must be recognized in the design and evaluation of public access systems.

References

Ashford, J. and Willett, P. (1989), *Text Retrieval and Document Databases*, Chartwell Bratt, Bromley.

Bailey, P. (1985), 'Speech communication: the problems and some solutions', in *Fundamentals of the Human–Computer Interaction* (ed. A. F. Monk), Academic Press, London.

Cakir, A., Hart, D. J. and Stewart, T. F. M. (1980), *The VDT Manual*, Wiley, New York.

Callahan, D., Hopkins, M., Weiser, M. and Shneiderman, B. (1988), 'An empirical comparison of pie versus linear menus', in *Proceedings CHI '88 Human Factors in Computer Systems*, ACM, New York, pp. 95–100.

Carroll, J. M. and Thomas, J. C. (1982), 'Metaphor and the cognitive representation of computer systems', *IEEE Transactions on Systems, Man, and Cybernetics*, SMC, **12** (2), 107–16.

Fox, E. A. (1987), 'Developments of the CODER system: a testbed for artificial intelligence methods in information retrieval', *Information Processing and Management*, **23**, 341–55.

Galitz, W. O. (1980), *Human Factors in Office Automation*, Life Office Management Association, Atlanta, GA.

International Typeface Corporation (1988), *The ITC Typeface Collection*, ITC, New York.

Jones, P. F. (1978), 'Four principles of man–computer dialog', *IEEE Transactions on Professional Communication*, **PC21**, 4 December, 154–59.

Margano, S. and Shneiderman, B. (1987), 'A study of file manipulation by novices using commands versus direct manipulation', Twenty-sixth Annual Technical Symposium, ACM, Washington, DC, June, 154–9.

McGraw, C. L. (1992), *Designing and Evaluating User Interfaces for Knowledge Based Systems*, Ellis Horwood, New York/London.

Mohan, L. and Byrne, J. (1995), 'Designing intuitive icons and toolbars', *UNIX Review*, September, pp. 49–54.

Negus, A.E. (1979), 'Development of the EURONET DIANE Common Command Language', in *Proceedings of the 3rd International On-line Information Meeting*, London, 4–6 December, Learned Information, Oxford.

Norman, D. A. (1988), *The Psychology of Everyday Things*, Basic Books, New York.

Norman, D. A. (1992), *Turn Signals are the Facial Expressions of Automobiles*, Addison-Wesley, Reading, MA.

Pace, B. J. (1984), 'Colour combinations and contrast reversals on visual display units', *Proceedings of the Human Factors Society Twenty-Eighth Annual Meeting*, Santa Monica, CA, pp. 326–30.

Rogers, Y. (1989), 'Icon design for the user interface', *International Review of Ergonomics*, **2**, 129–54.

Rowley, J. (1992), *Organizing Knowledge: an Introduction to Information Retrieval*, 2nd edn, Ashgate, Aldershot.

Salton, G. and McGill, M. J. (1983), *An Introduction to Modern Information Retrieval*, McGraw-Hill, New York.

Shneiderman, B. (1982), 'The future of interaction systems and the emergence of direct manipulation', *Behaviour and Information Technology*, **1**, 237–56.

Shneiderman, B. (1986), *Designing the User Interface: Strategies for Effective Human–Computer Interaction*, Addison-Wesley, Reading, MA.

Smith, S. L. and Mosier, J. N. (1984), *Guidelines for Designing User Interface Software*, Report ESD-TR-86-278, The Mitre Corporation, Bedford, MA.

Stewart, T. F. M. (1979), 'Displays and the software interface', *Applied Ergonomics*, **7**, 137–46.

Temple, Barker and Sloane Inc. (1990), 'The benefits of the graphical user interface', *Multimedia Review*, Winter, 10–17.

Treisman, A. (1982), 'Perceptual grouping and attention in visual search for features and for objects', *Journal of Experimental Psychology: Human Perception and Performance*, **8** (2), 194–214.

Chapter 6

Managing the creation of interfaces: information systems methodologies

The analysis, design and implementation of information systems in general, and the human–computer interaction more specifically, need to be managed if the system is to meet user requirements, be completed on time and within budget. Information systems methodologies comprise a series of stages, tools and methods that aid systematic information systems planning. Since the interface is an integral component of an information system it is useful to be acquainted with some of these methodologies. In this chapter we focus on those methodologies that are most appropriate in supporting the user-centred approach to analysis and design that is a prerequisite of interface design. As a precursor to the introduction of specific methodologies, key concepts relating to systems and the systems lifecycle are introduced.

By the end of this chapter, you will:

- appreciate the importance of systems concepts to interface design;
- be able to identify the place of interface design in the systems lifecycle;
- understand the values of an information systems methodology and its relevance to interface design;
- be aware of the stages and essential features of some key user-centred information systems methodologies;
- have considered some of the issues associated with the emerging methodologies to support design in object-oriented GUI and multimedia environments;
- be aware of the relevance of strategic information systems planning to public access systems.

Systems concept

What is a system? And why are systems concepts useful? The word system

123

is used to describe a set of components working together to achieve a common purpose. Society, organizations and nature abound with systems. Your body has a nervous system and a digestive system. Society organizes legal systems, political systems, educational systems and tax systems. Organizations have appraisal systems, information systems, production systems and service systems. A systems perspective of an information system aids in understanding of the whole system and its environment. It encourages an understanding of the system as a whole, giving a systems or holistic perspective.

Systems are made up of components known as elements and subsystems. Elements for the particular view being taken of the system need not be broken down into smaller components. Sometimes it is more appropriate to describe components as subsystems, which recognizes that the subsystems are systems in their own right, but systems whose function is defined by the overall system of which they are part.

Defining systems and subsystems implies that certain things are part of the system and others are not. A boundary can be drawn to identify which components are in the system and which are outside it. The concept of a system boundary is very important. For example, Figure 6.1 is two simple systems maps showing two different views of a computer system. One includes the user within the system boundary and therefore as part of the system, whilst the other excludes the user.

The environment of a system comprises all the entities outside the system boundary which influence directly or indirectly the activities in which the system is engaged. In Chapter 3 we have already drawn attention to the importance of the environment on the system design and performance.

One of the most valuable contributions of these basic concepts from systems theory is the opportunity that they offer to use a systems diagram, possibly in the form of a systems map, as shown in Figure 6.1, to record

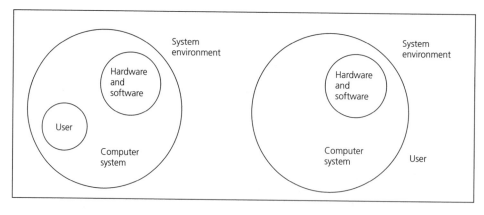

Figure 6.1   Two systems maps

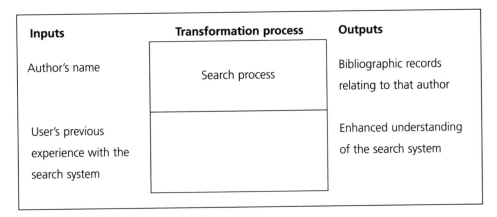

Figure 6.2   An input–output diagram for an author search in an OPAC

and share perceptions of the system amongst a group of people. Designers, evaluators and users may have different perspectives on where to draw the system boundary and how to resolve the system into its subsystems. Successful systems development depends on the identification of a shared perspective.

Review and apply:	Which of the two models in Figure 6.1 is most appropriate from the perspective of the interface designers?
Answer:	The one that includes the user since it acknowledges that a system is socio-technical and not just technical, and that a system must include the people who work with it.

Another useful concept from systems theory is the control system, with its feedback loop. We use this concept to start to explore the relationship between design and evaluation. A system can be represented as an input–output diagram, with inputs, a transformation process and outputs. Figure 6.2 shows a simple input–output diagram for a search for books by a specific author in an OPAC.

Analysing inputs and outputs can be a valuable way of identifying the key functions of a system. A feedback and control system also includes a feedback loop which feeds back a measurement of the output to control an input. Control is an action which a system or subsystem applies to its own activities in order to reach or maintain a desired state. Figure 6.3 shows the design and evaluation process for HCI as a feedback and control system. To explain Figure 6.3 more fully:

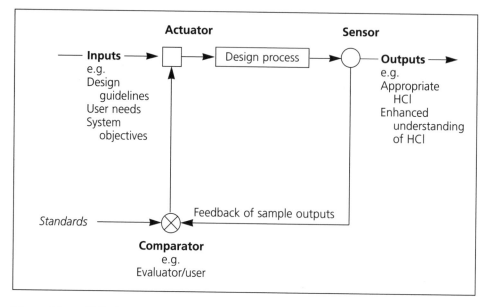

Figure 6.3   HCI design and evaluation as a control system

- Inputs, in the form of, for example, design guidelines, user requirements and system objectives are fed into the design process.
- The main output from the process is an appropriate HCI, but by-products of that process will include an enhanced level of HCI design skills for the designer, and a better understanding of the needs of systems users.
- The comparator, in this case the evaluator or user, will then test aspects of HCI design using, as appropriate, guidelines and standards, and feed these back into the next stage of the design process.
- Guidelines and standards should be the same in both the design and evaluation process.

An important message emerges from this diagram:

> **The inputs to the design process, in terms of user requirements, design guidelines and system objectives must be used in the evaluation process as metrics.**

However, as will be very evident in the later chapter on evaluation (Chapter 9), a simple mechanistic approach to evaluation is not sufficient, and user involvement in evaluation is critical. This is because the initial system inputs are based on an imperfect understanding of proposed system characteristics. Both the designers' and users' understanding of the requirements improve as the process continues. This is a result of the fact that any system that is under design is new and unknown and has associated uncertainty.

Finally, it is important to remember the danger of treating systems in isolation. At any one time an individual or an organization may be involved in several systems projects or be a user of a number of different systems. Some of these may be public access systems, whilst others will support the operation of the organization. Organizations, for example, need to operate and manage a range of information systems, including a personnel record system, production control system, a financial system and a marketing information system. Each of these systems is likely to be at a different stage in its lifecycle.

Review and apply: List all the systems of which you are a component.

Answer: This depends on the reader's role, and in what sense we define an individual as an element of, or a subsystem within, a wider system. Typically you are likely to be a user of information systems and be recorded as an entity in systems such as library record systems, financial and banking systems; you may access electronic documents, and create such documents using word-processing and spreadsheet software. You are probably also a member of other systems that seek to achieve their own objectives, such as the politico-legal system, the social system and the tax system. Note that all these systems have environments and boundaries.

The system lifecycle

Whilst the control and feedback system model in Figure 6.3 demonstrated the relationship between design and evaluation, these two activities need to be placed in the context of a wider system lifecycle. A system lifecycle is a summary of the main stages in the life of a system. Early systems methodologies, in an attempt to impose order on chaos and to get software projects to completion on time and within budget, viewed this lifecycle as having a number of discrete stages, each of which could be signed off and completed before the next stage was started. There is now widespread recognition that the development process needs to be iterative, particularly with the introduction of tools that accommodate the iterative process more readily, such as those associated with prototyping and object-oriented design. These allow greater user involvement in analysis and

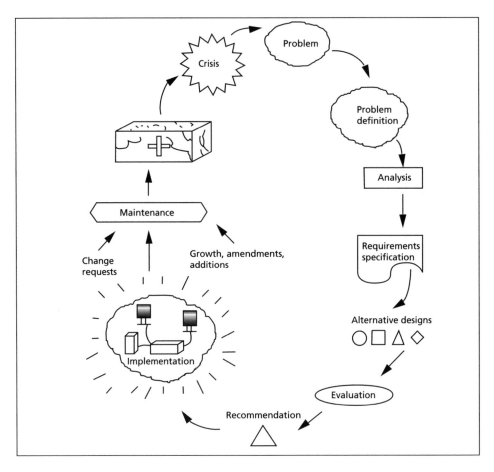

Figure 6.4   A rich picture of the system lifecycle

design and erode the boundary between the different stages in the life-cycle. Nevertheless, it is still important to recognize the stages in the life-cycle, and several different models are available. Preece et al. (1994), adapting Hix and Harston (1993), uses the star lifecycle (see Figure 6.10) which emphasizes the central role of evaluation in all stages in the life-cycle. Boehm (1988) proposes the 'spiral model of the software process'. This model still uses the main processes of systems development – require-ments gathering and design and implementation – but recognizes that several iterations are required. We propose a simple model (Figure 6.4) that embodies all the stages of the system lifecycle, yet recognizes the central role of evaluation and the iterative nature of this process. This model is used to guide the structure of those chapters in this book that are concerned with design and evaluation.

The model attempts to recognize the complexity of the system lifecycle, whilst avoiding excessive complexities that would cloud the message. Although this model is intended to reflect the lifecycle for the system as a whole, including the interface design, there are a few specific comments that should be noted in relation to public access systems:

1. Interface analysis, design and implementation is embedded in all stages of this lifecycle, and may be closely interlinked with other aspects of systems design, such as evaluation.

2. The training of users takes place after changeover (during implementation) and is embedded in their use of the system. In most instances training is achieved through help systems or other design features embedded in the interface and is context-sensitive in that training is given in the context of specific actions that the user is seeking to perform.

3. It may or may not be possible to distinguish the stages of logical, physical systems design and coding, depending on the tools available. Indeed, with some prototyping approaches, analysis and design may be closely interlinked. However, in contrast to some systems intended for a limited audience, there will be a distinct divide between design and implementation.

4. Only during the managing systems evolution phase will problems associated with the mass use of the system become apparent. This phase is likely to lead to a number of smaller projects to enhance or upgrade aspects of the original implemented design, which can be viewed as projects in their own right. This perspective is consistent with the concept of evolving information systems, and recognizes that at any given time different subsystems may be at different stages in their lifecycle.

5. In the design of public access systems, users are likely to be remote, and communication with users during design or analysis will often be with an alpha or beta test group of users or professional reviewers, acting as representatives of the wider user group.

6. Evaluation during implementation may embrace both the interface design and its effectiveness in a given location or application, as well as evaluation of the commercial or marketplace viability of the total system.

7. Design methodologies for some public access tools such as CD-ROMs and OPACs may be applied twice, once by the original supplier, and again later by the purchasing organization, acting as an intermediary for the end-user.

Review and apply:	What kinds of problems might become evident with mass use of a system, that might have been difficult to predict during design?
Answer:	• Too much complexity.
	• Ambiguous instructions.
	• Absence of necessary recovery routes.
	• Demand for actions that the system does not support.

Information systems methodologies

An information systems methodology is a methodological approach to information systems planning, analysis, design and sometimes implementation. Methodologies were introduced to support the efficient and effective completion of software projects.

The adoption of a systematic approach to information systems development offers a number of advantages. Broadly the advantages for the manager include:

- control over planning, since progress can be charted, and financial allocations can be predicted;
- standardized documentation which assists in communication throughout the systems planning and lifecycle;
- continuity provided as a contingency against key members of staff leaving the systems staff.

As far as those who are responsible for the system are concerned, a formal methodology encourages completeness. The need to produce formal written documentation encourages more careful consideration of each issue, which is more likely to lead to well-founded recommendations and conclusions.

An information systems methodology may be used in:

- the replacement of a manual system with a computer-based system;
- a changeover from one computer system to another computer-based system;
- modifications, upgrades and extensions to existing computer-based systems.

Most projects are concerned with the last of these. In this context the methodology may be used either:

- to aid in the choice and implementation of a commercially available system; or

- to aid in the design and implementation of a new, specifically tailored system.

For some systems, the path from conception to implementation and evaluation may involve several applications of methodologies. For example, a library management systems supplier will use a methodology in the creation phase of the OPAC product. Once that product is available to customers, libraries will undertake a further project which may lead to the implementation of that OPAC in a specific library and for a specific group of users. Two distinct projects are evident in this process, with distinct objectives; it would be appropriate to use a systems methodology in both these contexts.

Also, many organizations may conduct several systems projects, or parts thereof, at different points in time, and in relation to different areas of activity. Obviously, a relatively all-embracing analysis of the organization's operations helps the entire range of operations to be viewed as a whole, and increases the likelihood of the various subsystems which perform different functions being compatible with one another. Choice, design and implementation of a system are always time-consuming, and time must be allocated for these activities, even if the system being implemented is relatively modest.

Approaches to systems analysis and design have been divided into two categories: hard and soft. Typically, hard approaches seek to develop a technical solution to problems through the implementation of an information system. They assume the possibility of a clear and agreed statement of both the current situation and its problems, and of the desired state of affairs to be achieved. The problem for systems development is then seen as that of designing a solution that will take us from where we are now to where we want to be. Users are viewed as sources of information about the system, and are viewed in terms of their information requirements, and as devices for data input. The role of the analyst is that of the expert who is responsible for the design of the system.

Soft approaches recognize the impact of human beings within the area of systems analysis and design. First, these methodologies deny the premise that it is easy to specify current and desired solutions, and assert that problem situations are messy. Second, the role of the analyst is more as a participant in a team, and the role of the participants in the existing system is integral to successful system development.

In general, the interface designer will have a specific perspective on these methodologies. For example, Figure 6.5 demonstrates how elements of interface design are integrated into SSADM (structured systems analysis and design method) version 4, a well-established structured systems methodology.

Many of the traditional hard systems methodologies did not start from a user perspective; rather they focused on functional and technical aspects

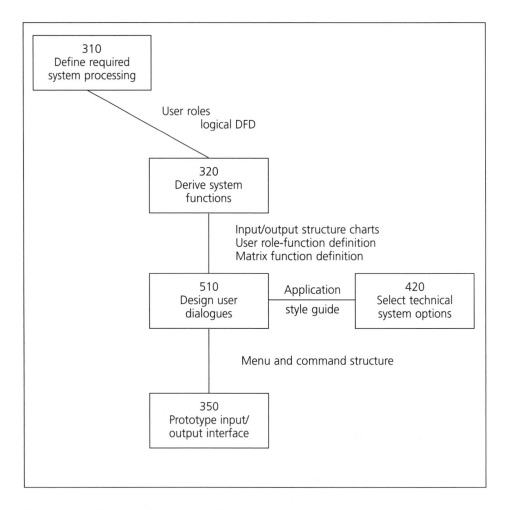

Figure 6.5   Interface design in SSADM version 4

of the system. Early systems were limited in the extent to which they could meet the needs of the user and were not user-focused. This means that these methodologies do not have a very evident focus on interface design. User-centred methodologies, commencing with some of the general approaches identified in soft systems methodologies, and progressing to some specialist HCI methodologies, are most appropriate for the user-centred focus that is implicit in HCI, and particularly important for public access interfaces. In addition, emergent methodologies that specifically accommodate analysis, design and implementation in object-oriented, GUI and multimedia environments are important.

There is no one methodology that will serve design in every environment and a systems designer needs to be aware of the range of options. Some the more significant methodologies that the interface designer is likely to encounter are reviewed below. A brief overview of hard methodologies is provided because the total design project, of which interface design is a part, may be contextualized in one of these. In addition, these methodologies have generated some of the tools for data and task analysis and design that are described in Chapter 7. Different methodologies have strengths focusing on different elements of the design process. Organizations often work with one or a limited number of these methodologies, and adapt them to suit their local context, or specific projects.

Review and apply: Why is an information systems methodology useful in an interface design project?

Answer: The methodology lends *communication* and *control*:

- *Communication* between team members, users, developers and managers.
- *Control*, so that it is possible to plan the project and measure progress against that plan.

Hard systems methodologies and structured systems analysis and design method (SSADM)

In order to illustrate the nature of structured methodologies in more detail we describe in outline the stages of one methodology. SSADM is probably the most widely used information systems method in the United Kingdom because it has been adopted by the UK Government. It was originally developed by Learmonth and Burchett Management Systems for the Central Computer and Telecommunications Agency (CCTA). SSADM is a data-driven methodology which places emphasis on data modelling, but also advises analysis and specification of process views with data flow diagrams, and behaviour using entity life histories (see Chapter 7). SSADM is structured in three phases: feasibility study, systems analysis and systems design. The first phase, feasibility study, may not be necessary for small projects. Each of these three phases is subdivided into a number of stages, which in turn are subdivided into a number of steps. SSADM comprises eight stages, 50 steps and about 230 tasks. The eight stages are, in outline:

1. *Problem definition*   The aim of this stage is to obtain a precise defini-

tion of the overall problem or resolution by the system to be developed. Overviews are created of the present systems and data structure, and current problems are identified.

2. *Project identification*   This stage aims to create a number of options for dealing with the problems identified in the first stage. The options are evaluated and formalized for inclusion in the feasibility report.
3. *Analysis of present system and problems*   This stage analyses the existing system and documents in the form of data flow diagrams and logical data structures. In addition, the identification of the problems is refined from the second stage.
4. *Specification of requirements*   In this stage the user requirements determined in the previous stage are defined more closely. A data structure is defined based on the logical systems description created in the third stage. Audit, security and control aspects are defined. The output is the systems specification.
5. *Selection from physical options*   This stage involves the users and system staff in selecting a suitable physical system. In most cases it is possible to decide on the hardware configuration and on the characteristics of the appropriate software.
6. *Data design*   Data structures for the proposed system are designed by combining the top–down view of the organization derived from the third stage with the bottom–up view of data groupings.
7. *Process design*   This stage is carried out in conjunction with the data design stage. The logical processing associated with enquiries and updating is defined. The logical design is then validated by means of a quality assurance review before proceeding to the physical design.
8. *Physical design*   The logical design is translated into programs and the database content. The data dictionary is updated and the design tuned to meet performance objectives. Programs and systems are tested. Operating instructions are created. The implementation plan is drawn up and the manual procedures defined.

Review and apply: In hard systems methodologies the user's role is to specify requirements. In which stages in an SSADM-structured project might this occur?

Answer: A number of the stages involve the user in requirement specification including stages 1, 2, 3 and 4. Later stages are not inherently user-centred.

User-centred design methodologies

A central aspect of user-centred design is the involvement of users or, in the case of public access databases, representatives of users, throughout the design process. In this section four user-centred methodologies are introduced: soft systems methodology, MultiView, effective technical and human implementation of computer systems (ETHICS) and open systems task analysis (OSTA).

Soft system methodology (SSM)

Soft approaches recognize the impact of human beings within the area of systems analysis and design. They are based on the premise that it is difficult to specify current and desired solutions, and recognize the inherent messiness of problem situations. Second, the role of the analyst or

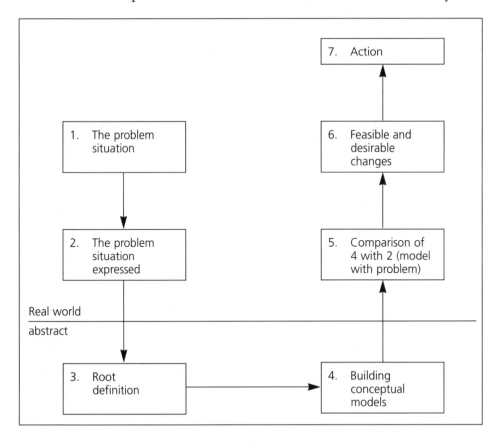

Figure 6.6   Stages in soft systems methodology

designer is as a participant in a team, and the role of the user is integral to successful systems development.

SSM is the foundation for the family of soft system methodologies. It was one of the early methodologies to recognize the importance of the construction of a systems perspective which embraced input from all stakeholders. SSM, as proposed by Checkland (1991), focuses not on finding a solution to a specific problem, but on understanding the situation surrounding the problem. In the context of human–computer systems, SSM is valuable in establishing the purpose, people, constraints and world-view of the system, and in the development of conceptual models of that ideal system.

The stages of SSM are shown in Figure 6.6. Stages 1 and 2 are concerned with drawing out a rich expression of the problem situation. The first stage identifies the problem in general terms. The next stage is the creation of a rich picture and the isolation of the primary task and issues. A rich picture is a pictorial representation of what the organization is supposed to be doing, what the current situation appears to be, and how the actors see things. Figure 6.4 shows a rich picture of the systems lifecycle. The objective of a rich picture is to suggest some ways of viewing the situation, and to elicit the conceptual views of the problem, which may in turn lead to possible solutions. This involves meeting with all stakeholders, so that their different views can be identified and reconciled. Stage 3 is concerned with the generation of the root definition, in order to generate appropriate conceptual models. Stages 3 and 4 are conducted away from the real world so that the definition is not hindered by real-world constraints. The generation of the root definition needs to take into account:

- Customers or clients – who is the system operating for?
- Actors – who is involved in carrying out the process?
- Transformation – what is the process supposed to do? What are its inputs and outputs?
- Weltanschauung (world-view) – what are the assumptions or attitudes under which the process is operating?
- Owners – who is the problem owner? Who is responsible if the system does not function properly?
- Environment – what conditions is the system experiencing that may have a bearing on its viability?

This CATWOE definition forces a consideration of missing or incomplete elements of the system. The root definition is completed by testing to see if the definition is internally consistent, is clear and unambiguous and generally understood and accepted.

Completion of the root definitions leads to the creation of logical models for each relevant system. The conceptual model specifies all the steps and activities needed to carry out the task specified in the root definition. The fifth stage compares the ideal solution with what is actually in place.

The outcome of this comparison will generate the next stage. Any variance between what exists and what is needed will throw up opportunities for action. There will normally be many possible actions and many possible ways of performing those actions. These need to be debated, with a view to reaching agreement on how to proceed with change. The final, seventh stage is concerned with taking action.

Review and apply:	What is the difference between an actor and an owner as the terms are used in SSM? Why is it important to make the distinction?
Answer:	The owner is responsible for the system. In a public access system this responsibility is likely to belong to the manager responsible for customer service in the context in which the system operates. Actors, in the context of information systems, are often those who operate or interact with the system. For public access systems this will be the customer base of the organization proving the system.

Cooperative design

Before moving on to describe other user-centred methodologies, we outline two approaches that are relevant to them. The two main bodies of methodologies differ in their underlying philosophy and the practices associated with user involvement. They are:

- Participative design, which takes as a starting-point the right of users to be involved in the design of systems that they will subsequently use. Users are responsible for analysing organizational requirements and planning appropriate social and technical structures to support both individual and organizational needs. ETHICS, as described below, is a good example of this approach.
- Socio-technical design, which focuses on the development of complete and coherent human–computer systems. The emphasis is on the consideration of social and technical alternatives to problems. A number of methods of socio-technical design have been proposed. The most significant of these, open systems task analysis (OSTA), is introduced below.

Whilst the user focus that is present in cooperative design is important, there is a particular challenge in applying these methodologies in the context of public access systems. The actual system users are unlikely to be available, and it may be necessary to work with representative users.

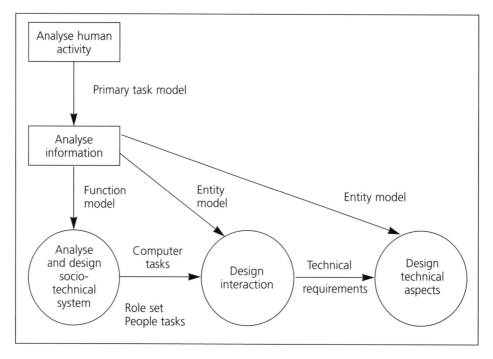

Figure 6.7   Stages in MultiView

Before we examine specific examples of participative and socio-techni-cal design, we introduce MultiView, which couples socio-technical and soft systems approaches.

MultiView

MultiView is an information system design methodology which combines socio-technical and soft systems approaches into a staged and controlled methodology. MultiView has five main stages. These start with the defini-tion of the purpose of the system, the stakeholders and the perspective of the system owners (the primary task model). This is followed by concep-tual modelling of information flows and information structure to produce the functional model (FM). The FM is then used as a basis for task alloca-tion; this part of the process uses strong socio-technical foundations. The socio-technical components, the people tasks (PT), role sets (RS) and com-puter task requirement (CTR), together with the entity model of the infor-mation structure, are used to drive the design of the interface. It is only once the interface has been designed that the technical aspects of the system are considered. The methodology uses entity relationship modelling and data flow modelling. More specifically, the stages in MultiView are:

1. *Analyse human activity*   This stage is heavily based on SSM, with its primary objective being the development of a world-view of views and the use of a rich picture of the problem situation to develop an agreed root definition. Finally, a conceptual model of the system is constructed and discussed by the design team until an agreed conceptual model emerges.

2. *Analysis of information*   Stage 2 focuses on the identification of the functions and entities in the system. Functional decomposition is conducted. The main function of the system is identified and broken down into subfunctions as far as is necessary. Data flow diagrams are then produced to show the system of events. These, together with the function charts, form the input to Stage 3.

3. *Analysis and design of socio-technical aspects*   Using the principles of the ETHICS approach (see below), both the technical and social systems are separately identified. The aim is to select the best system from the alternatives. This determines the people tasks, computer tasks, role set and social aspects of the system.

4. *Design of the human–computer interface*   Using the entity models from Stage 2 and the people tasks, computer tasks and role sets from Stage 3, the elements of the interaction are identified. These include distinguishing between batch processing and on-line tasks and an analysis of the dialogues between user and computer.

5. *Design and technical aspects*   Using the entity models and the technical requirements, this stage concentrates on technical implementation issues. The major outputs are the application database, and associated maintenance control, recovery and monitoring aspects of the system.

MultiView is attractive in the way in which it seeks to integrate hard and soft approaches, and acknowledges the central role of the user. However, despite this strength, it does not provide clear guidance on the detail of human–computer interface analysis and design. Use of some of the tools described in the next chapter, together with appropriate guidelines and standards within an overall project design methodology structured in accordance with the stages in MultiView, might alleviate this problem.

ETHICS

Effective technical and human implementation of computer systems (ETHICS) is a participative design methodology. ETHICS starts from the concept that a successful system will only emerge where the social and organizational needs of a work group are given equal weight with the technical aspects. Participation by users and potential users is regarded as a right. Different interest groups are represented in the design teams. In addition, two parallel strands of systems development – the technical and the social – move forward under the auspices of different design teams. These teams choose from a range of possible solutions by reference to pre-determined criteria. Where one proposed solution ranks highest on both technical and social criteria, it is adopted. Briefly, the stages in ETHICS are:

1. *Systems analysis*   The analysis stage involves the identification of the problem and the establishment of key objectives. Its unique feature is that two sets of goals – task and satisfaction goals – are created, and these are then ranked by all participants on a 5-point scale. Technical and business constraints are also identified.

2. *Socio-technical systems design*   Two groups are formed: one focusing on the technical issues and the other on the social issues. In each area the resources available are identified and the priority objectives are speci-fied. Once the social and technical objectives have been checked for compatibility, both technical and social decisions are taken.

3. *Set out alternative solutions*   The alternative social and technical solu-tions are each, in turn, evaluated against the criteria established earlier, in relation to priority, constraints and resources. The outcome of this stage is a shortlist of possible solutions.

4. *Merge social and technical solutions*   The two groups of solutions are merged in order to identify compatible socio-technical solutions.

5. *Rank solutions*   Solutions identified in Stage 4 are ranked using the criteria from Stage 3.

6. *Detailed design*   Once the outline of the design has been agreed, the normal process of systems analysis and design continues, except that at various points the earlier groups are consulted and continue to par-ticipate in the development process.

ETHICS focuses on developing a shared perspective, but needs adaptation to reflect the use of prototypes where this is necessary. Also, although it is systematic and thorough, the process is time-consuming, and may be expensive in both users' and designers' time.

Review and apply:	What problems would be posed by the use of ETHICS as a methodology in the design of public access inter-faces?
Answer:	A central focus of ETHICS is the negotiation of social issues. In public access interfaces these are of a differ-ent order to those in in-house systems. In public access

systems, the system generally only impacts on users' lives to a limited extent, and the tasks are normally concerned with simple transactions or retrieval. The user has choice about whether to use the system or not and, in avoiding the system, may seek to fulfil their needs through a different route, such as an organization's competitors. In addition, due to the unavailability of real users, the user perspective is often offered by experts. In summary, then, although it is important to be aware of methodologies such as ETHICS, and it is possible to use them with representative users, they have serious limitations in the context of public access systems.

Open systems task analysis (OSTA)

OSTA is a socio-technical system analysis methodology which, in a similar way to ETHICS, seeks to define technical requirements (in terms of systems structure and functionality) alongside social system requirements (such as usability and acceptability). It starts with a definition of the task to be performed by the system, and consideration of the system environment. The fundamental aim is to understand the transformation that occurs when a computer system is introduced into an environment (Eason, 1988).

The steps in OSTA are shown in Figure 6.8. They are:

1. Definition of the primary task of a system, from the user's perspective.
2. Identification of task inputs which affect the way in which the system achieves its primary task. These inputs can be variable and are usually from outside the system. Examples of inputs might be handwritten customer orders and telephone customer orders.
3. Establishment of the external environment, including the physical environment, economic and political conditions, and the nature and source of the demand for task output.
4. Description of the transformation process, which involves describing the functions that have to be undertaken to transform the inputs into outputs, so that the primary goal requirements are fulfilled. Analysis is aided by the construction of an object/action flow chart in which the objects to be transformed and the actions that bring this about are identified. The relations between the functions are also shown.
5. Analysis of the social system, in terms of the roles of people in an organization, and the characteristics and qualities of the people who will ultimately become the users of the new system.

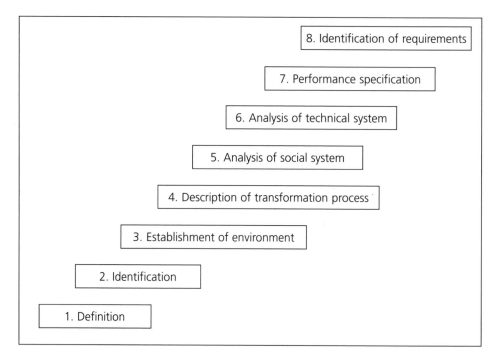

Figure 6.8   Steps in OSTA

6. Analysis of the technical system, particularly with regard to the integration of the new system with other systems and the environment.
7. Outline of performance specification, in terms of the requirements for the new social system, once the technical system has been introduced.
8. Identification of requirements for the new technical system, including aspects of functionality, usability and acceptability. The roles of technology and people in the new system are allocated. Statements are then made about the form of the interface, what changes are needed to the overall system, and training needs.

Review and apply: Draw up a table comparing ETHICS and OSTA

Answer:

ETHICS	OSTA
Focus on both social and technical aspects of the system	Focus on both social and technical aspects of the system
Participative methodology	Socio-technical methodology
User involvement in the analysis stage, particularly, underlies the approach	Social aspects are studied but there is no explicit commitment to user involvement

Parallel consideration of social and technical issues followed by a stage during which they are merged	A linear process which considers the social system first, followed next by the consideration of the technical system
Initial focus on task in terms of goals	Initial focus on task is developed further to consider task inputs and the transformation process

Task-oriented approaches to user interface design

All of the earlier methodologies focus strongly on users, but none offers a direct focus on the interface design process. A number of the tools described in the next chapter seek to analyse tasks. Macaulay (1995) offers a task-oriented approach to design which is not formally presented as a methodology, but whose steps might form the basis for practical project execution. We introduce this model with two objectives:

1. The model clearly identifies the stages necessary for a methodology that includes some of the tools described in the next chapter.
2. The model forms a useful basis for the comparison of a more conventional approach to interface design with that which might be proposed in a GUI environment, as described later.

The main stages of a task-oriented design are listed below and summarized in Figure 6.9.

- Understand users

- Task analysis and allocation of functions

- Identify interface tasks

- Dialogue specification

- Plan the design

- Produce a draft design

- Test the design with users

Figure 6.9   **Main stages in task-oriented user interface design**

1. *Understand users* This stage uses similar approaches to cooperative methodologies to build a shared vision, with input from a range of stakeholders in the future system. This involves understanding the business problem, the user environments, and the scope and boundaries of the proposed system.

2. *Task analysis and allocation of functions* Task analysis is the process of analysing the way that people complete tasks and the role of the system in the completion of those tasks. The designer needs to be aware of the objects that people use when carrying out their tasks. Users conduct tasks on an object. Chapter 7 explores some of the techniques for task analysis. Allocation of functions is concerned with whether the system or the user executes a function. For example, in an ATM the system performs the task on instruction from the user. The user indicates that they wish to withdraw cash and the amount that they wish to withdraw and the account from which it should be withdrawn. The ATM pays the money and also, automatically, without instruction from the user, records the withdrawal.

3. *Identify interface tasks* This is done on the basis of the task analysis and allocation of functions in Stage 2.

4. *Dialogue specification* Explore in detail the dialogue between the user and system that is necessary to achieve the identified tasks. Dialogue modelling techniques such as dialogue network diagrams, logical dialogue controls and logical dialogue outlines can support this process.

5. *Plan the design of the user interface* Planning the design has four aspects:

   - deciding what information to display in each window;
   - deciding how the information should be displayed;
   - deciding where each field will appear;
   - deciding what highlighting is required.

6. *Produce a draft design* This can be in the form of a mock-up, prototype or paper design.

7. *Test the design with users* Evaluate the design with users, employing one of the methodologies described in Chapter 9.

Holistic design and the star model

The star lifecycle, as shown in Figure 6.10, forms the basis for a methodology in which the ordering of stages and activities is inappropriate. System development may begin at any stage (indicated by the entry arrows) and may be followed by any of the other stages (indicated by double-headed

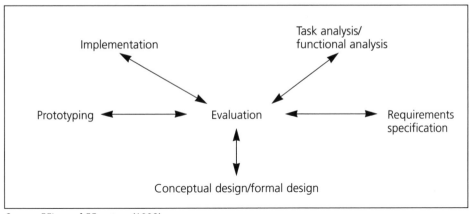

Source: Hix and Harston (1993)

Figure 6.10   The star lifecycle

arrows). The star model also recognizes the central role of evaluation. It is particularly appropriate to holistic methods of design, such as prototyping, where there is an incremental development of the final product, otherwise known as iterative design.

Holistic approaches seek to view design as a whole. Design is a loosely structured activity with no rigorous ordering of stages. Attention focuses on the appearance and presentation of the conceptual model, and then on working with manifestations of that model using actual examples. There is a strong focus on the visual appearance of the interface and its behaviour, coupled with the need for designers to exercise their creative skills.

In many instances, holistic approaches can be effectively integrated with more structured methodologies. For example, information gathered from task analyses may inform the design of a prototype. Alternatively, an initial holistic exploration of a proposed interface can form the basis for a more detailed task analysis. Prototypes and sketches, for example, provide a basis for early testing with users and allow an exploration of the way that new tasks might be conducted.

We explore prototyping, sketches, scenarios and storyboarding as tools in the design process in Chapter 7.

The object-oriented approach to GUI design

Many public access interfaces make use of graphical user interfaces. In this context a design that is sympathetic to the internal environment will focus on the objects in the GUI. Methodologies that embrace the object-oriented approach, including object-oriented analysis and design, are still being formulated. First some basic concepts concerning object-oriented approaches are introduced before proposing a possible methodology for object-oriented analysis and design.

Concepts in object oriented methods

Object-oriented (OO) programming has demanded the development of specific object-oriented systems analysis and design methodologies. These methodologies are relatively new, but may become increasingly important. In a sense object-oriented programming is an extension of structured programming. The fundamental motivation of OO methods is to facilitate development by creating software components that can be re-used. The basic approach of OO methods is to create objects, to group them in class hierarchies, and to associate attributes and methods to those objects. OO programming languages contain features such as inheritance, encapsulation and polymorphism (see explanations below) which make them particularly suitable for interface development. They allow easy construction of screen objects by the use of existing code, they are less error-prone and the programmer does not need to be familiar with the fine detail of how the code works. In visual direct manipulation environments this allows the developer to concentrate on the design of the interfaces.

Objects are a combination of entities with methods (see below). Thus an object includes both an entity and the processes to which it might be subject. An object might be a form, table, report or a control, such as a button on the screen, that can be manipulated as a unit.

Classes are groups of objects. Lower-level classes are specializations of higher-level classes, so that, for instance, a proforma order is a type or specialization of a general order, or a keyword is a specialization of a subject index term.

Attributes are data items which describe the object, as a button, for example, will have attributes relating to its colour and size.

Operations are actions which create, change or delete the object's attributes.

Methods (sometimes called services) are procedures, algorithms or calculations which carry out the activity inside objects. Methods are the processing part of objects, and are specified in structured English or pseudo-code. So, for example, clicking on a button will cause something to happen, such as a new dialogue box to be displayed.

Messages are communicated by objects. Messages may contain data to be processed by the object or requests for services.

The concepts of inheritance, encapsulation and polymorphism are also important in understanding object-oriented methods:

Inheritance Lower-level classes inherit properties (such as attributes, operations and methods) from higher-level classes; this facilitates the re-use of more general higher-level objects by specialization, which creates a new class by addition of further detail. So, for example, a code could be written for a NEXT button. The OK button can then simply be written by defining the OK button as an instance of the button class of objects, in which case it inherits all the properties of the button class. The code for a button needs to be written only once. If at a later stage the developer decides to change some characteristic of the buttons, such as their default colours, this could be achieved for all buttons by changing the properties of the button class definition.

Encapsulation is the concept that objects should hide their internal contents from other systems components to improve maintainability. The encapsulated parts of objects are hidden to insulate them from the effects of modifications to higher-level objects.

Polymorphism refers to the ability to define general processes such as PRINT without the need to define specify parameters. The same command is interpreted differently according to the context and the recipient of the command. Thus, although the detailed operations associated with printing, say, a chart, a spreadsheet or a text file are very different, in windows applications all these can be achieved by choosing the PRINT icon or option.

The virtue of OO methods is that the specification becomes the implementation. Analysis and design proceed by gradual addition of detail to the objects. The system is modelled as a collection of objects connected by message passing channels. Objects pass messages to each other to request a service, such as the updating of an object's attributes, or a request for a report. More detail is added to objects until the specification becomes sufficiently detailed to be programmed in an object-oriented language.

Objects are a mixture of programs and data structures, and do not therefore fit into the context of a relational database. This has led to the development of object-oriented databases that store data and programs as one component rather than, as in other database designs, as two distinct components.

A number of object-oriented methodologies have been proposed. These include object-oriented analysis and object-oriented analysis and design. Both of these methodologies start by defining objects and classes, and then define relationships to put objects and classes together to form a system-wide view. Object detail is added successively by specifying attributes, methods and the object life history.

Review and apply:	List some of the objects in a GUI.
Answer:	Buttons, windows, menus, dialogue boxes, icon buttons.

An object-oriented methodology

GUIs use an object–action paradigm where the user indicates an object first and then gives the command. The stages in one such approach are summarized in Figure 6.11 and described below. In contrast to the task-oriented approach to interface design, outlined in Figure 6.9, after Stage 1, Understand users, which is common to both approaches, 'objects' are central to most stages of this methodology.

1. *Understand users*   This stage is shared with many other methodologies. The unique feature is that the descriptions of what users do must be in a form that can be used for the later identification of objects.
2. *List objects associated with all users and workgroups*   Again, in the task-oriented approach Stage 2 was concerned with the user, task and objects. However, here the focus is on objects, with the outcome of this stage being a long list of potential objects.
3. *Decide on the role of the system and identify which objects will be visible at the user interface*   The scope and role of the system first needs defini-

- Understand users
- List objects associated with all users and workgroups
- Decide on the role of the system and identify which objects will be visible at the user interface
- Describe each visible object according to the interface metaphor
- Identify relationships between objects according to the interface metaphor
- Decide how to view each object
- Draw sketches of the interface design
- Test the design with users

Figure 6.11   Stages in an object-oriented user interface design process

tion. Next, objects need to be classified thus:

(a)   objects that are to be fully automated and will not be visible at the user interface;

(b)   objects that are visible and on which the user can perform actions;

(c)   objects external to the system which remain the user's responsibility.

Next, objects with classification (a) and (b) are examined to remove any redundant objects that can be viewed as attributes of other objects (for example, name and address may be viewed as belonging to customer) or different names for the same objects, or objects that can be generated from other objects.

4.   *Describe each visible object according to the interface metaphor*   Those objects with classification (b) need to be described, to include:
   - who has access?
   - who is responsible?
   - representation and quality;
   - descriptions according to the interface metaphor.

5.   *Identify relationships between objects according to the interface metaphor*   Relationships will show associations between objects and whether one object is contained within another.

6.   *Decide how to view each object*   The designer should produce lists detailing the contents of each menu bar, each pull-down menu, each form, table or list. Icons should be described in terms of allowable user actions and their consequences. For example, drawing a reservations icon on to the printer will cause the reservation form to be sent to the printer.

7.   *Draw sketches of the interface design*   Including hand-drawn mock-ups and prototypes.

8.   *Test the design with users*   User reactions are sought concerning the choice of objects, the views of each object, the allowable user action on each object and the representation of each object. Design needs modification to reflect user reaction.

Review and apply:	User participation is much less evident in this methodology than in some of those that we discussed earlier. Why do you think that this is the case? How might this be overcome?
Answer:	This methodology is primarily concerned with the technical aspects of design. User participation could be possible if it were used iteratively in a prototyping approach in the context of a holistic design methodology.

Designing multimedia GUIs

Methodologies for the design of multimedia GUIs are in their infancy. The object-oriented methodology described above is a good starting-point, but it is important to remember that the 'design process' in a multimedia context involves a technical team including project manager, multimedia designers (such as graphic designers, illustrators, animators, image processing specialists, instructional designers and interface designers), writers, video specialists, audio specialists and multimedia programmers. Vaughan (1994) offers a light-hearted checklist of action items which might be grouped to form a methodology with the stages in Figure 6.12. In addition, the list of action items is worthy of reiteration in its own right:

- design instructional framework
- hold creative idea sessions
- determine delivery platform
- determine authoring platform
- assay available content
- draw navigation map
- create storyboards

1	Market research
2	Design concept, including technical aspects
3	Identify resource, e.g. available content
4	Structure product
5	Design interface
6	Gather resources including team and content
7	Build prototype
8	User test
9	Revise design
10	Create multimedia components
11	Program and author
12	Test and fix functionality
13	Beta test
14	Create master
15	Deliver to the marketplace

Figure 6.12   **Stages in a methodology for multimedia interface design**

- design interface
- design information containers
- research/gather content
- assemble team
- build prototype
- user test
- revise design
- create graphics
- create animation
- produce audio
- produce video
- digitize audio and video
- take still photos
- program and author
- test functionality
- fix bugs
- beta test
- create golden master
- replicate
- prepare package
- deliver
- award bonuses
- throw party.

Significant aspects of this methodology which have a wider relevance for public access interfaces are:

- A user view of the system is neither feasible nor desirable at the beginning of the project. Designers decide what they want to create on the basis of the message to be communicated or the product to be delivered. Market research will probably include customer consultation in respect of the viability of the idea and its likely market success, but this focus is rather different from the direct involvement in interface design.
- A prototype is built and then tested on potential users or user representatives early in the process.
- Storyboarding (see Chapter 7) is necessary to identify how all the different media are to be integrated.
- There is significant design work involved in the creation of audio, video, photographs, graphics and animations.
- In many applications the interface design is constrained by the multimedia items that are available for inclusion; it can be difficult to distinguish between interface design and the creation of the product in its entirety – the two are intimately linked.

Strategic information systems planning

Public access systems may be strategic information systems, and it may, therefore be necessary to consider not only those methodologies that address technical issues and usability, but also those which consider the contribution that the system makes to the business. Here we introduce briefly the concepts of strategic information systems and competitive advantage as a prelude to the consideration of strategic information systems planning.

Innovative use of information systems in business has led to the creation of new products, improved service and dramatically reduced costs. In other words, the use of information systems has changed the way in which business is conducted and has altered the competitive position within the industry. For example, traditionally businesses pay bills on receipt of invoices by cheque. Using information systems technology it is possible for the purchaser to send an electronic payment instruction to their bank when the goods are received. The payer's account is debited and the payee's account is credited. These types of uses of information can be described as strategic, and are generally managed by strategic information systems. Strategic information systems allow the business to achieve competitive advantage.

Porter (1988) defines competitive advantage as coming

> fundamentally out of the value a firm is able to create for its buyers. It may take the form of prices lower than competitors' for equivalent benefits or the provision of unique benefits that more than offset a premium price. Competitive advantage is at the heart of the firm's performance in competitive markets.

Technically such systems may be very similar to traditional information systems, but they differ in that their focus is on treating information as a strategic resource. Strategic information systems are business-driven and focus on the environment in which the business operates. More specifically, strategic information systems are:

- outward-looking with a focus on the service to customers;
- able to offer real benefit to the customers;
- capable of changing the marketplace's perception of the firm.

Public access systems may be strategic information systems in the following senses:

1. New products such as CD-ROM versions of, say, a print encyclopaedia are affecting the players and structure of the publishing industry. The products offer new features over the print version and price may be competitive.

2. Public access systems are concerned with communication with customers and customer service. They may offer:

- enhanced customer service and market differentiation of the product on the basis of that service;
- better communications with customers, which leads to a better understanding of the benefits that a customer seeks from a business.

Strategic information systems planning (SISP) is a methodology which seeks to develop strategic information systems. SISP is the process of establishing a programme for the implementation and use of information systems in such a way that it will optimize the effectiveness of the organization's information resources and use them to support the objectives of the whole enterprise as much as possible. The outcomes of an SISP programme are typically a short-term plan for the next 12 to 18 months, as well as a longer-term plan for the next three to five years. SISP has a dual nature. It covers both detailed planning and budgeting for information systems at one level, and strategic issues and formulation at another.

SISP is a complex planning activity which requires a small project team, supported by input from a relatively large number of members of staff and possibly consultants. SISP is usually conducted as a project lasting from three to six months. It is important that the scope of the project is defined at the outset. The scope may be the whole organization or more narrowly focused on a specific product. SISP provides a broad context in which to examine and plan for information product development that will lend the organization a competitive advantage. Although, as Figure 6.13 demonstrates, SISP is concerned primarily with information systems within the organization, it can also be used to inform the planning of those systems or products that support customer service, because it includes consideration of marketplace factors such as critical success factors and cost–benefit analysis. For public access systems, SISP is likely to force a more evident focus on the corporate context of interface development, and commercial factors.

Summary

There is a wide range of information systems methodologies that can be used to assist in the structuring of a systems project. Hard systems methodologies have been widely used in systems analysis and design, and may well be used to structure the total systems project. However, they have little that is specific to offer to interface design, and need to be supplemented with other perspectives in this context. Soft systems methodologies recognize that situations are inherently messy and that there are a

1	Obtain authorization
2	Establish a team and arrange accommodation, tools, etc.
3	Allocate responsibilities and create a timetable
4	Determine the corporate goals, objectives, mission, etc.
5	Establish the firm's corporate strategy, explicitly or implicitly
6	Define the critical success factors
7	Establish the key performance indicators
8	Define the critical data set
9	Incorporate the firm's information technology architecture
10	Conduct a systems audit
11	Rank current system condition and prioritize current systems proposals
12	Brainstorm for new systems and create an IT opportunities list
13	Perform cost–benefit and risk analysis
14	Conduct filtering workshops
15	Produce an action plan
16	Communicate the action plan to all appropriate staff
17	Identify and appoint project champions
18	Arrange for top management to commit publicly to SISP
19	Create feedback mechanisms
20	Update SISP

Figure 6.13   Twenty steps to SISP

number of distinct perspectives on any situation, and offer approaches to eliciting and understanding these various perspectives. Yet, even soft systems methodologies do not offer very clear guidance on interface analysis and design. Borrowing some of the concepts from both schools of ought, a few methodologies have been developed that specifically focus nterface design, including MultiView and OSTA and other task-orient-roaches. These methodologies do not specifically consider GUI nd object-oriented approaches to design, special features of multi-rfaces, and the broader strategic issues associated with design-narketplace. There are some methodologies, or less formal t start to address these issues. Nevertheless, there is scope h in this area.

References

Boehm, B. (1988), 'The spiral model of software development and enhancement', *IEEE Computer*, **21** (5), 61–72.

Checkland, P. (1991), *Systems Thinking, Systems Practice*, Wiley, Chichester.

Eason, K. (1988), *Information Technology and Organisational Change*, Taylor and Francis, London.

Hix, D. and Harston, H. R. (1993), *Developing User Interfaces: Ensuring Usability through Product and Process*, Wiley, New York.

Macaulay, L. (1995), *Human–Computer Interaction for Software Designers*, International Thomson Computer Press, London.

Porter, M. E. (1988), *Competitive Advantage*, Free Press, New York.

Preece, J. et al. (1994), *Human–Computer Interaction*, Addison-Wesley, Wokingham.

Vaughan, T. (1994), *Multi-media; Making it Work*, 2nd edn, Osborne/McGraw-Hill, London.

Additional reading

Aktas, Z. (1987), *Structured Analysis and Design of Information Systems*, Prentice-Hall, Englewood Cliffs, NJ.

Avison, D. E. and Fitzgerald, G. (1988), *Information Systems Development: Methodologies, Techniques and Tools*, Blackwell, Oxford.

Clayton, M. and Batt, C. (1992), *Managing Library Automation*, 2nd edn, Gower, Aldershot.

Crinnion, J. E. (1992), *Evolutionary Systems Development*, Pitman, London.

Cutts, G. (1991), *Structured Systems Analysis and Design Methodology*, 2nd edn, Blackwell, Oxford.

Daniels, A. and Yeates, D. (1984), *Basic Systems Analysis*, 2nd edn, Pitman, London.

Downs, E. et al. (1988), *Structured Systems Analysis and Design Method: Application and Content*, Prentice-Hall, London.

Harbour, R. T. (1994), *Managing Library Automation*, Aslib, London.

Holloway, S. (1989), *Methodology Handbook for Information Managers*, Gower, Aldershot.

Hughes, M. J. (1992), *A Practical Introduction to Systems Analysis and Design: an Active Learning Approach*, DP Publications, London.

Lester, G. (1992), *Business Information Systems, Vol. 2: Systems Analysis and Design*, Pitman, London.

Mason, D. and Willcocks, L. (1994), *Systems Analysis, Systems Design*, Alfred Waller, Henley-on-Thames.

National Computing Centre (1990), *Systems Training Library*, 2nd edn, Blackwell, Oxford.

Olle, T. W. et al. (1988), *Information Systems Methodologies: a Framework for Understanding*, Addison-Wesley, Wokingham.

Remenyi, D. S. J. (1991), *Introducing Strategic Information Systems Planning*, NCC/Blackwell, Oxford.

Robb, A. F. (1992), *The Management Guide to the Selection and Implementation of Computer Systems*, 2nd edn, Blackwell, Oxford.

Rowley, J. (1990), *Basics of Systems Analysis and Design*, Library Association Publishing, London.

Skidmore, S. (1994), *Introducing Systems Analysis*, 2nd edn NCC/Blackwell, Oxford.

Skidmore, S. and Wroe, B. (1990), *Introducing Systems Design*, Blackwell, Oxford.

Ward, J. et al. (1990), *Strategic Planning for Information Systems*, Wiley, Chichester.

Wilson, B. (1990), *Systems Concepts, Methodologies and Applications*, Wiley, Chichester.

Chapter 7

Tools to support interface analysis and design

Chapter 6 described some of the key methodologies for interface design. When using these methodologies designers make use of a variety of different tools in the analysis of the situation, design of the interface and to support communication with users. Since a number of these tools are common to more than one methodology, they are collected together in this chapter, rather than being described in the context of the specific methodologies. By the end of this chapter, you should:

- be familiar with the analysis and design tools used in functional and data modelling, usability modelling, task modelling and interface modelling;
- understand the need to create an environment in which analysts, designers and users can work effectively together;
- be able to identify when to use which tools;
- be able to experiment with the application of analysis and design tools to support your analysis of problem situations;
- understand the models and diagrams that are created by other analysts, designers and users.

Tools and models

Most of the tools described in this chapter can make a contribution to a number of stages in the systems lifecycle, including analysis, design and evaluation. These tools may be used to specify requirements and objectives in analysis, to guide the design process, and as a framework for evaluation. They are essentially used to describe systems and the way they work. They may be used in:

- analysis to describe an existing system prior to the development of a new system, or the requirements for a new system;
- design to describe a proposed system as a basis for the creation of the proposed system;
- implementation and evaluation, initially to match the completed system against the models for the proposed system to ensure that the system matches the specification developed during design; later, the models may be amended after evaluation to describe enhancements to an existing system.

In general, the tools are aids to thinking, creativity, communication and the testing of potential performance. All the tools that support interface analysis and design are modelling techniques which generate a series of models, or simplifications of the real-world situation, as an aid to enhanced understanding of that situation. There are a number of characteristics that all good models exhibit. These include:

Simplicity   All models are simplifications of the real world, where the essential or key features of the real-world systems have been identified. Systems models should convey the key features simply, yet without overlooking necessary details.

Consistency   The symbols and terminology used to represent and describe aspects of information flow, and organizational structure. These should be used consistently.

Completeness   Models need to be complete in the areas that they cover, and not to overlook essential processes or entities.

Hierarchy   Models must have some means of representing several levels of detail, so that they support both a more detailed and a holistic view of the real-world situation. A hierarchy of models is likely to be necessary to reflect these levels.

The tools focus on logical analysis and design, in terms of what the system can do and will look and feel like. Finally, this chapter reviews some of the contextual features that support effective analysis and design.

System description typically uses a range of the tools described in this chapter to provide a holistic perspective on the system. For example, since tools associated with functional and data modelling derive largely from the hard systems methodologies and are therefore prone to exhibit a focus on the system rather than the user, it is important that they be coupled with tools that take into account the user perspective, tasks and the environment in which the system will be used, such as those tools associated with usability modelling, task modelling and interface modelling.

The tools and models introduced in this section can be divided into those associated with:

- functional and data modelling;
- usability modelling;
- task modelling;
- interface modelling.

Functional and data modelling is concerned with what the system must do, and the data that are available for processing.

Usability modelling encompasses tools associated with task, user and environmental analysis, which focus on user performance and satisfaction with the system.

Task modelling is concerned with the tasks that the user will complete in order to achieve their goals in using the system.

Interface modelling is concerned with the look and feel of the interface.

Throughout analysis, design, implementation and evaluation it is necessary to consider the system in its entirety and not just the computer system. Early decisions will need to be made concerning system boundaries and the necessary level of detail in system specification; these may need to be revisited during the course of analysis and design.

Functional and data modelling

The result of analysing and collecting functional and data requirements is a representation of the system known as the functional specification. This formal document records a model of what the system is to do, what data the system processes, how data are processed by the system and the relationships between the data elements. Functional and data requirements are usually specified with the aid of some of the variety of charting techniques, such as data flow diagrams, coupled with a natural or structured description of the details of the functional component, as might be recorded in a data dictionary. These charting techniques are widely used with a number of the structured systems methodologies to support systems analysis and design in general. Further details can be found in any of the many textbooks on the subject. Here we briefly introduce data flow diagrams, data dictionaries and entity relationship diagrams in order to provide a flavour of the nature of such tools.

Data flow diagrams

Data flow diagrams (DFDs) are central to most structured systems analysis and design methodologies. The notation varies between methodologies. DFDs can be used to show both current physical activities and to summarize the logical model of the system. DFDs have the following components (see Figure 7.1):

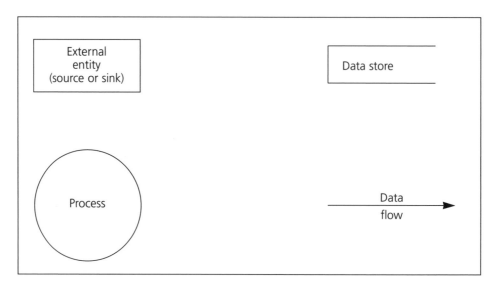

Figure 7.1   Data flow diagram

- A data flow is a route which enables packets of data to travel from one point to another. Data may flow from a source to a process, or to and from a data store or process. The flow is depicted by an arrowed line, with the arrowhead pointing in the direction of flow. Data flows should be labelled with names that clearly describe the flows, and which are unique. Data flows moving in and out of stores do not need names, the store names serve to describe them.

- A process represents a transformation, where incoming data flows are changed into outgoing data flows. Processes must also have clear, informative names. Appropriate labels often include an active verb (for example, compute, retrieve, store and verify) followed by an object or class.

- A data store is a repository of data such as a database file. Stores, again, should have clear names. If a process merely uses the contents of a store and does not alter it, the arrowhead goes only from the store to the process. If the details in the store are altered by the process, then a double-headed arrow is used.

- A source or sink is a person or part of an organization which enters or receives data from the system but is considered to be outside the context of the data flow model. Sources and sinks force useful consideration of the boundaries of the system.

- A physical flow shows the flow of material.

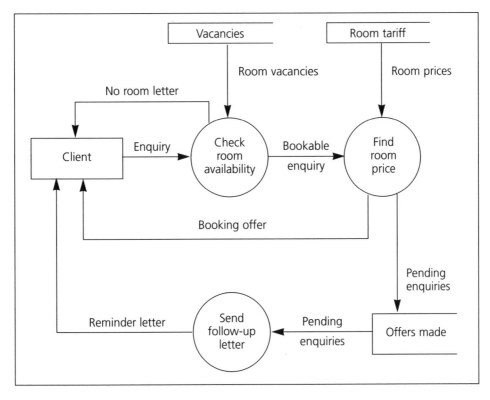

Figure 7.2   Data flow diagram for booking a hotel room

Figure 7.2 is an example of a simple data flow diagram. It shows the flow of information in the activity of booking a hotel room.

Review and apply:	In the data flow diagram in Figure 7.2 identify:
	• a data flow
	• a physical flow
	• a process
	• a data store, and
	• a source or sink.

DFDs should be used in a hierarchical structure to represent models showing different levels of detail. For example, the top level DFD, conventionally labelled 0, can be used to give a system overview, whereas the subsequent levels 1, 2, 3, and so on, can be used to show more detailed aspects of the system.

DFDs give a useful picture of how data pass through a system and define the relationships between processes, data flows and data stores. They form a useful basis for discussion with users and are useful in performing structured walkthroughs.

Data dictionaries

A data dictionary is simply a definition which provides the information concerning the data in a system. The data dictionary holds data concerning all:

- data stores
- processes
- data flows
- data elements
- data structures.

We have already defined data stores, processes and data flows.

A data element is an item of data which has been decomposed as far as is appropriate for the task in hand. Precisely what constitutes a data element will vary from one system to another. A data element is a named item of data which cannot be decomposed into any other logically meaningful data items. Examples might be a department name or a product name.

A data structure is a collection of data elements that regularly appear together. Thus a data structure can be used as a shorthand reference in flow, process and store definitions. Any group of data that has been named will be defined as a data structure. Examples might be an order, or a reservation for an item in the stock of a library.

The structure of the data dictionary entry for the various different types of components will vary. Figure 7.3 shows the components of an entry for

---

- Name description of the data element
- Aliases – alternative terms used for the same data element
- Type, i.e. numeric, character or alphanumeric
- Format
- Values – the range of values that the element may take
- Security – who is allowed to modify, add or delete a given data item
- Editing
- Comments – any special information

Figure 7.3   Components of an entry in a data dictionary in respect of a data element

a data element. This includes names and definitions of allowable formats, values and associated editing and security features. The dictionary is dynamic, and is built up as the designers learn more about the system. The data dictionary supports a complex web of interrelationships. A single element may appear in many data structures, data flows, data stores and processes. When an element is amended, the implications of the amendment must be traced through the various structures, flows, stores and processes. Data dictionary software or systems are specifically tailored to support this process. The functions of a data dictionary can be summarized as:

- Consistency checking, for example in a data flow diagram, to ensure that all flows have sources and destinations and all data elements in stores have a means of arriving in the store.
- Testing – data descriptions and ranges of values can allow test data to be automatically generated.
- Coding – the description of data structures may be sufficient to support the generation of data descriptions in the host language or data manipulation language (DML) through a pre-compilation pass of the dictionary.
- Change – data dictionaries are invaluable in tracing the effects of change in, say, the range of values that a data element can take, through a complete system.

Entity relationship diagrams

In addition to identifying the flow of data it is important to define the meaning and structure of the data and agree these with users. Data dictionaries help to define the meaning of data, but there is also a need to specify entities and their relationships. Logical structure diagrams or entity relationship diagrams complement the data dictionary definitions by providing a graphical model of entities, their attributes and the relationships between them.

Entity relationship modelling highlights the entities that are important in the context of the system, identifies the attributes of those entities and summarizes the relationships that exist between them. To define these terms:

An **entity** is something about which it is desirable to store data. An entity must be uniquely defined, but may vary from a physical object (such as a bouquet of flowers or an item of furniture) to a more abstract concept such as a sales area, or a subject index term. Distinctions can be made between entity type and entity occurrence. For example, the entity type might be 'book', whereas the entity occurrence is a specific book. An entity must be capable of being uniquely identified, that is, it must have an identifying attribute or combination of attributes, which are termed the entity identifier.

An **attribute** is a property or characteristic of an entity. For example, the entity 'book' may have the attributes title, author and date of publication. Note that none of these attributes is unique to a specific book, since the same title may be shared by different books, and by different editions of the same book. Similarly publication dates and authors are not unique identifiers. The unique identifier for a title is its ISBN, and this is widely used in bibliographic databases. However, even the ISBN is not a unique identifier in a library circulation control system which may need to handle the circulation control of several copies of the same title; here a unique copy number or stock number will be necessary.

Relationships link entities. So, for example, the entity supplier may be associated with the entity order by a relationship that might be called 'placed with'. The entity 'book' might be linked to the entity title by the relationship 'named'. The degree of a relationship is an important property of a relationship. Relationships may be 1:N (one-to-many) or M:N (many-to-many). A 1:N relationship is one where the relationship occurrences fan out in one direction only. For example, the relationship between order and supplier is many-to-one, in that a given order can be placed with only one supplier, but a supplier may receive many orders. In M:N relationships several relationship occurrences fan out in both directions to link, for example, many book entities to many order entities. Thus an order may include several books, whilst a book may be itemized on several orders. The degree of the relationship is shown in the entity relationship diagram as shown in Figure 7.4.

The process of creating an entity relationship diagram is concerned with

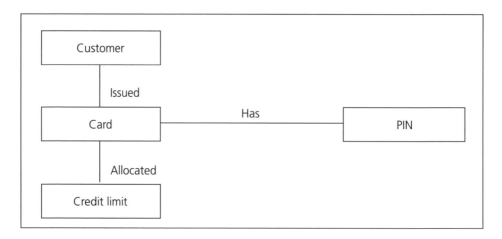

Figure 7.4   An entity relationship diagram for a cashcard withdrawal

identifying the main entities in the system, defining the relationships between them and assigning attributes to them.

Review and apply: List the entities in the entity relationship diagram shown in Figure 7.4.

Usability modelling

Entity relationship modelling, data flow diagrams and data dictionaries are key tools in structured methodologies, but their focus is on the system and not on users. The concept of usability was introduced earlier (Chapter 1) as it underlies the design of interfaces. In order to embed usability in a system it is necessary to seek to define usability requirements. These may be collected by the various data gathering techniques, such as interviewing and observation. The activity of gathering user requirements can be termed a usability study. A usability study has three main components:

- A **task analysis** (see below) to determine the characteristics required by users of the system, such as the search strategy required.
- A **user analysis** to determine the user population, including aspects such as their intellectual ability, cognitive processing ability, previous experience, physical capability, and any other salient characteristics. This can be conducted using user modelling techniques, though to date no established techniques exist. Most user modelling relies upon checklists of user characteristics.
- **Environmental analysis**, including aspects of both the physical environment and the user support environment.

In addition, by being expressed in a functional specification using some of the tools described above, usability requirements are often expressed in terms of performance measures or usability metrics, which are detailed in a usability specification. Tyldesley (1988) lists 22 possible metrics or measurement criteria as shown in Figure 7.5. Designers need to select appropriate criteria on the basis of the type of system being tested.

   Below we briefly introduce some of the models and tools used in usability modelling. These focus on task analysis, because the development of tools for user analysis and environmental analysis is still in its infancy. Nevertheless there is a limited number of tool sets which seek to embrace task analysis, user analysis and environmental analysis, with a view to the identification of requirements. We introduce these first.

1	Time to complete task
2	Percentage of task completed
3	Percentage of task completed per unit time (speed metric)
4	Ratio of successes to failures
5	Time spent in errors
6	Percentage number of errors
7	Percentage number of competitors that do this better than current product
8	Number of commands used
9	Frequency of help or documentation used
10	Time spent using help or documentation
11	Percentage of favourable:unfavourable user comments
12	Number of repetitions of failed commands
13	Number of runs of successes and of failures
14	Number of times the interface misleads the user
15	Number of good and bad features recalled by users
16	Number of available commands not invoked
17	Number of regressive behaviours
18	Number of users preferring your system
19	Number of times users need to work around a problem
20	Number of times the user is disrupted from a work task
21	Number of times the user loses control of the system
22	Number of times the user expresses frustration or satisfaction

Figure 7.5   Usability metrics – possible measurement criteria

Tool sets for usability modelling

The most significant work in this area is that conducted at the HUSAT Centre at Loughborough University as part of the Human Factors in Information Technology (HUFIT) project. HUFIT consists of a number of tool sets. The planning, analysis and specification (PAS) tool set was developed as a method for gathering information about human factors including users, tasks and environments. The result of this analysis is a summary of user requirements and a functionality matrix (Catterall et al., 1991). This functionality matrix is used as the basis for informed task allocation and evaluation. Figure 7.6 shows an example of the HUFIT functionality matrix.

System features	Elemental system features						Compound system features		
	VDU			Keyboard	Hard copy	Audible alarms	Relative position	Layout		
Task elements	Graphics		Technology					VDU format	Keyboard	Hard copy printer
	Text	Symbol								
System requirements										
Information processing										
Direct access										
Navigation										
Alarm handling										
Logs										

Figure 7.6   **The HUFIT functionality matrix**

<table>
<tr><td>Review and apply:</td><td>List some usability metrics that might be appropriate with an on-screen site map of a university.</td></tr>
<tr><td>Answer:</td><td>● Number of users completing the task within 3 minutes.
● Frequency of successful location of required building or room, expressed as a percentage.</td></tr>
</table>

User specification must include success criteria for each usability objective. It must be evident what needs to be measured, so, for example, if user satisfaction is a success criterion, a means of measuring user satisfaction must be specified. Accordingly, we might set a criterion such as 85 per cent of users enjoy using the system. An appropriate criterion for effectiveness might be that staff can learn to perform all the common functions in one hour to retrieve all records on a specific subject.

The usability statement including usability objectives and the things to be measured provides the designer with clear design objectives. It is developed during specification, guides design and is revisited as a basis for evaluation later in the systems lifecycle. Guidance on specifying and measuring usability is available in Part II of the ISO 9241 Standard Ergonomic Requirements for Office Work with Visual Display Terminals.

Task modelling and task analysis

Task analysis is concerned with what people do when they are going about their activities, the way that tasks are broken down or decomposed into subtasks, what knowledge users need to complete their tasks, and the objects, actors and actions that are involved in the task.

Task analysis (TA) describes a range of techniques designed to elicit descriptions of what people do, represent those descriptions, predict difficulties and evaluate systems against usability or functionality requirements. Chapter 4 explored aspects of the searching task, which is a central concern in public access systems. The techniques of task analysis extend beyond the search task to encompass all tasks that users might complete with systems. They are nevertheless also applicable in this more specific context.

The terms goal, task and action are used differently by different authors. Here we adopt the following definitions:

A **goal** is a state of a system that the human wishes to achieve. It is achieved by using an action, which is able to change the system to the desired state. Often goals can be achieved using more than one device, such as a keyboard or a mouse or menus on a touch screen.

A **task** is the activity required, used or believed to be necessary to achieve a goal using a particular device. This definition includes a number of differing perspectives on tasks:

- required tasks emerge from the system and designer perspective;
- used tasks relate to what the users actually do;
- believed tasks are what the user thinks that they should do.

Differences may arise between these different perspectives on tasks.

An **action** is a simple task that involves no problem-solving or control structure component, such as touching a touch screen or clicking a mouse. A series of actions is usually necessary to complete a typical task, such as recording the loan of a book.

Users alternate between forming goals and determining tasks, based on their conceptions of the devices and interface available. In addition, it is important to remember that what to an expert user is an action may be considered by a novice user as a complex task. Many public access systems that involve complexity in, say, search strategy or location of appropriate databases, need to accommodate these differing perspectives.

Hierarchical task analysis

Hierarchical task analysis (HTA) is one of the oldest and best-established forms of task analysis and accordingly there are several different types. Using structure chart notation (see Figure 7.7), HTA decomposes a high-level task into its constituent subtasks of operations or actions, on the basis of the logic or practice of a task. It centres on an iterative process of identifying tasks, categorizing them, breaking them down into subtasks and checking the accuracy of the decomposition. Information about tasks is collected and checked using a variety of sources, including conversations with users, observations of users working, job descriptions and operating manuals. Walkthrough techniques are one means of checking the decomposition. The ultimate aim is to establish an accurate description of the steps that are required to complete a task, with a view to informing the design so that appropriate steps can be reflected in design.

Review and apply:	Consider the task of searching all the newspaper articles dealing with mergers and acquisitions in the pharmaceutical industry over the past six months, on say a CD-ROM version of *The Guardian*. Conduct a hierarchical task analysis.

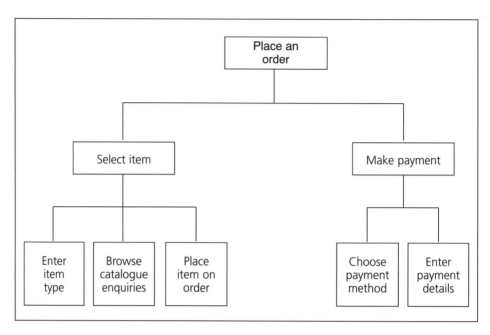

Figure 7.7   **A structure chart showing hierarchical task analysis (HTA) for placing an order on a multimedia kiosk**

Command language grammar (Moran, 1981) is another attempt to provide designers with a model of the tasks that users need to perform. These tasks are then broken down into subtasks and descriptions of necessary actions. CLG produces a task hierarchy model with tasks broken into subtasks in a structured way, similar to a structure chart. The model is then represented at three higher levels (this first being the task level). At the semantic level, pseudo-code is used to describe entities and permissible actions. The syntactic level uses commands which describe arguments, which refer to the entities. The interaction level specifies commands that are available in that context or screen. It provides the rule structure and command set for the user interaction.

This division of the interaction into task, semantic, syntactic and interaction levels has been widely adopted within HCI. The purpose of the approach was to distinguish the conceptual model of a systems from the command language, and so to reveal the associations and connections between the two. The grammar itself provides a way of working through different parts of a system, making explicit both the relationships between the different components and the different levels of the system. In practice, it can be difficult to separate semantic and syntactic aspects of interactions. The approach nevertheless provides a way of analysing what users do at the interface, and is a useful basis for the development of other tools.

Task–action language (TAL) seeks to build on CLG, but introduces a more formal production rule grammar. Predictions about ease of use can be made on the assumption that good design is concerned with minimizing the number of rules, the length of the terminal symbols (the words in the language) and the number of terminal symbols. **Task–action grammar** is a further development of TAL which attempts to evaluate the consistency of an interface. Its underlying assumption is that inconsistencies make an interface more difficult to learn.

Cognitive task analysis

Cognitive task analysis (CTA) is a group of techniques that seek to capture some representation of the knowledge that people have or that they need to have in order to complete the task – these techniques seek to inform the design process through the application of cognitive theories. The underlying assumption is that humans perceive the world and produce some representation of it in their mind. They then manipulate this perception and produce some output or behaviour that can be observed. CTA attempts to model this internal representation and processing in order to design tasks that can be undertaken more effectively by humans. There are a number of cognitive analysis techniques which focus on different aspects of the cognitive processing assumed to be necessary for a person to complete a task. Here we briefly look at two levels of cognitive activity: task–action representation and mappings and goal–task representation and mappings.

Task–action representations and mappings are concerned with the procedural or 'how-to-do-it' knowledge possessed by users. The focus is on the actions that need to be completed to accomplish a given goal. The best-known of these representations is the GOMS (goals, operations, methods and selection rules) model (Card et al., 1983), which consists of descriptions of the methods (that is, plans) needed to accomplish specified goals. The GOMS model works by breaking the task down into a goal stack, and specifying the operators, methods and rules for selecting between alternative methods. Thus the model can be used to predict times and users' routes through tasks. The methods comprise a series of steps consisting of operators (or actions) that the user performs. When there is more than one method available to accomplish a goal, the GOMS model includes selection rules which choose the appropriate method, depending on the context. A GOMS analysis, like an HTA, can be applied at different levels of abstraction: general methods, unit task and keystroke.

The GOMS model is intended to provide an appropriate cognitive model of human information processing. However, GOMS is limited in application, because it assumes expert behaviour, and error-free performance. The GOMS model is important because it was one of the first cognitive models of HCI.

The **keystroke level model** (KLM) is based on GOMS and describes the time taken to execute a subtask using the systems facilities. Cognitive complexity theory (CCT) is an extension of GOMS which attempts to predict how difficult a system will be to learn and use. CCT uses a GOMS model of the task and its required knowledge, a model of the user's current knowledge and a list of the items of knowledge to be learned in order for the user to make error-free use of the system.

Although attractive from a theoretical perspective, in practice, GOMS and its variants are difficult to use. In addition, GOMS relies upon a very simplistic model of human task performance, and seeks to model the actions of expert users who act rationally at all times in pursuit of clear goals and make no errors in performance. The techniques are useful for, say, comparing mouse actions with keyboard short cuts, and other alternative ways of performing the same task, that might be designed into software. In addition, as software tools for prototyping become more important it will be less necessary to undertake the predictions of performance from specifications for which these tools have been primarily developed. Nevertheless, GOMS makes a valuable contribution by drawing attention to the need to examine task–action mapping in design. There is some development of tools that automate these approaches which may make this type of analysis more straightforward (for example, Laird et al., 1987; Anderson, 1987).

Goal–task representations and mappings take into account the previous knowledge that users have, both of the specific task and generic tasks. People may often have knowledge about a generic task, such as keyword searching on a kiosk, but may not know how to perform the task using a particular computer system (that is, a particular device). The ease of learning a new system depends on previous knowledge and the extent to which that previous knowledge can be applied to the new situation. Various methodologies have been developed to aid in the exploration of the knowledge that users call upon when they encounter a new problem. Here we briefly describe two such approaches, knowledge analysis of tasks (KAT) and cognitive dimensions:

Knowledge analysis of tasks (KAT) (Johnson, 1992) is a technique concerned with identifying knowledge relevant to the task. Requirements gathering techniques are used to identify the task knowledge structures possessed by users. KAT involves the following stages:

- identify the person's goals, subgoals and subtasks;
- work out the order in which subgoals are to be carried out;
- identify task strategies;

- identify procedures;
- identify task objects and actions.

KAT takes into account the fact that different individuals perform differently, and recognizes the need to take into account organizational and environmental factors. Sampling of users is central in the gathering of task data, through a wide variety of different techniques, including interviews, observation and rating scales.

HTA and other task analysis approaches can be used in various parts of the design process. They can be used to analyse old and new tasks and to identify areas where training is required.

Cognitive task analysis can reveal difficulties with specific designs, support choices between designs or inform the design process by removing anticipated problems.

Although the fine-grained techniques described in this chapter might seem important to an understanding of the effectiveness of interfaces, the increasing complexity associated with modelling tasks at a detailed level, and the need to accommodate a wide range of different, non-expert users is making them increasingly difficult to apply, in general, although they may have some application in very simple public access kiosk interfaces. Another danger of task analysis techniques is that designers can become too tied to current processes and task structures. Understanding the content and structure of the knowledge used in interaction can be a better basis for innovative design. The structure of people's knowledge can be represented using techniques such as entity relationship diagrams, and their knowledge of procedures can be represented using data flow diagrams. Rigidity in design is not appropriate and should be avoided – analysis and design needs to accommodate the fact that any computer system will change the tasks that users perform to accomplish their goal.

Cognitive dimensions

One alternative approach to the detailed task analysis approaches described above is the cognitive dimensions approach proposed by Green (1989). Cognitive dimensions are a vocabulary for describing aspects of the information structures. Some cognitive dimensions are:

- Viscosity – or resistance to change, and the ease with which change can be made to aspects of the artifact.
- Delayed gratification, which is the effort required to meet a goal; goals that the user perceived to be easy may be difficult to achieve with a given interface.
- Premature commitment, where the user is forced to makes choices too soon in the dialogue.

- Hidden dependencies – links between items in the artifact which are not easily visible.

ERIMA (entity relationship modelling for information artifacts) (Green, 1991) employs entity relationship notation to represent the information structure of a screen display or other artifact and allows the cognitive dimensions to be described and analysed.

Task allocation

Once the necessary tasks have been identified it is important to allocate them between the system and the users. This allocation is concerned with whether the user or the system is to provide the data or knowledge necessary to accomplish a task and whether the system or user is going to accomplish the task, or whether and how the systems might support the user in accomplishing it. For example, in searching an OPAC, a user might start to type in an author name. This might trigger the display of the author name in its index sequence in another window, so that the searcher is alerted to author variants. The allocation must take into account the feasibility of obtaining data from the two different sources and the desirability of doing so, in the light of the cognitive loading, or the amount of learning and knowledge required of the user. Task analysis techniques and, in particular, cognitive task analysis can be used for this purpose.

Review and apply:	What is the difference between CTA and HTA?
Answer:	• CTA is a group of techniques that seek to model the knowledge that people have or need to have in order to complete the task. Different models seek to analyse the actions required to complete different goals (for example, GOMS), and the previous knowledge that users have of the specific and generic tasks, for example, KAT.
	• HTA decomposes a high-level task into its constituent subtasks or actions, on the basis of the logic or practice of a task. Information is collected from users about tasks, but no attempt is made to investigate the knowledge that the user needs to bring to the task.

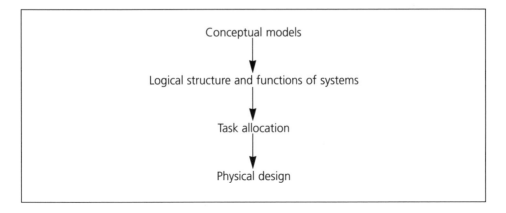

Figure 7.8   A multi-layered approach to design

Interface modelling

Physical design or the design of the interface attempts to draw together all the preparatory work that may have been conducted during the earlier stages of analysis and design into a completed interface. Figure 7.8 shows a multi-layered approach to design which starts with conceptual models, moves through the logical structure and functions of systems and then task allocation to physical design. In approaches to design that rely heavily on prototyping, physical design may be intimately interlinked with, say, the development of conceptual models. However, these processes nevertheless need to occur, and on occasions the tools from all the layers shown in Figure 7.8 will be appropriate.

Physical design attempts to embed the conceptual model of a system in a physical structure. There are two aspects to physical design: operational and representational. Operational aspects are concerned with the dialogue structure and the information that is displayed on the screen as a result of user interaction. Operational specification of systems needs to cover:

- how the system can reveal the state it is in;
- how the system makes it clear what actions the user can take;
- system responses and feedback to user.

It is necessary to choose input devices and the type of interaction style. Both must be appropriate for users, tasks and the environment. Closer specification covers the flow of control and the logical dialogue. These can be represented using flow charts, data flow diagrams, state transition diagrams or structure charts, or the methods based on user interface design environment (UIDE) outlined below.

Representational aspects include details such as where to position items on the screen, how to use colour, display actions taken by the system, and dialogue conventions and the way in which they are translated into a set of keystrokes, touch screen actions or mouse movements.

Sketching and metaphor

The concept of metaphor, as a way of explaining something new by focusing on its similarities with a familiar object, has been explained in the context of user conceptual models of the system. Here we consider sketching and other approaches that support the development of a system metaphor. A good system metaphor is one which has meaning for users, and therefore it needs to align to a sufficient extent with the user's metaphor.

Metaphors can be used to present a coherent image of the whole system, as in the desktop metaphor, or to deal with specific functions or parts of the system. A commonly used metaphor is 'cut and paste' in word processing. This metaphor has now become so much part of the system that its metaphorical links have faded into history. Indeed, the desktop metaphor is widely used. Langford and Jones (1994) propose a metaphor based on the kitchen interface, arguing that 'not all potential users now possess the office experience upon which depends the desktop metaphor'. It may be that a new metaphor is required for public access systems. Metaphor is also culturally dependent. For example, the metaphor of a mailbox may need to be represented in different ways in the United States, the United Kingdom and Germany, where mailboxes take on a different shape.

Sketching, initially on paper, and subsequently, with the creation of cardboard representation, can be used as a basis for visual brainstorming in the exploration of alternative designs. These early prototypes can be used as the basis for the creation of software or video prototypes. Sketching requires the creative development of metaphors.

Review and apply:	Give some examples of how the windows interface uses the desktop metaphor.
Answer:	• Overlapping windows containing overlapping documents. • Cut and paste. • File to store a document.

Review and apply:	Look at the icons on a GUI-based system to which you have easy access. Which icons have never made any sense to you? Experiment with drawing alternative icons.
Answer:	There is no standard answer to this question. The answer will depend on the metaphors held by different readers.

Storyboards and scenarios

Storyboards are screen designs without any actual functionality. They are working screens that can be evaluated by users in terms of features such as language, screen messages, screen layout and use of colour. They may be produced 'by hand' or with graphics packages or screen or form design packages. A set of these designs can be animated to provide an idea of the sequence of the screen displays to the user, using, for example, slide show facilities. Storyboards are particularly used in the design of a multimedia package where it is necessary to decide at an early stage how the various media will be integrated.

Scenarios are fictional stories with characters, events, products and environments. They support the designer in their exploration of ideas and the ramifications of design decisions. Scenarios should encourage the designer to think about the range of users, and the context in which they will use the system. So, for example, for the use of a kiosk in a catalogue shop the scenario will paint in the social environment, the on-system tasks, success with the task, and the subsequent actions associated with payment and/or collection of items purchased.

Prototypes

The sketches and storyboards discussed above are a series of pictures produced either on screen or as simple paper-based prototypes. Software prototypes are versions of the system with limited functionality. For example, a prototype might show an opening screen with menus, but the screen might not do anything or only respond in a limited way to user input. Typically, prototypes:

- do work, but have limited functionality;
- will be iteratively developed;
- must be quick and cheap to build;
- will differ from the final system in size, reliability, robustness, completion and construction materials.

Prototyping allows early user testing of the usability of certain features of the interface, and then subsequent re-testing (providing the users are willing and available). Prototypes allow designers to collect information with respect to:

- necessary system functionality and user goals;
- action/operation sequences;
- user support needs;
- acceptable metaphors and their representation;
- look and feel.

Not all aspects of usability can be tested with a prototype. Notably, reliability and performance times will differ between a prototype and the real system because the two systems are likely to be implemented on different hardware and software platforms. If these are important parameters, they will need to be tested with a test version of the real system unless evolutionary prototyping is being used.

There are a number of different kinds of prototyping. Although in some types of prototyping it is possible to divide the prototype from the eventual system, some prototypes and the full system are more closely linked. Some common types of prototyping are:

Rapid prototyping, in which the prototype is discarded, and only used as a development tool.

Incremental prototyping, in which large systems are installed in phases to avoid delays between specification and delivery. The implementation is phased and the phased implementation is a live prototype. The early version of the system is a skeleton with the core features. Requirements are checked in the field, and changes made to the core features. Once the core features have been refined sufficiently, features that are more peripheral are added and tested in the same way.

Evolutionary prototyping, in which the initial prototype is constructed, evaluated and evolved continuously until it forms the final system.

Using prototyping and design

Prototyping is useful at several stages in the design process, including product conceptualization, task-level prototyping and screen design prototyping, as follows:

1.   **Product conceptualization.** Here prototyping is used to gain a better understanding of the nature of the product requirements. Several different sketch designs can be presented to users and to members of the development team for comment and improvement. These activities aid communi-

cation and decision making, and help designers to conceptualize their design.

2.   **Task-level prototyping.** Prototyping can help in the assessment of whether the user can perform the necessary tasks, and task sequences can be completed easily and efficiently. Tasks and scenarios need to be carefully designed to ensure that they are representative of the system's anticipated use. System tests and acceptance tests which might be generated through software engineering could be used in such scenarios. Developing early versions of documentation and help systems may also assist in the identification of usability problems.

3.   **Screen design prototyping** concentrates on icons, menus and screen layouts. This looks, for example, at the suitability of icons and screen layouts, the use of colour, visual and audio effects and grouping of commands within menus.

Review and apply:	We have placed prototyping in the section on interface modelling. Does it also have relevance in the context of task modelling and functional and data modelling?

Answer:	Yes.
	    In the product conceptualization stage, prototyping can be used to identify relevant entities, data flows and processes with users, and provide input to functional and data modelling.
	    In task analysis, prototyping can help in the assessment of whether the user can perform the necessary tasks and whether the task sequences can be completed easily and efficiently.

Software prototyping tools

There are a number of software prototyping tools available to support the creation of prototypes. Designers need to select prototyping tools to match the prototyping method chosen, and the purpose for which the prototype is to be employed. A key feature of any prototyping tool is that it should require only limited programming skills and be quick and easy to use, so that prototypes can be generated speedily by designers who have either little training in the specific tool or in programming in general. There are two types of prototyping tools:

Production tools have to be comprehensive and must impose constraints so that complete, reliable, robust and maintainable software is produced.

These constraints are not compatible with prototyping, and so prototyping with productions tools can be slow.

Special prototyping tools have therefore been created to support the speedy construction of a prototype. These tools are likely fully to automate code management at the expense of efficient maintainable code and, for example, remove the enforced quality checks that would be a feature of a compiler in a production tool. Special purpose prototyping tools may, however, limit what can be configured and the match between these tools and the eventual system can sometimes be difficult to achieve.

Hypermedia systems, such as HyperCard for the Apple Macintosh, can be particularly useful interface prototyping tools. Help systems often feature some kind of hypertext system to support users in jumping between related subjects at the click of a button, rather than having to scroll through linear documents; this can be emulated effectively with a hypermedia tool.

Interface modelling tools

There is a range of different tools that can be used in interface development. The time devoted to interface design is a significant proportion of the total design time, so any tools that support and accelerate the interface design process are particularly valuable. User interface functions were originally supported by general input and output models or programming language features. However, the advent of graphic output and non-textual input required that special interface development tools be developed. These can be divided into stand-alone tools, toolkits and integrated environment (as in user interface management systems – UIMS – see below).

Stand-alone tools fall into three categories: graphics tools, modelling and diagramming tools, and visualization tools. Graphics tools, allow designers to create and manipulate drawings, icons and other graphics images; they include icon editors, menu builders, window managers, screen painters and report generators. Modelling and diagramming tools may be either graphically or text-based. They check and maintain the syntax and semantics of a model, so that users can be sure that diagrams are syntactically correct and adhere to appropriate diagramming rules. Visualization tools offer a visual representation of a program code, in order to facilitate understanding of the code. Stand-alone tools are flexible and are not specific to any given environment. However, the designer needs to take responsibility for ensuring that the tools chosen for a project will work together. Transferring data between tools can be difficult, and a lack of consistency between tools may mean that a house style and internal interface standards cannot be easily enforced.

User interface toolkits are a library of interface objects and related information, such as buttons, menu bars, scroll bars, icons, error messages and help messages. The toolkit supplies the objects, but the designer needs to write the control sequence to organize and invoke the relevant interface elements. Toolkits are useful in that they provide the screen items, but it may be difficult to change the look or behaviour of the items supplied. An interface builder also allows the behavioural aspects of the system to be specified.

Integrated environments, sometimes referred to as system shells, incorporate a collection of tools together with, for example, configuration management (to support configuration to reflect in-house standards), version control, a body of knowledge about the system (for example, as in the data dictionary) and accommodation for other tools. Tools are often specific to given methodologies such as SSADM, which was described in Chapter 6.

There are two terms that are used to refer to integrated environments.

User interface management systems (UIMS) and user interface design environment (UIDE). A UIDE is an integrated environment that offers facilities for designing the interface. The environment allows application programmers and interface designers to create interfaces without programming and without learning the details of underlying toolkits. Through the UIDE the designer creates an interface by describing the application at the semantic level, in terms of functionality, using objects and operations. A UIMS, strictly, focuses on the problems associated with interface execution, by mediating the interaction between the end-user of an application and the application code itself; the application carries out the tasks while the UIMS handles all details of communication with the end-user. A UIMS is a software tool that supports designers in the creation of a complete and working user interface, without having to program in a traditional programming language. Programming languages may be used to implement additional functions, such as database search and network communication, but the user interface can be created, reused and maintained in a higher-level language, via menus, forms and direct manipulation actions.

For development tools, in general, but particularly those for GUI development, there are a number of mini-markets. Content providers and source material experts with no programming expertise seek tools offering relative ease of use. Professional programmers, on the other hand, are looking for tools to support the integration of applications, some of which will be in existing code.

Supporting design

The design process has shifted from the earlier focus on programming and attempts to get the system to perform in a way that minimizes user-unfriendliness, with the focus now on usability. Designers now have tools at their disposal which make technical and physical design relatively straightforward. In addition to their skills in using these tools, they now need a host of skills which facilitate designs that meet customer needs, whether those customers be within the organization, or in the wider business or consumer marketplace. Some prerequisites for the design of ever better interfaces are:

1. Guidance, including guidelines, style guides, and so on, either in the form of specific house style guides or those provided by IBM, Motif, Apple or Microsoft, or other general purpose guidelines.
2. Acceptance criteria, which govern when the iterative process of software development should stop and the product be delivered to the marketplace.
3. Measures of usability, including those embedded in health and safety and ISO standards.
4. Support for communication, both within the design team and with users. This implies the availability of time and appropriate space with, if necessary, a good recording system. Video-conferencing facilities may support communication with geographically scattered team members or users.
5. Software for capturing ideas, exploring alternatives, recording decisions and converting them into programs or prototypes. UIMS are useful in this context.
6. Access to examples of other systems. Interfaces with good usability provide valuable inspiration for the creation of ever better interfaces. Review of a good range of alternative systems will suggest a wide range of design options.
7. Standardized notations and conventions for diagrams, such as data flow diagrams, entity relationship diagrams and data dictionaries, which support communication and the identification of what is required.
8. Understanding the context, which covers both an appreciation of the business objectives of the system, and the environment in which the system will be used.
9. Support for communicating and recording the decisions made during the design process. Too many systems are poorly documented. The maintenance of records of decision making during design forms a foundation for the development of appropriate documentation.
10. Support for collaborative working, ranging from e-mail and whiteboard to sophisticated workstations on which two or more designers can work at the same time, and teleconferencing.

11. Effective procedures for documenting design decisions and the key characteristics of the final design. These procedures need to address the generation of documentation which through its various generations may also act as a record of software maintenance.

Summary

For some methodologies it is not only difficult to differentiate design from evaluation, but also to separate the methodology from the tool. Accordingly, Chapters 6 and 7 should be used together to contribute to a complete understanding of design methodologies and their tools. Any organization involved in design will draw upon a wide range of methodological approaches and tools in structuring the methodology that is most appropriate for a specific application. Analysis and design tools to support functional and data modelling, usability and task modelling and interface modelling have been explored here. Physical design of the interface attempts to draw together all the preparatory work that may have been conducted during the earlier stages of analysis and design. Research must continue into the various tools and environmental factors that contribute to effective design.

References

Anderson, J. R. (1987), 'Skill acquisition: compilation of weak-method solutions', *Psychological Review*, **94**, 192–211.

Card, S. K., Moran, T. P. and Newell, A. (1983), *The Psychology of Human–Computer Interaction*, Lawrence Erlbaum, Hillsdale, NJ.

Catterall, B. J., Taylor, B. C. and Galer, M. D. (1991), 'The HUFIT planning, analysis and specification toolset: human factors as a normal part of the IT product design processing', in *Taking Software Design Seriously* (ed. J. Karat), Academic Press, London.

Green, T. R. G. (1989), 'Cognitive dimensions of notations', in *People and Computers IV* (eds A. Sutcliffe and L. Macaulay), Cambridge University Press, Cambridge.

Green, T. R. G. (1991), 'Describing information artifacts with cognitive dimensions and structure maps', in *People and Computers VI*, Proceedings of the 6th Conference of the British Computer Society Human–Computer Interaction Specialist Group (eds D. Diaper and N. V. Hammond), Cambridge University Press, Cambridge.

Johnson, P. (1992), *Human–Computer Interaction: Psychology, Task Analysis and Software Engineering*, McGraw-Hill, London.

Laird, J., Newell, A. and Rosenbloom, P. (1987), 'SOAR: an architecture for general intelligence', *Artificial Intelligence*, 33, 1–64.

Langford, D. and Jones, C. (1994), 'The kitchen interface – a lateral approach to GUI', *SIGCHI Bulletin*, **26** (2), 41–5.

Moran, T. P. (1981), 'The command language grammar: a representation of the user interface of interactive systems', *International Journal of Man–Machine Studies*, **15** (1), 3–50.

Tyldesley, D. A. (1988), 'Employing usability engineering in the development of office products', *Computer Journal*, **31** (5), 431–6.

Chapter 8

On-line help facilities and user support

The purpose of this chapter is to examine design and evaluation issues related to on-line help and user support in public access information databases. Specifically by the end of this chapter, you will:

- understand the role of on-line help and user support;
- be acquainted with some of the principles for the design of on-line help;
- have considered how on-line help can be used in a variety of different public access systems and contexts.

Help and support

Public access information systems are designed to be used by clients of an organization or information seekers in order to obtain information or the answer to a specific query. These users come with a primary task – to find the information or the answer they require. However, they also have a secondary task, which is to be able to use the searching tools of the public access information system to help them find the answer. Every public access system, no matter how intuitive or user-friendly, must provide a minimum amount of on-line help. This is necessary to support a first-time or novice user; a user carrying out a new task; or a user who has made a mistake in entering the query. Different levels of help are required in different systems and these will be considered in this chapter. However, as a minimum, on-line help should provide the user with information on how to start to use the system, how to enter the query, how to correct a mistake and how to exit from the system.

On-line help is provided in public access information systems in a variety of ways, both explicit and implicit. The most common methods of providing explicit help are:

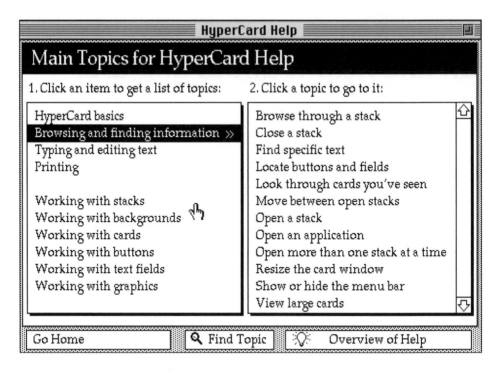

Figure 8.1   Part of a HyperCard help index

- messages available to a user when they choose a help option on a menu or a specific (often F1) button;
- dialogue boxes which provide contextual help;
- general help indexes, developed as part of the software (Figure 8.1).
- on-line documentation and electronic manuals;
- on-line tutorials and training.

Implicit help is provided for users in a number of ways; in the general text of the interface, in the design of the system itself and, in a public access system, it should provide the greatest part of the guidance to help users use the system.

In addition to on-line help and other electronic assistance, users can also be supported by printed documentation, printed instructions positioned around the terminal and training sessions provided by expert users or by the information providers. For novice or occasional users of complex bibliographic or full-text databases, training sessions are essential for effective searching by the users. However, users of tourist information systems, for example, can normally search successfully when guided by printed instructions close to the terminal.

Types of help and support facilities

Users require help to answer a number of their difficulties in using the public access information system. Preece et al. (1994, p. 314) categorizes these requirements as:

- goal exploration – 'What can I do with this system?'
- definition and description – 'What is this? What is it for?'
- task achievement – 'How do I do this?'
- diagnostic – 'How did that happen?'
- state identification – 'Where am I?'

Help facilities and user support should provide information which guides users through these requirements. Users need to know what to do next when they find themselves in difficulty. A request for on-line help should be answered with an explicit screen; if there is no specific request for help, implicit instructions embedded in the text should guide the user to a remedy. In certain situations, perhaps where an error is repeated, a 'pop-up' help screen will appear to show the user a route through the task.

General help

General help is normally information available from the top screen of the public access system. It contains details as diverse as the opening hours of the organization or the structure of the database. General help answers the user's requirements for goal exploration information and for definitions and descriptions of the system. Information for task achievement may also be provided, but general help will not normally answer diagnostic or state identification problems.

This type of help is accessed by a menu selection, a command such as HELP or '?', the F1 key or an icon and is normally displayed following a specific request from the user. On-line help in public access information systems can range from short prompts of less than one screen to 150 screens of information (Trenner, 1989).

Contextual help

Contextual help, or context-sensitive help, provides assistance and guidance to a user at a specific location or event in the searching task. The help facilities of the public access system take into account the context of the application at the time that the user requests help and so guide the user through the process in which they are engaged. For example, when a user of a banking ATM has made an error in selecting an option a dialogue box will appear which asks the user to press the Cancel Request button. This then interrupts and cancels the erroneous transaction and allows the user to proceed with the correct transaction.

Good context-sensitive help will assist not only the first-time user, but also the occasional user who may need to relearn specific operations, and the frequent user who is using an unfamiliar function in the system. In some public access systems, such as OPACs and CD-ROMs, contextual help provides hyperlinks or other facilities which allow the user to obtain more information on the task or function if it is required (Crawford, 1992). Contextual help provides information on task achievement, diagnostic and state identification problems.

Tutorials

A number of public access information systems allow users the opportunity to use an on-line tutorial before beginning a search on the system – these systems tend to be bibliographic or full-text databases on OPACs or CD-ROMs and so require more complex searches than the queries entered into a catalogue store kiosk or a tourist information service. Tutorials are a useful means of providing goal exploration, definition and description, and task achievement information. A well-designed tutorial will also give some assistance in diagnostic and state identification problems, but the user may not be able to memorize this information to use when a real, rather than simulated, problem arises.

On-line tutorials provide the users with a simulation of a searching task and guide them through the stages of entering and refining search terms and retrieving information. Tutorial facilities should be well designed and present a realistic simulation of a search. Discussing OPACs, Crawford states that 'tutorials should offer information about the online catalog, possibly at various levels of specificity' (1992, p. 67). The same applies to CD-ROM services and full-text databases, as users with all levels of experience may need to use a wide range of search functions in the database. However, a user may decide that a tutorial will take too long to carry out and may skip the tutorial in favour of continuing with the search. Therefore, while there is a place for on-line tutorials in a good public access system, they should not be seen as substitutes for an effective help facility.

Training and documentation

Users of public access information systems rarely experience any kind of training before carrying out the task because such systems are ideally designed to be intuitive, user-friendly and forgiving of errors. However, users of large complex database systems as described above, and in particular those databases provided through on-line hosts, do require prior training to carry out effective and efficient searches. This is especially important where the cost of telecommunication connections must be accounted for. On-line providers will run training sessions for library and information professionals who act as search intermediaries within their organizations. Training sessions are also provided in libraries and information units for users who wish to use CD-ROMs, OPACs or the Internet. Users are then issued with documentation which enables them to carry out their own searches more effectively. This documentation would be expected to complement, not replace, on-line help (Dohar, 1993). Both training and documentation are useful for goal exploration and task achievement, and documentation also provides definitions and descriptions.

The focus of research and practice in the USA has been on ways of teaching users, particularly in academic institutions, to use OPACs effectively. It is believed that this type of bibliographic instruction, learned while still in education, equips students with the ability to become efficient users of technology and searchers for information in the wider public arena. This is perhaps one reason why the spread of public access information systems, and especially the Internet, has been so rapid throughout the North American continent.

Review and apply:	Why may external training sessions not provide effective user support for public access information systems?
Answer:	In locations where any member of the public may use an information system, such as in a shopping centre, at an airport or in a museum, it is impossible to insist that users undergo a training session before using the public access system. However, in locations where there is an identifiable clientele, such as in a library, users can be offered specific training in using OPACs and CD-ROM services.

Summary of research and practice

An early description of on-line help systems was a paper by Houghton (1984) which discussed the type of on-line help provision on mainframe computer systems. The attributes required for effective on-line help, that is, 'availability, accuracy, consistency, completeness' (pp. 128–9) were listed, as were other elements which should be avoided, such as solid blocks of text, 'documentation overload' and 'anthropomorphization' (p. 129), that

- *Slash the verbiage.* Less to read can mean better training
- *Force coordination of the system and the training.* Training designs must impel the learner to attend to the system during the course of training
- *Expect every possible error.* Training should be designed with this understanding
- *Focus on real tasks and activities.* New users of application systems are generally not in the position of learning for learning's sake
- *Let the learner lead.* The expert perspective counts very little within the context of real learning

Source: Carroll (1984, pp. 129–30)

Figure 8.2   Minimalist training

is, the computer being presented as if it were human. Implementations of on-line help as contextual assistance; by means of natural language; and as a software simulation were described, and the results of experiments on different types of help systems were discussed. Houghton concluded that more research was needed to determine the effectiveness of on-line help for different user groups and to see how on-line help compared with assistance provided in the form of manuals and other documentation.

Another early paper, frequently cited by writers on on-line help and training facilities is 'Minimalist training' by John Carroll (1984). In it he reviewed common errors made by users in training and stated that 'people learning to use an office application system want to do real work, immediately' (p. 126). His 'minimalist' design principles proposed a number of measures, shown in Figure 8.2.

Although principally aimed at designers of user training tools, these general principles could equally be applied to the design and evaluation of on-line help facilities in public access information systems where users need to learn quickly how to carry out their intended tasks. Experiments carried out using 'minimalist' training produced encouraging results, where learners 'got started faster, produced better work, and spent less time ... on ... errors' (p. 136). Help systems are 'an essential part of the human–computer communication' (Fischer et al., 1985, p. 161), but 'providing help is a complex cognitive process' (Hancock-Beaulieu and Mitev, 1989, p. 113).

Shneiderman (1986) discussed a number of methods of providing help to users. In discussing on-line assistance he commented that 'there is limited understanding of what constitutes effective design for novices, intermittent knowledgeable users, and experts' (p. 30). To provide different levels of on-line help, Shneiderman suggested that users should be able to control for themselves the amount of 'informative feedback' (p. 55) which they received. Inexperienced users would need on-line help to confirm their actions, whereas regular users of the system would require assistance less frequently. However, it was also Shneiderman's contention that this was just 'helpful medicine' (p. 63) and that it would be more efficient to design a system where users would not make mistakes. In the second edition of his text, Shneiderman (1992) offers the following guidelines from Kearsley (1988):

- Make the help system easy to access and easy to return from.
- Make helps as specific as possible.
- Collect data to determine what helps are needed.
- Give users as much control over the help system as possible.
- Supply different helps for different types of users.
- Make help messages accurate and complete.
- Do not use helps to compensate for poor interface design.

Users and on-line help

While a great deal has been written about human–computer interaction, relatively little has been concerned with the provision of on-line help to end-users. It seems that although most writers recognize the need for a clear and adequate on-line help facility, little research has attempted to discover the attitudes of users to the on-line help provided. Use of on-line help takes place in between only 5 per cent and 20 per cent of interactions (Slack, 1991; Preece et al., 1994), so a considerable amount of data needs to be collected in order to examine the use of on-line help. There are a number of reasons why users do not request help, including the fact that use of help interrupts their search and users think that they might not be able to resume their search after they have consulted the help screen (Lipow, 1991). Crawford points out that 'if there is one thing we know about almost all user interfaces and their Help systems, it is that most people will not ask for help even when they need it and it is clearly labeled' (1992, p. 74).

Slack (1991) examined the use of help facilities by end-users while carrying out subject searches on academic library OPACs and recommended five guidelines for on-line help and instruction facilities:

1. Improving general instructions so that the user did not have to break off from a search to use a help screen.
2. Development of the GUI to provide novel help and instruction messages, particularly through the use of windows and icons.

In 1990, when this research was carried out, GUIs were only available on a limited number of facilities, mainly in the Apple Macintosh environment. Since then developments have meant that both OPACs and

CD-ROM services have incorporated some or all of GUI attributes into their interfaces.

3. Provision of 'pop-up' help screens which would appear after a certain number of errors, or in a particular state of searching activity.
4. Use of multiple interfaces and different levels of help to serve the wide range of users.
5. The use of 'Hints for subject searching', that is, embedded conceptual help 'hints' displayed in rotation whenever a user selects the Keyword or Subject search options.

Review and apply:	Consider a public access system which you have used. Which of these guidelines have been incorporated in the design of the interface? Are there design difficulties associated with any of the guidelines?
Answer:	GUIs which embed general help are now commonplace in many public access environments. More specialized information retrieval systems, such as CD-ROMs and OPACs, frequently offer different interfaces or different search strategies for different levels of user. The use of overlapping windows to display contextual help is desirable, but not that easy to provide. However, Crawford makes the point that 'requiring the user to escape out of Help before issuing the new command is just plain rude, albeit easier to implement' (1992, p. 69).

On-line help in public access systems

Much of the research into aspects of on-line help and user support has concentrated on the assistance required by users of task-oriented systems such as word processors. Carroll and Kay (1988) worked on the minimal manual and the scenario machine to train users of office technology where repetition, summaries, reviews, exercises and indexes were eliminated and explanations unrelated to practical action were omitted. Learners were asked to try out things and see what happened, and information on error recovery was greatly increased. The principles developed in this environment were useful to the designers of user interfaces for public access information systems.

It can be seen that different users carrying out different tasks in different contexts are likely to benefit from different types of help. However, in the case of public access systems, the interface tends to be designed with minimal or embedded help in place and relies on clear instructions to support the user. The minimal instruction approach to both electronic and printed documentation has been shown to speed learning for some tasks. However, there is a difference between true public access where a user may be any member of the public, and locations such as libraries where users can be trained or offered on-line tutorials.

On-line help systems are weakest when users are unable to conceptualize their questions, and conceptual difficulties are particularly common in public access systems, especially when the search is for a subject rather than a known item (Slack and Wood, 1990). In public access information systems conceptual navigation concerns navigation through the ideas represented by the material; physical navigation concerns navigation between items of information as presented. This demonstrates the difference between contextual help and general help; between goal exploration and task achievement. The tools, aids and metaphors provided in the system for physical navigation should fit the users' models of the concepts they are investigating (see also the section in Chapter 2 on mental models).

Review and apply:	What is the minimum amount of help required on a public access information system?
Answer:	How to start the system; how to enter the query; how to correct a mistake; how to exit from the system.

Design and evaluation of on-line help systems

Guidelines for the evaluation of on-line help facilities may also be employed by user interface designers. There is no ideal help facility for public access information systems in the same way that there is no ideal user and no ideal searching task. However, there are a number of standards by which on-line help can be measured. Trenner (1989) suggested a list of guidelines which she developed through her research. Although the research was carried out some time ago, the guidelines are still relevant in public access systems today:

- On-line help should be available at all times.
- It should be easy both to enter and exit the help facility.
- The help facility should be well constructed and reveal its structure to the user.
- Help should be well presented.
- Help information should be well written and the language used should be friendly.
- Help should accommodate more than one user level.

In addition to Trenner's guidelines, Crawford (1992) offers the advice that the word 'error' should never appear in on-line text!

The two types of on-line help which are required in any system are described here. Operational help corresponds to general help and covers the definitions and descriptions of the system. It also provides some measure of task achievement information. Conceptual help corresponds to contextual help and supports the user in task achievement, in diagnostic problems and in state identification.

Operational help

Operational help supports the mechanical operations that need to be performed by the user in terms of keystrokes, form of commands and meaning of specific menu options. It is relatively easy to write and easy to understand – therefore operational help is seen as being effective. Operational help is provided explicitly through the on-line help facility and implicitly through the system's instructions and on-screen presentation.

The first five guidelines should be met by operational help. As soon as a user accesses the information system a reminder of how to obtain on-line help should be displayed on the screen at all times. Entering the on-line help facility by means of a menu option, a command, the F1 button or an icon should be simple to carry out and users must be able to return to their previous position when they exit from help. The help facility should be structured in such a way that it presents a logical appearance to the user and that relationships between elements can be identified. Space and text should be well balanced on the help screens and users should not feel that they are receiving too much information. The language used on the help screens must be appropriate, accurate and impersonal but polite.

Figure 8.3 shows an operational on-line help screen which gives definitions of the services provided by the system.

Conceptual help

Conceptual help is concerned with understanding the task and the way in which the system breaks the task down into subtasks. For example, in the catalogue store multimedia kiosk users need to understand the sequence of tasks to place an order (see Figure 7.7). In searching a bibliographic database, however, the user needs to understand the nature of the indexing and search terms and the precision and recall that can be expected to be achieved with different search strategies, and then what strategy to try next if the first attempt is unsuccessful. A search for 'great barrier reef' as a phrase will yield very different results from a search where the terms great, barrier, reef may be implicitly ANDed by the system. Conceptual help must assist the user in addressing these concepts.

Gift Selector   Internet Store   Services at Argos   HomeHelp   Special Offers & LinksHelp

Services at Argos

Here you can find out where your nearest store is, how our delivery service works, a list of your most frequently asked questions (and an opportunity to ask your own) and an application to ensure that details of our wedding list service get to someone you know who is getting married. There are also details about Argos Premier Incentives.

back to Help index   View order   Go to checkout

Figure 8.3   **An operational help screen**

Trenner's (1989) six guidelines apply to conceptual help, particularly the advice that help should accommodate more than one user level. However, a number of help requirements are related to conceptual information and this is a much more difficult area in which to provide on-line help. In a library context, for example, when a user is experiencing difficulty with an OPAC or a CD-ROM database, support may be better provided by means of printed documentation, a training manual or a tutorial session, rather than by on-line explicit conceptual help. Implicit conceptual help, however, may be provided by any sequence of operations that the system forces the user through. For example, Figure 8.4 shows a Boolean search screen where implicit help is given to the user by requiring the radio buttons to be used to combine terms.

Review and apply:	At what stage in the system lifecycle should the design of the help and support facilities for public access information systems be carried out?
Answer:	This should be done alongside software development and should use prototyping with potential users as part of the development.

Help and support for on-line databases

On-line databases are traditionally searched by expert intermediaries who are familiar with the services provided and can search efficiently at a minimum cost of telecommunication charges. Most users prefer printed documentation to any form of electronic help (Harris and Oppenheim,

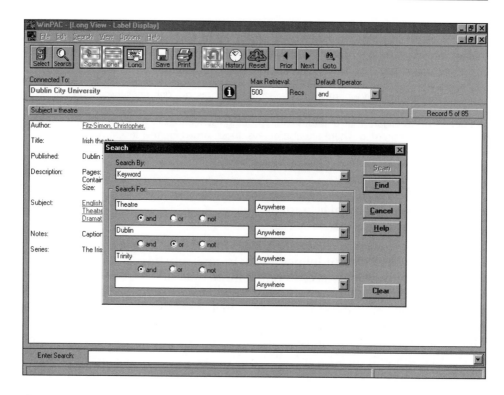

Source: Dynix Library Systems (UK) Ltd

Figure 8.4   Implicit conceptual help in a Boolean search

1996), although amounts of printed documentation are increasing. The emphasis of help and support has traditionally been on the contents of databases, for example, the structure of records and commands, possibly with some advice of the optimum search strategies. Training sessions and on-line tutorials are an important part of the user support for on-line databases.

Help and support for CD-ROM services

General help and contextual help are required on CD-ROM services to support users. Feinberg (1991) suggested that contextual help be provided for every screen with instructions, tips and warnings for both novice and expert users, together with dialogue boxes which pop up to support Boolean searches. Harris and Oppenheim (1996) found that CD-ROM users searching bibliographic databases, however, did prefer printed documentation. On GUI-based services Bosch and Hancock-Beaulieu

(1995) recommended that explicit general help and explicit contextual help be provided throughout the CD-ROMs in separate windows, although care should be taken in the design to avoid cluttered screens. On-line tutorials and training sessions are also required by novice users (Large, 1991; Keylard, 1993). A number of public library authorities have been training their users on CD-ROM services and this has met with some success (Batterbee, 1996).

Help and support for OPACs

Research for the Council on Library Resources project in the USA investigated the provision of general off-line and on-line user assistance (Markey, 1984). It was found that most users learned to use the OPAC from printed material and that most users obtained help during their searches by using printed instructions. Although the OPAC systems studied at that time have now been superseded, an important finding from Markey's work still applies to current systems. It is vital for users to be able to relearn use of public access systems, as their use of the system is not an everyday occurrence. The provision of implicit general help in the instructions of the OPAC and contextual task achievement help screens remind users of how to perform searches. In some OPACs on-line help is provided in a separate window so that both the help and the task can be seen at the same time (Beaulieu, 1997).

There is a new challenge in library-based public access information systems that provide access to OPAC, community information, various Internet resources and the catalogues of other libraries. In public (rather than academic) libraries this creates a demand for very complex help as many users with different levels of experience, different languages and different backgrounds are accessing the systems. End-user training is needed to enhance and complement the on-line help provided on the OPACs.

Help and support for multimedia and hypermedia systems

The current research on help and support in multimedia and hypermedia systems is based on four main areas (Liu and Wheat, 1995):

1. **Instructional** – dealing with instructional strategies used in the systems. These are the basis for the approaches used and the philosophies reflected in the system.

2. **Branching** – how to navigate through a system and how much user control should be provided.
3. **Affective** – dealing with learning styles and motivation factors, which are critical perceptual aspects of the learning environment.
4. **Media** – the different types of media used, such as interactive videodisk, CD-ROM, CD-I and DV-I.

These issues are important in the design of multimedia systems and in the provision of help and support to users. Because multimedia kiosks and hypertext systems appear to be user-friendly it is vital that such systems are well designed. They should be capable of satisfying a user's need by presenting information in such a way that a user will find it interesting and motivating enough to use again. They should also support a user's navigation strategy and ensure that a user does not get 'lost in hyperspace' while having total control of the system.

Implicit help, designed into the system can provide an overview, or holistic view, of the system and allow the user to know: Where have I been? Where am I going next? What else is there to see? Figure 8.5 shows the overview screen of the Celtic Museum, a HyperCard museum information system (Newton, 1991). From this screen the user can see all the

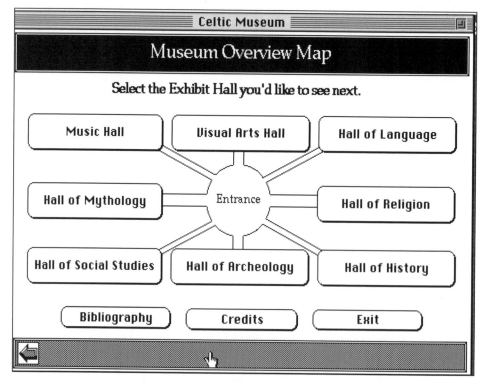

Figure 8.5   Navigation in a hypertext system

parts of the museum system and can move straight to one gallery simply by clicking on one area of the map.

Help and support for systems on the Internet

Different Internet sites run different types of software for accessing their catalogues and databases. This results in two issues:

1. Since different sites may have different search capabilities, the screen for different sites may vary. The structure of the search screen should be designed to give the user an intuitive feel for the kinds of searches that can be conducted. For example, some sites allow for searching across multiple term types. In other words, it is possible to enter both author and subject search terms, thus allowing a user to search for all references to a particular subject written by a particular author. Sites which allow this sort of searching typically provide implicit help by means of a search screen which provides for entering multiple search term types during a single search. Sites which do not allow multiple-term searching provide implicit help by means of a screen which allows the entry of only one term type at a time.

2. Different sites, databases and catalogues may display data in a variety of forms or at various levels of completeness. This results in the display of data from a particular search being different in different catalogues. For example, some catalogues may return complete location information, while others do not. This help is provided implicitly in the way that the output screen is designed.

Explicit help screens on the Internet give information and support in:

*   Goal exploration – 'What can I do with this system?'
*   Definition and description – 'What is this? What is it for?'
*   Task achievement – 'How do I do this?'

Figure 8.6 shows the explicit general help screen of The Internet Antiques Shop which defines and describes the site, indicates what can be achieved and what aspects of the site can be explored.

Explicit help screens on database or catalogue sites are used to guide a user through the process of entering a search term into the appropriate search term fields. Once the terms have been entered, it is necessary to press the Submit button in order to execute the search. Subsequent sets of records can be retrieved easily from the screen presented in response to a search. Thus it is possible to view all the entries for a particular search by retrieving subsequent sets of records. The next set to be retrieved is determined automatically, and can be retrieved by pressing the Retrieve button from the Search Results screen.

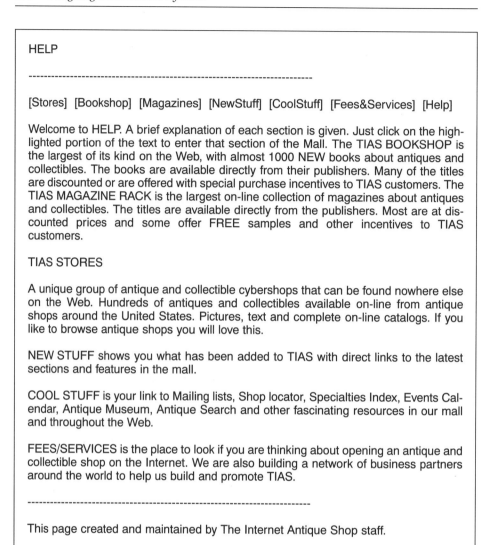

Figure 8.6   **An Internet help screen**

Some searches provide implicit help to allow for the specification of special attributes to be associated with search terms. These attributes are typically selected by toggling a radio button under the search term boxes (see Figure 8.4). Often the default values for these attributes will give good results, but the user may need further guidance to improve the search.

At this point some systems refer the user to their printed documentation which is not restricted by the size of the screen and can give more detailed explanation and illustration. This is appropriate when the user is in a library or information unit, or has the documentation ready to hand. However, if the user is searching an Internet system in the home or in an office where the documentation is not available, the system support may not be sufficient to help the user.

Summary

In using public access information systems the requirement for most members of the public is to be 'fast in and fast out'. They do not wish their primary task – to obtain information – to be subsumed in their secondary task – using the information system effectively. This chapter has shown that on-line help and user support falls into a number of categories and is provided both explicitly and implicitly. Operational and contextual help, on-line tutorials and off-line training and documentation should all be provided where appropriate to support users in their seeking task. Research has shown that on-line help is used by very few people, but Crawford states that there is a need for 'effective online Help, even if the people who need it most may not use it that much' (1992).

References

Batterbee, C. (1996), 'Case study 2: public libraries', in *The End-user Revolution: CD-ROM, Internet and the Changing Role of the Information Professional* (ed. R. Biddiscombe), Library Association Publishing, London, pp. 110–18.

Beaulieu, M. (1997), 'Experiments on interfaces to support query expansion', *Journal of Documentation*, **53** (1), 8–19.

Bosch, V. M. and Hancock-Beaulieu, M. (1995), 'CD-ROM user interface evaluation: the appropriateness of GUIs', *Online and CD-ROM Review*, **19** (5), 255–270.

Carroll, J. M. (1984), 'Minimalist training', *Datamation*, **30** (18), 125–36.

Carroll, J. M. and Kay, D. S. (1988), 'Prompting, feedback and error correction in the design of a scenario machine', *International Journal of Man–Machine Studies*, **28** (1), 11–27.

Crawford, W. (1992), 'Starting over: current issues in online catalog user interface design', *Information Technology and Libraries*, **11** (1), 62–76.

Dohar, J. (1993), 'Documentation for novice computer users', in *Toward New Horizons, ACM SIGUCCS*, ACM, pp. 437–9.

Feinberg, S. (1991), 'Helping the user retrieve data from a CD-ROM', in *9th Annual International Conference on System Documentation*, pp. 3–4.

Fischer, G., Lemke, A. and Schwab, T. (1985), 'Knowledge-based help systems', in *Human Factors in Computing Systems II*, Proceedings of the CHI '85 Conference, San Francisco, 14–18 April 1985 (eds L. Borman and B. Curtis), Elsevier, Amsterdam, pp. 161–7.

Hancock-Beaulieu, M. and Mitev, N. N. (1989), 'Online library catalogues: the interactive dimension', in *Perspectives in Information Management 1*, (ed. C. Oppenheim), Butterworths, Oxford, pp. 89–118.

Harris, S. and Oppenheim, C. (1996), 'Does machine-readable documentation on online hosts and CD-ROMs have a role or future?', *Journal of Information Science*, **22** (4), 247–58.

Houghton, R. C. (1984), 'Online help systems: a conspectus', *Communications of the ACM*, **27** (2), 126–33.

Kearsley, G. (1988), *Online Help Systems: Design and Implementation*, Ablex, Norwood, NJ.

Keylard, M. (1993), 'CD-ROM implementation in developing countries: impacts and pitfalls', *IFLA Journal*, **19** (1), 35–49.

Large, A. (1991), 'The user interface to CD-ROM databases', *Journal of Librarianship and Information Science*, **23** (4), 203–17.

Lipow, A. G. (1991), 'Instructional impact of the online public access catalog', in *Think Tank on the Present and Future of the Online Catalog: Proceedings* (RASD Occasional Papers: 9), ALA Midwinter Meeting, Chicago, 11–12 January (ed. N. van Pulis), RASD/ALA, pp. 85–96.

Liu, M. and Wheat, J. (1995), 'Designing effective multimedia kiosks', in *Educational Multimedia and Hypermedia Conference*, pp. 401–6.

Markey, K. (1984), 'Offline and online user assistance for online catalog searchers', *Online*, **8** (3), 54–66.

Newton, M. (1991), *Celtic Museum*, HyperCard stack, 40522 Eady Lane, Boulevard, CA 91905.

Preece, J. et al. (1994), *Human-Computer Interaction*, Addison-Wesley, Wokingham.

Shneiderman, B. (1986), *Designing the User Interface: Strategies for Effective Human-Computer Interaction*, Addison-Wesley, Reading, MA.

Shneiderman, B. (1992), *Designing the User Interface: Strategies for Effective Human-Computer Interaction*, 2nd edn, Addison-Wesley, Reading, MA.

Slack, F. E. (1991), 'OPACs: using enhanced transaction logs to achieve more effective online help facilities for subject searching', PhD thesis, Manchester Polytechnic (unpublished).

Slack, F. E. and Wood, A. J. (1990), 'Subject searching on British OPACs: problems and progress', *Library Review*, **39** (6), 41–9.

Trenner, L. (1989), 'A comparative survey of the friendliness of online "help" in interactive information retrieval systems', *Information Processing and Management*, **25** (2), 119–136.

Chapter 9

Evaluation

Evaluation is central to the design process, since it informs the design team of the fit between the system and the needs of users in terms of user characteristics, the tasks for which the system will be used, the environment and the supporting technology. By the end of this chapter, you will have acquired a familiarity with some of the established evaluation methodologies and be able to conduct evaluation studies as well as critically appraise studies conducted and reported by others. Specifically, you will:

- understand the role of evaluation and its place in the design process.
- be familiar with methods for collecting usage data.
- appreciate the value of and procedures associated with experiments and benchmarking.
- be able to select appropriate evaluation methods.
- be able to conduct effective and efficient evaluation.

The role of evaluation

Evaluation is typically the 'Achilles heel' of public access systems. In most cases such systems are developed by commercial organizations with little sophistication in research design and under intense time pressure to complete the job. (Kearsley and Heller, 1995)

The star life cycle (Hix and Harston, 1993) was introduced in Figure 6.10 as a model for one possible design methodology. The strength of this model is the central role that it accords to evaluation. Evaluation in the most general of terms is involved with gathering data about the usability of a design or product for a specific activity within a specific environment. Why conduct evaluation? In general, the objective of evaluation is to find out what users want, and what problems they experience, with a view to improving product design. For public access systems it is important to consider both formative and summative evaluations, as described below.

Hewett (1986) distinguishes between formative and summative evaluation by focusing on their purpose:

Formative evaluation helps the designer to refine and form the design. Formative evaluation therefore needs to have an emphasis on qualitative information, which can be used to assist the designer in the identification of problems, and to identify appropriate changes.

Summative evaluation involves assessing the impact, usability and effectiveness of the system, and is concerned with the overall performance of the user and the system. The focus here may be more strongly on quantitative data.

The relationship between summative and formative evaluation is different for public access systems to that in other information systems. Taking formative evaluation as that which is conducted before the system 'goes live', all the usual formative evaluation techniques will be used during the development phase. However, summative evaluation is equally important and is the norm with public access systems. Summative evaluation leads to the development of a later version of the software or the interface, possibly over a period of months or years. Summative evaluation is important because:

1. As has been emphasized throughout this book, it is not possible to evaluate the interface in isolation from its environment. An interface for, say, a multimedia CD-ROM that might be acceptable in the home may be less appropriate in an airport departure lounge. Typically such an interface may require less complexity, and needs to be multilingual. Retailers recognize the importance of location and are currently trialling kiosks in different stores with a view to identifying the impact of location on the nature and volume of use of the kiosks.

2. Interface evaluation cannot be separated from evaluation of the use of the device as a whole. Businesses and public sector organizations that are involved in access to information via public access avenues, such as kiosks and CD-ROM access in public libraries, need to ask whether people will use this technology, what they will gain from that use and, in general, is the public access technology worth the investment?

Related to the type of evaluation being performed is the issue of who is conducting the evaluation. There are three main categories of evaluators:

● End-users and their representatives in the form of experts, both explicitly during the design and evaluation process, and implicitly in their use and selection of the interface.

- Designers, in reflecting on comments from users and reviewers, and in formulating their own evaluation of the effectiveness of the interface.
- Intermediaries, such as library and information professionals, where these professionals will evaluate a product on behalf of the end-user.

There are four general reasons for conducting a formative evaluation:

1. To understand the uses for which the system will be employed, including users, activities and context.
2. To compare two alternative designs, in order to select the best design or design idea.
3. To benchmark against competitors to ensure that aspects of the design are at least as good and preferably better than those of competitors.
4. To check conformance to a standard, for instance, with respect to screen legibility.

The reasons for performing a summative evaluation are:

- to complete the evaluation and selection process when choosing between information products such as different CD-ROMs.
- to collect data on user perceptions that will inform enhanced design of later products, either through user evaluation of existing products or through evaluation of competitors' products.

Evaluations may occur at different points in the design and selection process. Specifically, within design, evaluation may be conducted to:

- check the design team's understanding of users' requirements by examining how an existing system is being used in the field;
- predict features that will be important to incorporate for good usability;
- identify user difficulties so that the product can be more finely tuned to meet their needs;
- improve an upgrade of the product.

Review and apply:	Is a research study which seeks to evaluate the interfaces of seven CD-ROM products performing formative or summative evaluation?
Answer:	In simple terms, summative evaluation, but in the sense that this evaluation may inform later designs, it is difficult to distinguish between formative and summative evaluation.

Irrespective of whether formative or summative evaluation is being conducted, it is important to consider:

- the characteristics of the users or predicted users, including experience, age, gender, psychological and physical characteristics;
- the activities or proposed activities that the users will perform;
- the environment of the study, which could range from a controlled laboratory to a natural work or leisure or public setting;
- the nature of the artifact being evaluated; evaluation may be performed on the finished product, but also on a series of sketches or a working prototype.

Different evaluation objectives will demand different approaches to evaluation. Most approaches to evaluation can be classified into one of the following categories:

- **Observing and monitoring users' interaction**, both in a laboratory and a natural setting, with a view to gaining an insight into users' performance.
- **Eliciting users' opinions** because, very simply, if users do not like using an interface they will not do so.
- **Experiment or benchmark tests** where the experimenter attempts to control some variable whilst examining the effect of varying others. These tests are often conducted in a usability laboratory.
- **Interpretative evaluation**, which investigates how the system integrates with other activities in its natural setting.
- **Predictive evaluation**, concerned with predicting the usability of a product without direct feedback on users' opinions. Prediction may be based on a psychological modelling technique, such as keystroke analysis, or by using expert reviewers.

Often more than one method will be used in order to yield a multi-dimensional perspective on the design. Any evaluation method, or combination of methods, must be:

- valid, so that the evaluation is measuring what is required given the purpose of the evaluation;
- thorough, so that the scope of the investigation is appropriate;
- reliable and consistent, so that the same results would arise, with the same test conducted again on subsequent occasions, under the same conditions.

Most of the above methods involve users. User involvement in testing provides important insights and user testers must be regarded as a valuable resource. In a testing context, it is important therefore to ensure that users are relaxed and natural so that they can be reflective and objective. Designers need to cultivate environments in which this is likely to be possible. Specifically it is useful to remember that:

- users have other things to do and their time is precious;

- pilot studies can assist in refining the observational or data gathering process;
- users need reassuring that it is the system that is under test and not them;
- confidentiality with respect to observations and comments should be paramount at all times;
- users should be informed of the objective of the test and in some instances it will be courteous to inform them of the outcome.

Above all else, designers need to remember that they may want to go back to the same users for later evaluations and that they need to cultivate their relationships accordingly.

Review and apply:	Why are users a valuable component of the evaluation process?
Answer:	Because collectively they have greater familiarity with the task, and the knowledge and experience that users bring to the system. A properly constituted test panel draws on a variety of different perspectives, which it is difficult for the designer to anticipate without such consultation.

Observations

The methods in this section focus on the observation of users when they are interacting with systems. Observations may be used to investigate how a specific task, such as searching for the location of a specific product in a large shopping mall, is performed, or to examine how the technology is used in different environments. For example, are multimedia kiosks generally used by individuals, couples or families, and how does the absence of seating affect the way in which users use an OPAC?

Review and apply:	Comment on the user characteristics, environment and tasks associated with a bank ATM machine.
Answer:	User characteristics: general population, wide age range, but no children and a smaller percentage of the over 60s, population all has money, and is seeking a fast and convenient transaction.
	Environment: exposed in some situations and therefore vulnerable to assault and theft, adverse weather conditions and passing traffic noise and movement. Environments include: shopping mall, high street, station, airport and other public arenas.
	Tasks: Typically, withdrawing money, inspecting account balances, and ordering a statement.

Observation may take a number of different forms ranging from the informal to the formal, but in all cases it is important to be aware that physiological and psychological factors may determine the way in which an observer interprets their observations. Observation is not always as straightforward as it may seem (Diaper, 1989). Observers bring a range of preconceptions which influence the way in which they observe. Cross checking of these perceptions, by using other methods of evaluation or observation performed by other evaluators, should be carried out to contribute to the minimization of bias. There are a number of observational techniques, as specified below.

Direct observation

Users may be observed conducting specially designed tasks or in their natural setting. The observer may take notes. There are three main disadvantages of direct observation:

- It is very difficult to conduct unobtrusive observations; the sense of being watched may influence people's actions.
- Notes will always be selective and subjective. Unless the types of actions to be noted are carefully specified in advance, it is likely that the note keeping may be somewhat random since it is difficult to distinguish key activities and interactions.
- Cognitive information such as attitudes, beliefs, motivation or perception cannot be observed.

One strategy for overcoming this last limitation is active observation, where the observer first watches and then later asks questions about why a particular behaviour has been adopted.

Despite these limitations, observation is a widely used means of investigation and can provide valuable informal feedback which may support the design of other more structured evaluation experiments.

Indirect observation: video recording

Video recording or video logging is preferred to direct observation in many circumstances because it provides a permanent record which can be revisited and reviewed by others in addition to the original observer. Video logging is also a little less intrusive than direct observation, although users may still be uncomfortable with 'being on camera'.

Again, the effectiveness of video logging depends on having a clear understanding of what it is that is being examined. This will determine when a video recording is made and will be important in analysing the video data. For example, a small sample of a series of users using an encyclopaedia on CD-ROM might facilitate the investigation of the sections in the encyclopaedia that attract attention and the way in which users move between different sections, whereas an extended video of the general environs of a multimedia kiosk for ordering goods from a catalogue might be necessary to investigate general reactions to the kiosk, and the way in which family groups might handle such transactions.

There are two formal approaches that are widely used in analysing video data:

1. **Task-based analysis**, which seeks to determine the way in which users tackle given tasks, to identify the difficulties and reflect on means for alleviating any problems. This might, for instance, study the search route for locating a specific document in a library catalogue, or the way in which users browse or surf the Internet.

2. **Performance-based analysis**, which seeks to obtain performance measures. Typical measures are drawn from the general metrics that were introduced in Chapter 7:
   - frequency of correct task completion;
   - task timing;
   - use of commands;
   - frequency of user errors;
   - time taken for specific cognitive activities, such as reading sections of the screen;
   - frequency of errors.

Reliability of video logging is important across several test groups and evaluators. In addition, analysis of video can be time-consuming. Some projects have sought to develop tools to support this analysis. These include the European ESPRIT Project MUSiC and VANNA (Video ANNotation and Analysis) (Harrison, 1991), which is a tool produced at the University of Toronto.

Review and apply:	Why is video recording preferred to direct observation in most interface evaluations?
Answer:	Video recording produces a permanent record which can be revisited and re-analysed by the original evaluator and other team members. The record is less selective, and there is time for the evaluator to undertake more reflection in their analysis.

Indirect observation: verbal protocols

The audio record that often accompanies a video record is known as a **verbal protocol** (Ericsson and Simon, 1988). These protocols are particularly valuable if it is possible to encourage users to include spoken observations on the tasks that they are involved in completing; such a protocol is sometimes called a **think-aloud protocol** (for example, Carroll and Mack, 1984). Verbal protocols can be enhanced by encouraging some interaction. This interaction may take the form of a dialogue between two users, or a question-asking situation where the user is permitted to request assistance from the evaluator when problems arise. **Post-event protocols** are obtained by asking the user to view a video and to provide a commentary on their actions after the event. When using post-event protocols evaluators need to be alert to the 'wisdom of hindsight'!

Review and apply:	What effect do you think that the 'wisdom of hindsight' might have on the data available from post-event protocols?
Answer:	In general, users may seek to view themselves in a more favourable light, so, for example, they may rationalize earlier mistakes in the light of knowledge that is acquired later in the process.

Indirect observation: software or data logging

Software logging is an unobtrusive way of monitoring how the interaction works. Software logging has been widely used in investigating design issues in OPACs. For example, Slack (1996) describes the use of data logging in the investigation of the use of help systems in OPACs.

There are two types of software logging:

1. **Time-stamped key presses** – which provide a record of each key that the user presses and records the time of each event. These provide a limited perspective on the interaction, which only reveals part of the picture when assessing search paths or in the evaluation of GUI-based system.
2. **Interaction logging** – where the recording is made in real time and can be replayed so that the observer can see the interaction. The combination of video, audio and key presses or interaction logging allows evaluators to relate data about body language, comments on audio protocols and records of the actual interaction. Such models are

common in usability laboratories, but in other contexts are expensive to establish, and may yield complex multi-dimensional data which presents real challenges in analysis.

Review and apply: Draw a table summarizing the strengths and weaknesses of data logging.

Answer:

Strengths	Weaknesses
Unobtrusive observation	No information on why actions were performed
Collects detailed data on search strategies and key presses	Need to establish logging facilities and sample logs at appropriate times
	Yields a lot of data requiring significant analysis of effort
	No easy tools for analysis of the recorded logs

Case study: Museum database – data logging (Schneiderman et al., 1989)

Field testing of three museum databases made use of data logging. In two of the museums, a database describing the work of the photographer David Seymour was used. Data were collected by data logging. These data included the time that each user session began, the name of the database article accessed, and the number of seconds spent in using each article. From these data, the developers were able to determine the most popular articles and access patterns. They were also able to compare the nature of the usage in the two museums, which reflect the differences in interests and backgrounds of the visitors to each museum. In a third museum, a different database on volunteer groups in archaeology was involved. In the evaluation, observation and interviews preceded the use of data logging. Problems with hardware, the hypertext system and the organization of the database were quickly identified. After correcting these problems, data logging was used to study the nature of the system usage, including the popularity of the different interfaces and the use of the index.

Users' opinions: interviews and questionnaires

Interviews and questionnaires are the two standard methods for collecting data on users' preferences and attitudes. Whilst such information is valuable, it should not be used uncritically. The literature on the concept and measurement of quality in the service experience (for example, Gronroos, 1988; Parasuraman et al., 1988) draws attention to the difficulty of defining the concept of quality. Although the debate continues around the precise formulation of service quality (for example, Cronin and Taylor, 1994; Teas, 1993), the relationship between expectations and perceptions that underpins this debate is sufficient to alert a researcher or evaluator to the role of expectations in the formulation of quality judgements. Equally, perceptions are found to be influenced by a variety of factors that are extraneous to the direct service experience, such as the environment (for example, Bitner, 1992) and customer-to-customer compatibility (for example, Rowley, 1996).

This section explores the use of interviews, including individual interviews and focus groups, and questionnaires, both in postal and telephone surveys and in usability assessment, as means of gathering data on users' preferences and attitudes.

Individual interviews

Interviews are useful for gathering facts and opinions; the data collected are generally qualitative in nature. The two-way communication that is a feature of interviews should lead to provide a more multidimensional analysis of the situation, yielding qualitative data concerning not only what a user does, but also why they do it.

There are two main types of one-to-one interview: **structured interviews** and unstructured or flexible interviews, sometimes called **in-depth interviews**. Structured interviews are guided by a set of predetermined questions often recorded on an interview checklist. Structured interviews are easier to analyse, and comparing the comments made by different people is more straightforward. Flexible interviews are guided only by a list of set topics; the interviewer allows the interview to develop in response to the interviewee's comments. Such interviews are useful for 'discovering the unknown' and identifying facts or attitudes that might not have been recited by the evaluator as being an issue, and therefore would have been omitted from a more structured interview based on a predetermined checklist. The main disadvantages of this type of interview are that they are time-consuming, need to be conducted by a trained interviewer and consequently can be very expensive. **Semi-structured interviews** are guided by a list of topics, but the way in which this list of topics is used depends upon the interviewee's responses; accordingly, different interviews may progress along different routes.

Focus groups

Focus groups are group discussions with between eight and ten people, specially selected in accordance with a set of predetermined criteria. The members of the groups exchange attitudes, experiences and beliefs about the particular topic. The advantages of focus groups are that:

1. Respondents feel safety in numbers and therefore greater willingness to express insights and greater spontaneity.
2. The process highlights the possible range of different attitudes and behaviours in a short time.
3. The group can be observed with the aim of yielding data on reactions, vocabulary and perceptions.
4. Group discussion triggers counter-responses, which might not surface in individual discussion.

The disadvantages of focus groups are that:

1. They may inhibit frank and confidential exchanges on sensitive issues.
2. Minority viewpoints and less dominant personalities may be lost.
3. Group leadership and facilitation requires training and expertise.

Projective techniques

Within the context of individual interviews or focus groups, a wide range of projective techniques can be used to elicit responses. These provide an indirect means of questioning that enables respondents to 'project' beliefs and feelings on to a third party, an inanimate object or a task situation. The underlying theory is that while it is sometimes impossible to obtain accurate information concerning what a person thinks and feels by asking them to explain their own thoughts and feelings, this information can be obtained by allowing a respondent to project these on to some other person or object. There are a number of different techniques, including:

*   sentence completion exercises, where a respondent is given the first part of a sentence and asked to finish it off;
*   word association tests, where a series of words are fired at the respondent, and they are expected to say immediately another word that comes into their mind;
*   psychodrama, which involves people in an imaginary situation, where they are asked to act out their anticipated behaviour.

In conducting an interview, whether it be an individual interview or a focus group, it is important to:

- undertake appropriate planning, including defining objectives, duration, venue and background information.
- gain authorization for the interview.
- control the interview so that it achieves its objectives, but without stifling unexpected information.
- use questions and terminology that the users understand.
- remain impersonal and objective.
- listen and watch!

Interviews can be recorded using a video or tape recorder or notes may be taken by the interviewer.

Review and apply:	Describe how you would establish a structured focus group interview to evaluate an interface for a public library OPAC.
Answer:	The key issues that must be considered include:
	• planning, including interview objectives and list of topics to guide a structured conversation.
	• selection and encouragement to participate in relation to user group.
	• authorization.
	• acknowledgement of the focus group members' contribution.

Questionnaires and surveys

Questionnaires can either be used to conduct a wider survey than might be possible with other methods or as part of a usability evaluation to collect subjective data, such as user attitudes (Alty, 1992; Lewis, 1995). If users are scattered and it is impossible to conduct interviews, a questionnaire may elicit a quick response from a large number of people. Questionnaires may also be used to identify 'key' individuals, so that interviews can be focused on these individuals. Questionnaires provide quantitative data. This means that analysis is likely to involve at least some basic statistical processing. The nature of these analyses must be determined at the questionnaire design stage, and not after the data have been collected.

Questionnaire design is a skilled activity and the development of an appropriate questionnaire may take a considerable period of time. Several drafts, followed by pilot trials, will be necessary.

Questions can be **open** or **closed**. Closed questions, which list the range of potential answers tend to reduce ambiguity and misinterpretation and are quicker to answer and analyse. These are often preferred but their effective use depends critically upon the appropriate selection of questions and potential answers. Open questions are useful where the range of possible responses cannot be readily predicted, and can assist in collecting ideas.

The selection of the sample who will receive the questionnaire is important. In a large-scale study, where it is important that quantitative data can be generated which are a reliable measure of population variables, appropriate sampling techniques must be used. However, for most of the evaluation conducted in relation to public access interfaces, a sample that can be expected to exhibit the range of perceptions of the user population is often regarded as the only realistic option. A strictly statistical random sample is neither desirable or possible.

Questionnaires may be used in:

- **Postal surveys**, in which respondents are requested to complete and return a questionnaire through the post. Non-response is a big concern with postal questionnaires. The advantages lie in the ease with which confidentiality can be maintained and the absence of interviewer bias. Postal questionnaires are also a reasonably cheap means of gathering feedback from a relatively large number of people.

- **Telephone surveys** use a questionnaire as a basis for a telephone interview. These surveys are more flexible than postal surveys and can use semi-structured questions, but do require an input of interviewer time and skill.

- **Usability assessment scenarios**, in which users complete a set of tasks which involve realistic problems, such as how to create and print a document or how to compose and send an item of electronic mail, may use questionnaires. Researchers may use questionnaires as one means of collecting quantitative data. Figure 9.1 includes two questionnaires which have been used in usability studies.

Before and after questionnaires enable researchers to measure the change in attitudes and performance between two versions of a system or when switching from one system to another. Zorn and Marshall (1995) report a small questionnaire-based survey which sought to compare the GUI-based Dynix Marquis with the text-based Dynix Classic OPAC.

Once questionnaires have been completed and returned to the researcher, any rating scales are converted to numerical values and appropriate statistical analysis is performed. Typically this may involve the calculation of means and standard deviations and other summary statistics. More sophisticated analysis, such as that which sought to examine the key variables in user satisfaction, might use multivariate analysis.

The short form of a generic user-evaluation questionnaire for interactive systems. (Copyright © 1988, 1989, 1991 Human–Computer Interaction Laboratory, University of Maryland. All Rights Reserved.) (This QUIS is available for licence in paper, IBM PC, and Macintosh forms from the University of Maryland's Office of Technology Liaison.) (Shneiderman, 1992, pp. 485–7)

Questionnaire for User-Interaction Satisfaction 5.0 - S

Identification number:_____

Age: _____

Sex: _____male_____female

PART 1: Type of System to be Rated

1.1   Name of hardware: _____

1.2   Name of software: _____

1.3   How long have you worked on this system?

_____ less than 1 hour   _____ 6 months to less than 1 year

_____ 1 hour to less than 1 day   _____ 1 year to less than 2 years

_____ 1 day to less than 1 week   _____ 2 years to less than 3 years

_____ 1 week to less than 1 month   _____ 3 years or more

_____ 1 month to less than 6 months

1.4   On the average, how much time do you spend per week on this system?

_____ less than one hour   _____ 4 to less than 10 hours

_____ one to less than 4 hours   _____ over 10 hours

PART 2: Past Experience

2.1   How many different types of computer systems, including mainframes and personal computers, have you worked with (e.g. Macintosh, DEC VAX)?

_____ none   _____ 3–4

_____ 1   _____ 5–6

_____ 2   _____ more than 6

Figure 9.1   **Questionnaires used in usability studies**

2.2 Of the following devices, software and systems, check those that you have personally used and are familiar with:

_____ keyboard	_____ text editor	_____ color monitor
_____ numeric key pad	_____ word processor	_____ time-share system
_____ mouse	_____ file manager	_____ workstation
_____ light pen	_____ electronic spreadsheet	_____ personal computer
_____ touch screen	_____ electronic mail	_____ floppy drive
_____ track ball	_____ graphics software	_____ hard drive
_____ joy stick	_____ computer games	_____ compact disk drive

PART 3: Overall User Reactions

Please circle the numbers which most appropriately reflect your impressions about using this computer system. Not Applicable = NA. There is room on the last page for your comments.

3.1 Overall reactions to the system

terrible   wonderful

1 2 3 4 5 6 7 8 9 NA

3.2

frustrating   satisfying

1 2 3 4 5 6 7 8 9 NA

3.3

dull   stimulating

1 2 3 4 5 6 7 8 9 NA

3.4

difficult   easy

1 2 3 4 5 6 7 8 9 NA

3.5

inadequate power adequate power

1 2 3 4 5 6 7 8 9 NA

3.6

rigid   flexible

1 2 3 4 5 6 7 8 9 NA

PART 4: Screen

4.1 Characters on the computer screen

hard to read   easy to read

1 2 3 4 5 6 7 8 9 NA

Figure 9.1 *continued*

4.2 Was the highlighting on the screen helpful?   not at all   very much

1 2 3 4 5 6 7 8 9   NA

4.3 Were the screen layouts helpful?   not at all   very helpful

1 2 3 4 5 6 7 8 9   NA

4.4 Sequence of screens   confusing   clear

1 2 3 4 5 6 7 8 9   NA

PART 5: Terminology and System Information

5.1 Use of terms throughout system   inconsistent   consistent

1 2 3 4 5 6 7 8 9   NA

5.2 Does the terminology relate well to the   unrelated   well related

work you are doing?   1 2 3 4 5 6 7 8 9   NA

5.3 Messages which appear on screen   inconsistent   consistent

1 2 3 4 5 6 7 8 9   NA

5.4 Messages which appear on screen   confusing   clear

1 2 3 4 5 6 7 8 9   NA

5.5 Does the computer keep you informed   never   always

about what it is doing?   1 2 3 4 5 6 7 8 9   NA

5.6 Error messages   unhelpful   helpful

1 2 3 4 5 6 7 8 9   NA

PART 6: Learning

6.1 Learning to operate the system   difficult   easy

1 2 3 4 5 6 7 8 9   NA

Figure 9.1   *continued*

6.2	Exploration of features by trial and error	discouraging	encouraging
		1 2 3 4 5 6 7 8 9	NA
6.3	Remembering names and use of commands	difficult	easy
		1 2 3 4 5 6 7 8 9	NA
6.4	Can tasks be performed in a straight-forward manner?	never	always
		1 2 3 4 5 6 7 8 9	NA
6.5	Help messages on the screen	confusing	clear
		1 2 3 4 5 6 7 8 9	NA
6.6	Supplemental reference materials	confusing	clear
		1 2 3 4 5 6 7 8 9	NA

PART 7: System Capabilities

7.1	System speed	too slow	fast enough
		1 2 3 4 5 6 7 8 9	NA
7.2	How reliable is the system?	very unreliable	very reliable
		1 2 3 4 5 6 7 8 9	NA
7.3	System tends to be	noisy	quiet
		1 2 3 4 5 6 7 8 9	NA
7.4	Correcting your mistakes	difficult	easy
		1 2 3 4 5 6 7 8 9	NA
7.5	Are the needs of both experienced and inexperienced users taken into consideration?	never	always
		1 2 3 4 5 6 7 8 9	NA

Figure 9.1   *continued*

PART 8: User's Comments

Please write any comments you have in the space below

_____

_____

_____

_____

_____

_____

_____

_____

_____

_____

_____

_____

_____

_____

_____

_____

_____

_____

_____

_____

_____

_____

_____

Figure 9.1   *continued*

THE IBM QUESTIONNAIRES (Lewis, 1995, p. 75)

The After-Scenario Questionnaire (ASQ)

Administration and scoring. Give the questionnaire to a participant after he or she has completed a scenario during a usability evaluation. Average (with the arithmetic mean) the scores from the three items to obtain the ASQ score for a participant's satisfaction with the system for a given scenario. Low scores are better than high scores due to the anchors used in the 7-point scales. If a participant does not answer an item or marks N/A, average the remaining items to obtain the ASQ score.

Instructions and items. The questionnaire's instructions and items follow. For each of the statements below, circle the rating of your choice.

1. Overall, I am satisfied with the ease of completing the tasks in this scenario.

strongly agree   ◄---------------►   strongly disagree

                        1 2 3 4 5 6 7   N/A

Comments:

2. Overall, I am satisfied with the amount of time it took to complete the tasks in this scenario.

strongly agree   ◄---------------►   strongly disagree

                        1 2 3 4 5 6 7   N/A

Comments:

3. Overall, I am satisfied with the support information (on-line help, messages, documentation) when completing the tasks.

strongly agree   ◄---------------►   strongly disagree

                        1 2 3 4 5 6 7   N/A

Comments

Figure 9.1   *continued*

Review and apply:	What are the limitations of postal questionnaires in interface evaluation?
Answer:	In specific terms this depends upon the type of product undergoing evaluation, but typically:

- there may be difficulty in identifying an appropriate user population to whom to dispatch the questionnaire;
- the pre-structuring inherent in a questionnaire may eliminate some possible and relevant responses;
- in order for a user to make any specific comments concerning interface design they need to have access to a prototype or a previous system, to provide a framework for their comments.

Experiments and usability engineering

This section briefly introduces the main issues involved in planning and executing laboratory experiments, as a precursor to exploring the concept of usability engineering. These are techniques that depend to some extent on access to appropriate laboratory facilities. In addition, because well-designed experiments involve careful control of most variables so that other variables can be isolated, most experiments have a very narrow scope, such as to investigate the optimum design of icons in relation to metaphor, size and colour. These facilities will not be available to most readers of this book. Nevertheless, a critique of these approaches as valuable is supporting readers in the critical analysis of the experimental evaluation performed by others, particularly where that work seeks to establish general theories and principles.

Experiments need the following components:

1. A specified area of focus.
2. A hypothesis, or speculation, stated in terms that can be tested.
3. Variables, including those to be changed and those that are held constant, or controlled.
4. Statistical tests.
5. Experimental subjects, who must be selected in such a way that bias is avoided.

Experiments in laboratory settings are very powerful in identifying the effects of various changes on user preferences and performance. Even a simple experiment can be very time-consuming, and therefore expensive, and may take time that is difficult to fit into the tight schedule of a development project. Accordingly, whilst retaining the basic scientific approach, in many experiments in human–computer interaction some rigour is exchanged for practicality or reality. This is the approach adopted in usability engineering.

Review and apply:	Give an example of an issue in human–computer interaction that might merit investigation using the experimental approach – explain why.
Answer:	A typical situation where an experimental approach might be appropriate is where an attempt is being made to identify some general principles concerning interface design. Possible examples might be:

- seeking to determine the optimum size of icons;
- investigating whether experienced users make use of menu options or memorize key presses and use those;
- investigating circumstances under which users seek assistance from help systems.

Case Study: Railway Ticketing ATM – Experiment (Felix, Graf and Kreuger, 1991)

Two alternative designs for a railway ticketing ATM were investigated. One design presented all options on a single screen, whilst the other presented sequenced options on successive screens. The study was conducted on a German railway station with actual passengers who were buying tickets; the program alternated between designs for each successive user. The time to complete the transaction as well as errors made was measured. Data were collected by on-line tracking as well as videotaping. The results indicated that the sequential approach seemed to be best for most people, although there was a difference depending upon their level of education and their computer experience.

Usability engineering

Usability engineering seeks to provide a systematic procedure for testing the usability of a product during its development. Usability engineering was defined by Tyldesley (1988) as 'a process whereby the usability of a product is specified quantitatively and in advance'. Another important facet of usability engineering is the close relationship between design and evaluation in cycles of design: design–evaluate–redesign. The term 'engineering' is used to describe the iterative nature of this development and the fact that many characteristics of the product are specified quantitatively and in advance.

Testing is usually conducted in a purpose-built laboratory and follows a procedure that recognizes the essential features of experimental design, as far as this can be achieved in an environment where it is not possible to control all of the variables not directly of interest.

Usability engineering comprises the following steps (Good et al., 1986):

1. Defining usability goals through usability metrics.
2. Setting the levels of usability to be achieved.
3. Analysis of the impact of possible design solutions.
4. Incorporation of user-derived feedback in product design.
5. Iteration through the design–evaluate–redesign loop until the planned levels are achieved.

Usability metrics are the measures that are used to describe the various levels of acceptability of the key design features. These metrics are recorded in a usability specification, as described in Chapter 7. Figure 9.2 shows examples of metrics which may be measured in usability testing (Hill, 1995; Dix et al., 1993).

Users' performance is measured using standard tests called **benchmark tasks**. Examples of such tasks might be the translation of a 3-D object, or the selection and printing of records from a bibliographic database in a specified format. Typically, benchmark tasks are elements of real-life tasks. These activities may be logged using software or data logging and video and/or audio recording as described earlier in this chapter. Data from questionnaires and interviews may also be used to produce any attitude metrics that might be part of the usability specification.

Usability objective	Effectiveness measure	Efficiency measure	Satisfaction measure
Suitability for the task	Percentage of goals achieved	Time to complete a task	Rating scale for satisfaction
Appropriate for trained users	Number of power features used	Relative efficiency compared with an expert user	Rating scale for satisfaction with power features
Learnability	Percentage of functions learned	Time to learn criterion	Rating scale for ease of learning
Error tolerance	Percentage of errors corrected successfully	Time spent on correcting errors	Rating scale for error handling

Figure 9.2   Usability metrics

Usability engineering is valuable in structuring interface design and setting common explicit and agreed goals. The usability specification is a document that aids communication between systems designers and users. On the negative side, the laboratory setting is recognized to be artificial, and usability engineering is therefore appropriately supplemented with other methods, such as observation and contextual enquiry.

Review and apply:	What is a usability metric? What is the relationship between a usability metric and a benchmark task?
Answer:	1. A usability metric is one of a series of measures used to describe the various levels of acceptability of key design features. 2. Benchmark tasks are designed to assess whether an interface meets the performance standards specified in the usability metric.

Case study: SilverPlatter's search adviser — drawing the tools together (Morley, 1995)

SilverPlatter needed to translate their search adviser software from a DOS environment to a windows environment. The search adviser provides a means for librarians to write search scripts to simplify searching for their novice users. The project started with the formulation of a project team representing development, marketing and product design/usability. This group started work on the definition, technical design and presentation of features. Conversations were documented and later evolved into functional and technical specifications. Usability was considered at the earliest stages of system design. Once initial specifications had been developed, prototypes in the form of paper prototypes, computerized slide shows and screen shots were created and shared with users. Next, a user profile and searching scenario was created to set the context for user tests. The profile outlined users who had some computer and mouse experience, but no search experience. The scenario described search requirements and listed specific tasks, beginning with identifying the appropriate script for the requirements and including limiting search results, marking records and starting a new search. The usability test was itself pilot-tested on SilverPlatter staff. The full usability test was conducted with volunteers from the Graduate School of Library and Information Science at Simmons College in Boston, Massachusetts. On average four test subjects were used for each round of tests. Usability testing was conducted in a laboratory-type environment at the SilverPlatter office, as well as in the actual library setting. Each session was videotaped and analysed, and embedded in an actual piece of software, and a further round of testing was undertaken. Some features were available for the first time during this round of testing. Appropriate amendments were made, and finally, after more testing, the software was released.

Interpretative evaluation

Interpretative evaluation techniques recognize the limitations of the objective evaluation inherent in usability engineering, and the artificial divide between designer and user. In interpretative evaluation, the agenda for evaluation arises out of the context of study and is jointly decided by users and evaluator. 'Interpretative methods of research start from the position that our knowledge of reality, including the domain of human action, is a social construction' (Walsham, 1993). Interpretative evaluation is particularly helpful in understanding the complex interaction in natural environments. It is very useful in the feasibility study, design feedback or post-implementation review stages of the lifecycle. This identification of stages may not be appropriate in end-user computing and prototyping where the user plays a major role in the design process. Interpretative evaluation methods recognize the limitations of the artificial context of usability engineering and seek to conduct evaluation and to identify usability problems within the normal working environment of the user. They include contextual enquiry, ethnography and participative and cooperative evaluation.

Review and apply: Draw up a table to show the essential differences between interpretative evaluation techniques and usability engineering. Which do you think is most likely to yield the greatest insight for public access systems?

Answer:

Interpretative evaluation	Usability engineering
Greater subjectivity	Greater objectivity
Designer and user work together	Rigid distinction between designer and user
Yields understanding of complex interaction in natural environments	Laboratory context which gives greater control of variables

---

In summary, interpretative approaches are important because the context of use of public access systems is central, but the public access environment does not feature captive users, so some laboratory testing might be appropriate at a preliminary stage during design.

Contextual enquiry

Contextual enquiry is one of the interpretative evaluation approaches.

Usability issues are identified and shared collaboratively between users and evaluators whilst users are working in natural environments conducting 'normal' tasks in relation to the system. This discussion between user and evaluator can be termed 'contextual interview'. This interview may be recorded on video for later joint viewing. The theoretical standpoint of contextual enquiry is appropriately summarized by Whiteside et al. (1988):

> Contextualism ... implies that interpretation is primary (rather than data); knowledge lives in practical action (rather than being based on representation) and it is assumed that behaviour is meaningful only in context (rather than that behaviour can be studied scientifically).

The key differences between the laboratory and the normal working environment include the work, time, motivation and the social context.
The evaluator in contextual enquiry is concerned to explore (Holtzblatt and Beyer, 1993):

- the structure and language used in the (work);
- individual and group actions and intentions;
- the culture affecting the (work);
- explicit and implicit aspects of the (work).

In seeking to understand these aspects of the context it is important for evaluators to:

- understand the (work) as well as possible;
- uncover any implicit or hidden (work) practices;
- create interpretation with users, including allowing users to define their own agendas.

Some evaluators may be uncomfortable with contextual enquiry because there are no metrics to support the identification of clear design issues, and the interpretation of the data must be done with reference to the wider work context and the users' aims. In the context of public access systems there is, in addition, a need to identify the system boundaries since there is not normally one clearly defined work environment as is implied in Holtzblatt and Beyer's (1993) perspective. Nevertheless, contextual enquiry is particularly useful in eliciting requirements for a new product.

Ethnography

Ethnography has recently been used to give a sharper focus to contextual enquiry. Ethnographic researchers immerse themselves in the situation that they want to learn about and seek to understand as much about the 'natives' as possible from the natives' own point of view. This perspective implies:

- the 'holistic' perspective in which everything is of interest;
- the use of a wide range of methods including observation, interviewing, participation, and watching and learning.

A video tends to be the primary recording mechanism, but notebooks, snapshots and artifacts may also be used. The important difference between ethnography and some of the approaches described earlier is in the analysis. The video and other data are viewed and reviewed and analysed in depth to generate multiple views of the activities. Ethnography is relatively new, but promises useful insights into how systems are used in the cultural, political and social environments.

Review and apply:	What insights might ethnographic evaluation of the use of an encyclopaedia on CD-ROM by children in a school classroom reveal? How might these insights differ from those associated with access to the same CD-ROM in an airport departure lounge?
Answer:	Some suggestions of factors that might vary between the two environments include:
	• the environment itself – noise, alternative activities, choice, tiredness, excitement, focus of interest (tasks in school, travel in departure lounge);
	• company – other children, age range, parents.

Cooperative and participative evaluation

Cooperative evaluation moves one step further along the spectrum from contextual enquiry. In cooperative evaluation users have significant involvement in determining the evaluation issues and in the techniques for collecting and analysing video protocols. Mack and Nielsen (1993) describe cooperative evaluation thus:

> Co-operative evaluation is a technique to improve a user interface specification by detecting the possible usability problems in an early prototype or partial simulation. It sets down procedures by which a designer can work with the sort of people who will ultimately use the software in their daily work, so that together they can identify potential problems and their solution.

Cooperative evaluation is an explorative technique that can be used by designers and users without specialist interface design knowledge. The procedure involves the following stages:

- One or more users who are typical of eventual users of the final product are recruited.
- Representative tasks are selected.
- As users work with the system they verbalize any problems, whilst the evaluator makes notes.
- A debriefing session serves to clarify any potential misunderstandings.
- The designer summarizes the notes and reports the problems to the design team.

Review and apply:	What is the essential difference between contextual enquiry and cooperative evaluation?
Answer:	The user involvement in the identification of evaluation issues and techniques in cooperative evaluation.

Participative evaluation and cooperative prototyping

Participative evaluation integrates the design and evaluation process, and shares the same philosophy and techniques as participative design (see Chapter 6). Participative evaluation and participative design are closely coupled and need to be considered together. Participative evaluation differs from cooperative evaluation in that it is subject to greater control by users. The approach relies heavily upon prototyping or mock-ups which are described in Chapter 7.

Case study: Olympic message system – prototyping (Gould et al., 1987)

Prototyping was used in the final stage of development of the Olympic message system for the 1984 Olympic Games in Los Angeles. The OMS was a multilingual voice messaging system in the form of 25 kiosks located around the Olympic village which allowed athletes, officials, friends and families to keep in touch with each other during the one-month period of the games. Some of the prototyping activities included:

- printed scenarios of people sending and receiving messages used as specifications of how the system would work;
- development and tryout of user guides to obtain feedback on system operation prior to development;
- simulation of the system on a mainframe computer;
- placement of mock-up kiosk in a limited public access position;
- bullet-proofing exercises in which groups of users were invited to try to crash the system.;
- a field test at pre-Olympic trials;
- final prototype testing with a large number of users.

Predictive evaluation

Predictive evaluation is evaluation that does not involve user testing. Usability testing which involves users can be expensive and users may not always be available or willing. Predictive methods attempt to predict aspects of usage rather than observing it directly. They:

- are comparatively fast.
- are low-cost.
- do not require specialist equipment.

Some methods do not even need a prototype system and can be conducted on a specification.

The methods are usually conducted by experts and are sometimes described as expert review. Inspection methods involve the inspection of aspects of technology by experts who have the knowledge of both the technology and the intended users. The goal is to generate a list of usability problems. Often these will be addressed early in the design process.

Predictive evaluation is often based on expert reviews and usage simulations, heuristic evaluation, discount usability evaluation and walkthroughs, as well as analytic evaluation. These may use a variety of different techniques to embed structure into the process.

Review and apply: Why is predictive evaluation attractive to designers?

Answer: Predictive evaluation:

- is appropriate in contexts where user involvement is not feasible; this applies in many public access situations;
- is comparatively fast;
- is low-cost;
- requires no specialist equipment.

Expert reviews and usage simulations

Usage simulations are reviews conducted by experts, who simulate the behaviours of less experienced users and seek to anticipate the usability problems that they might encounter. Such reviewers should be experts in interface design and systems and be able to identify usability issues associated with inconsistency, poor task structure and confusing screen design. Feedback from such experts should be more focused and require fewer trials than direct user evaluation. Good reviewers can identify a range of user problems in a single session, which might take many sessions to emerge with users. In addition, experts are in a more informed position to offer advice on improving the interface. Good reviewing depends critically upon:

- the impartiality of the experts; the use of a number of experts should reduce the impact of individual bias;
- the extent and nature of the reviewer experience of interfaces and the specific application;
- the definition of the role of the reviewers, and the ability of the reviewers to adopt the role of different types of users;
- the coverage of the tasks undertaken, and the availability of prototype or system and support materials that are truly typical of those likely to be made available to users.

Reporting from experts can be structured to a lesser or greater extent. The following terms are useful in this context:

Structured reporting – where reviewers report observations in a standardized format which might, for example, ask for the nature of problems, their source, importance to the user and proposed remedies. This approach may focus on system conformance where the system is evaluated using established standards and guidelines.

Unstructured reporting – in which reviewers report their observations and a *post hoc* categorization of problems is established. This is often termed 'expert opinion'.

Predefined categorization – where reviewers are given a list of problem categories and asked to report the occurrence of problems in these categories.

In formative evaluation expert reviewing is useful during the early stages of development. It may also be used in summative evaluation to predict aspects of the usage of a system prior to observing it directly in an experimental or operational setting.

Review and apply:	Under what circumstances do you think that unstructured reporting would be useful?
Answer:	It would be useful:
	- when experienced reviewers are available;
	- early in the design process when it is important to gather qualitative data concerning how and why users function with a given design;
	- novel applications, which, because of their inherent novelty, may have associated and unpredictable problems, are under development.

Heuristic evaluation

Heuristic evaluation is a type of usage simulation but, in this context, inspection is guided by a set of high-level heuristics that focus on key usability issues. These heuristics are applied by an expert or a group of experts who have internalized knowledge of good design (Johnson, 1992). There is no general agreement as to the definition of heuristic design and there is debate about whether explicit or implicit guidelines should be used in this process. There is, however, a growing body of evidence to suggest that criteria increase the evaluation performance of experts (for example, Bastien and Scapin, 1995; Jeffries et al., 1991). However, these guidelines must be closely related to the design guidelines. Molich and Nielsen (1990) identify nine general heuristics:

1. Use simple and natural dialogue.
2. Speak the user's language.
3. Minimize user memory loads.
4. Be consistent.
5. Provide feedback.
6. Provide clearly marked exits.
7. Provide short cuts.
8. Provide good error messages.
9. Prevent errors.

Other potential heuristics, at more specified levels and in respect of specific interface features are shown in Chapter 5 on interaction styles.

Heuristic evaluation comprises a number of sessions, during which each reviewer conducts a study, and examines both the flow of the interface from screen to screen and individual screens against the heuristics. A session lasts one to two hours.

The effectiveness of heuristic evaluation depends upon:

- the identification of appropriate heuristics during the design or evaluation phases;
- each reviewer spending sufficient time with the interface to uncover all the issues;
- the number of reviewers. Nielsen (1993) suggests that five reviewers provide a high level of cost effectiveness, although Nielsen (1992) determined that when the heuristic evaluators were 'double specialists' (that is, usability experts, also with experience of the kind of interface under evaluation) a group of two to three evaluators would be sufficient to locate most of the usability problems.

Case study: Evaluating Microsoft's Art Gallery – heuristic evaluation
(Garzotto et al., 1995)

Microsoft's Art Gallery is a hypermedia guide to the National Gallery in London. Initially designed for the museum's visitors, it is now widely available on CD-ROM. The researchers sought to perform a heuristic evaluation of a hypermedia application by coupling a systematic analysis of the application based on a hypermedia design model with general usability criteria, which were independent of the specific application area, user profile and user tastes. The method, based as it is upon heuristics, evaluated the internal strength of the design underlying the hypermedia application.

Discount usability evaluation

Discount usability evaluation (Nielsen, 1989; Potosnak, 1990) is a hybrid of usability testing and heuristic evaluation. Nielsen (1989) introduced the method for organizations that do not have the time or the resources to perform more controlled empirical evaluations. The focus is on detecting usability errors with designer observations, instead of using performance measures. The features of the method are as follows:

- Scenarios are created as the basis for usability testing. Users work through these scenarios and talk through their actions and thoughts in think-aloud protocols. These protocols are then analysed by the evaluators.
- Scenarios are modified on the basis of the first test, and then used again for subsequent tests.
- Scenarios are tested using heuristic evaluation.

Walkthroughs

Walkthroughs are a further type of review, but are characterized by the need for a more detailed prior understanding of potential user behaviour.

In designing a walkthrough an expert determines the exact task, context and important characteristics of the user population. The evaluator then 'walks through' the necessary action or tasks that take users towards their likely goals with a view to identifying the problems likely to be encountered and strategies used to solve the problems. This process is guided by a list of questions about the interface which seek to investigate the match between actions and goals. Results are recorded using a checklist. Two specific types of walkthroughs are:

- **Cognitive walkthroughs**, which focus on the cognitive needs of the intended users. The cognitive walkthrough was originally developed in the context of ATMs but has more recently been applied in other contexts (for example, Karat et al., 1992; Wharton et al., 1992).
- **Pluralistic walkthroughs** (Bias, 1991), in which users, developers and HCI specialists all participate. Pluralistic walkthroughs are less formal than cognitive walkthroughs. They are typically used to check that the interface is consistent with the relevant interface standards or guidelines.

Review and apply: Identify the tasks that would be needed in a walkthrough to locate all books by a specific author on a CD-ROM bibliographic database to which you have access.

Answer: Typically:

1. Select the database.
2. Select author search.
3. Key in author's name.
4. View hits available.
5. Choose to display records.
6. Scan records to locate relevant records.
7. Display full record format.
8. Mark relevant records.
9. Choose print or save format.
10. Print or save to file relevant records.

Analytic evaluation

Analytic evaluation models are based upon a pre-analysis of the way in which an interface might be used. These methods fall into two categories:

- those based on psychological models of user behaviour towards goals, as exemplified by GOMS (see Chapter 7);
- those based on linguistic models that attempt to evaluate the complexity of tasks by constructing a task grammar which can then be used to evaluate the task complexity, as exemplified by command language grammar (CLG) or task action language (TAL) (see Chapter 7).

Analytic evaluations do not involve use of prototypes, but are based on interface specification. As such they may be useful in the early stages of design, for example, to identify the quickest way to perform a task by an experienced user using that particular interface specification. Alternative specifications can be compared in terms of the predicted time to conduct

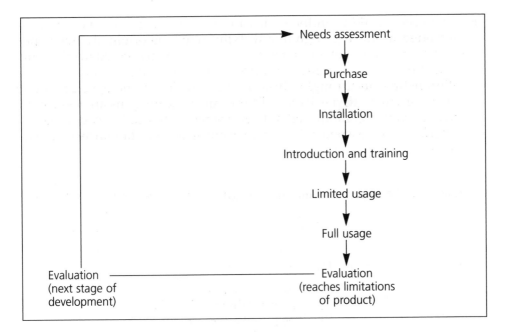

Figure 9.3   **Customer usage cycle**

identical tasks and the best (fastest) interface design selected. Such methods may be useful in comparing alternative designs, but their limitations rest with their underlying assumptions that all users are expert users who act rationally at all times in pursuit of clear goals, and who make no errors of performance. In addition, they ignore context and are difficult to use. With the advent of expert evaluation methods and prototyping opportunities, the interest in these methods is declining.

Evaluation from the customer perspective

Much of the literature on interface specification and systems analysis and design pays only scant attention to the wider context in which the system must function and assumes a close link between evaluation and design and an intimate relationship between the designer and the user.

Figure 9.3, based on Macaulay (1995, p. 175), identifies the stages in the customer experience of a system. Initially, the customer will define the system required, and during this stage, the supplier will need to be able to demonstrate the system to the customer with a focus on key features. Both purchase and installation need to be straightforward and quick. After installation, at the introduction and training stage, the system must be easy to learn and supporting materials will be critical. At the limited-use stage users will seek to perform their job with the system, and ease of use and speed in respect of frequently completed jobs will be essential. In full use, users will make use of all the system features provided and exploit the full potential of the system. Users need to be able to explore system features that are new to them. Once they have fully exploited the features of the system, and their job needs to change and develop, another stage of evaluation takes place. At each of these stages the user will have a different perception or perspective on what constitutes a usable system. Evaluation should embrace all these stages.

Case study: Museum information system

A large national museum is designing a computerized information kiosk that provides access to information on many of its exhibits, including pictures, short video inserts and text in four languages. The information will be presented on large, flat touch screens. The museum has developed a full specification and an initial prototype and wishes this to be evaluated before developing the database further and making the system available at a number of workstations and ultimately over the Internet. The museum is interested in the presentational aspects of the systems, such as the use of graphics, colours and symbols, how easily tourists can access relevant information and the suitability of the touch screens, as well as whether the information in the system is appropriate.

Evaluation could make use of a variety of different approaches:

- Expert review may be used to obtain feedback on the basic screen presentation. This might then be followed by:
- Laboratory tests with a number of typical users to perform usability tests in which they carry out prescribed tasks and observe or collect video data.
- Attitude data could be collected by questionnaire.
- Field testing, with prototypes in a few key sites, to observe how the system is used by the public with hidden video equipment and key logging.
- The data thus collected might use an ethnographic approach and in-depth analysis of videos.
- Additionally, some of the users might be interviewed.

Evaluation of competitive advantage

Chapter 6 introduced SSIP as a design methodology that encouraged consideration of the business benefits of an information system, with a particular focus on competitive advantage and marketplace factors, such as critical success factors and cost–benefit analysis. These approaches can be used as the basis for the evaluation of specific projects, such as the use of

Category	Major benefit	Effectiveness measure
ATMs	Convenience	Increased transactions ($)
POS	Convenience	Increased sales ($)
Information	Availability	Greater satisfaction
Exhibits	Involvement	Longer visit
Catalogues	Accessibility	Increased circulation
Message	Accessibility	More messages

Figure 9.4   Benefits of public access systems

multimedia kiosks in retailing, or a portfolio of CD-ROMs marketed by one publisher. Competitive advantage in the marketplace is the key consideration. In other applications, such as in libraries and employment offices, optimization of access to and exploitation of public service is a key factor. Retailers have, for example, been concerned with return on investment (ROI) associated with multimedia kiosks. Retailers expect kiosks to improve customer service without increasing labour costs (Fox, 1993). It can be difficult to identify the effect of kiosks on bottom line results; is any increase in sales due to the kiosks, or have other factors intervened? Those public access systems that result in better services, improve a learning experience or customers' enjoyment of, say, a museum visit lead to even more intangible benefits. Users' perceptions of such benefits can be measured by the use of questionnaires and surveys. Kearsley and Heller (1995) provide a useful list of benefits (see Figure 9.4).

Review and apply:	Why are cost–benefit analyses often difficult to perform for public access systems?
Answer:	<ul><li>Benefits are not quantifiable.</li><li>There is difficulty in measuring the extent of use.</li><li>In many contexts the impact of the terminal can only be measured as part of the total service package of which it is part.</li><li>Costs include ongoing and initial costs and it may be difficult to decide on an appropriate methodology for the allocation of the initial development costs.</li><li>It is difficult to isolate the role of the interface in determining system use.</li></ul>

	Observing, monitoring and logging	Experiments and benchmarking	Users' opinions	Interpretative	Predictive
Purpose	Understanding the real world, comparing designs and adapted for engineering towards a target	Standards conformance, comparing designs, adapted for engineering towards a target (i.e. benchmarking)	Can be used for many different purposes	Only understanding natural usage	Engineering to a target and conformance testing
Interface development	Any level of development	Likely to be at least a working prototype	Any level of development	Likely to be a working system	Usually early at specification or mock-up stage
User involvement	Yes, some control of tasks by users	Yes, little or no control	Yes, often no control	Yes, considerable control	No
Type of data	Quantitative and qualitative	Emphasis on quantitative	Quantitative and qualitative, but more emphasis on quantitative	Qualitative	Some qualitative but emphasis on quantitative
Practical considerations	Special equipment useful, but not essential	Laboratory conditions preferred	None	Little or no equipment needed Video may be used	No equipment needed

Figure 9.5   Comparing evaluation methods

Summary

Within the range of different evaluation techniques, the level and nature of user involvement varies from none to the definition of the agenda for evaluation and full participation in the evaluation process. Different methods are appropriate at different stages in the evaluation process. Figure 9.5, based on Preece et al. (1994, p. 696), summarizes evaluation methods in terms of purpose, interface development stage, user involvement, type of data and practical considerations. In any instance a well-designed evaluation programme involves the use of a number of different methods, as exemplified by the case study on SilverPlatter's search adviser (Morley, 1995).

Both quantitative and qualitative methods are important in eliciting different perspectives of the interaction and are often used in conjunction with one another (Lewis, 1995). Quantitative data are particularly valuable in accurately assessing the usability of a system, but it is the qualitative information that informs designers as to how to change an unusable system. There has been some limited investigation of the comparative contributions of different techniques. Jeffries et al. (1991) compared heuristic evaluation, usability testing, evaluation against guidelines and cognitive walkthrough methods. Cuomo and Bowen (1994) compared cognitive walkthroughs, heuristic evaluation and the Smith and Mosier (1986) guidelines in the context of a GUI. They noted that the cognitive walkthrough method identifies issues almost exclusively with the action specification stage, while guidelines covered more stages. The walkthrough was best, and the guidelines worst, at predicting problems that caused users noticeable difficulty.

There has been some work on standardized evaluation plans (StEP), which are methodologies that deal with usability evaluation. Such plans typically embrace more than one approach to usability evaluation. For example, Grissom and Perlman (1995) describe the development of a StEP for three-dimensional interaction techniques which combines performance-based evaluation with a use satisfaction questionnaire. Essentially, an evaluation plan describes what to evaluate and why. It also provides the step-by-step procedure necessary to accomplish the plan (Spencer, 1985). A StEP is designed to evaluate or compare a wide variety of systems that share certain capabilities. A StEP must have clear objectives and a specific scope, such as 3-D interaction techniques, or text editors. The StEP includes:

1. Benchmark tasks that are appropriate for most of the systems that fall within the scope of the methodology.
2. Participants who are able to perform the tasks, with few significant errors.
3. Test materials, so that tasks are complete in a consistent manner.

4. Usability measures, such as performance time and user satisfaction.
5. The procedure to be conducted in the informal use environment and recorded appropriately, with, say, a video camera.

Finally, evaluation is only as good as the evaluation process and associated usability goals. Unfortunately the question of who sets usability goals and how they are set has received less attention (Booth, 1989). Although usability evaluation has offered a more rigorous framework for, and approaches to, improving real systems, it does not constitute a rigorous theory. The usability approach offers no real explanatory framework for understanding human–computer interaction, and much is still left to intuition and judgement.

References

Alty, J. L. (1992), 'Can we measure usability?', in *Proceedings of the Advanced Information Systems 1992 Conference*, Learned Information, London.

Bastien, J. M. C. and Scapin, D. L. (1995), 'Evaluating a user interface with ergonomic criteria', *International Journal of Human Computer Interaction*, 7 (2), 105–21.

Bias, R. (1991), 'Walkthroughs: efficient collaborative testing', *IEEE Software*, September, 94–5.

Bitner, M. J. (1992), 'Servicescapes: the impact of physical surroundings on customers and employees', *Journal of Marketing*, 56, 57–71.

Booth, P. (1989), *An Introduction to Human–Computer Interaction*, Lawrence Erlbaum, Hove.

Carroll, J. M. and Mack, R. (1984), 'Learning to use a word processor: by doing, by thinking, by knowing', in *Human Factors in Computing Systems* (eds J. Thomas and M. Schneider), Ablex, Norwood, NJ, pp. 13–52.

Cronin, J. J. and Taylor, S. A. (1994), 'SERVPERF versus SERVQUAL: reconciling performance-based and perceptions minus expectations measurement of service quality', *Journal of Marketing*, 58, 125–31.

Cuomo, D. L. and Bowen, C. D. (1994), 'Understanding usability issues addressed by three user–system interface evaluation techniques', *Interacting with Computers*, 6 (1), 86–108.

Diaper, D. (1989), *Task Analysis for Human–Computer Interaction*, Ellis Horwood, Chichester.

Dix, A., Finlay, J., Abowd, G. and Beale, R. (1993), *Human–Computer Interaction*, Prentice-Hall, Englewood Cliffs, NJ.

Ericsson, K. A. and Simon, H. A. (1985), *Protocol Analysis: Verbal Reports as Data*, MIT Press, Cambridge, MA.

Felix, D., Graf, W. and Kreuger, H. (1991), 'User interfaces for public information systems', in *Human Aspects of Computing* (ed. H. Bullinger), Elsevier, New York.

Fox, B. (1993), 'Still experimental: kiosk ROI remains unproven', *Chain Store Age Executive*, **69** (6), 57–8.

Garzotto, F., Mainetti, L. and Padini, P. (1995), 'Hypermedia design, analysis, and evaluation issues', *Communications of the ACM*, **38** (8), 74–86.

Good, M., Spine, T. M., Whiteside, J. and George, P. (1986), 'User driven impact analysis as a tool for usability engineering', in *Human Factors in Computing Systems CHI '86 Conference Proceedings* (eds M. Mantei and P. Oberton), ACM Press, New York, pp. 241–6.

Gould, J. D., Boies, S. J., Levy, S., Richards, J. T. and Schoonard, J. (1987), 'The 1984 Olympic Message System: a test of behavioral principle of system design', *Communications of the ACM*, **30** (9), 758–69.

Grissom, S. B. and Perlman, G. (1995), 'StEP3D: a standardised evaluation plan for three-dimensional interaction techniques', *International Journal of Human–Computer Studies*, **43**, 15–41.

Gronroos, C. (1988), 'Service quality: the six criteria of good perceived quality service', *Review of Business*, **9** (3), 10–13.

Harrison, B. L. (1991), 'Video annotation and multimedia interfaces: from theory to practice', in *Proceedings of the Human Factors Society 35th Annual General Meeting*, pp. 319–22.

Hewett, T. T. (1986), 'The role of iterative evaluation in designing systems for usability', in *People and Computers: Designing for Usability*, Proceedings of the 2nd Conference of the BCS HCI Specialist Group (eds M. D. Harrison and A. F. Monk), Cambridge University Press, Cambridge.

Hill, S. (1995), *A Practical Introduction to the Human–Computer Interface*, DP Publications, London.

Hix, D. and Harston, H. R. (1993), *Developing User Interfaces: Ensuring Usability through Product and Process*, Wiley, New York.

Holtzblatt, K. and Beyer, H. (1993), 'Contextual design: integrating customer data into the design process', in *Bridges between Worlds*, INTERCHI '93 Tutorial Notes: 6 (eds S. Ashlund, K. Mullet, A. Henderson, E. Hillagel and T. White), Addison-Wesley, Reading, MA.

Jeffries, R., Miller, J. R., Wharton, C. and Uyeda, K. M. (1991), 'User interface evaluation in the real world: a comparison of four techniques', in *Proceedings of ACM HCI '92 Conference on Human Factors in Computing Systems* (eds P. Bauersfield, J. Bennett and G. Lynch), ACM, Monterey, CA, pp. 117–24.

Johnson, P. (1992), *Human–Computer Interaction: Psychology, Task Analysis and Software Engineering*, McGraw-Hill, London.

Karat, C. M., Campbell, R. and Fiegel, T. (1992), 'Comparison of the empirical testing and walkthrough methods in user interface evaluation', in *Proceedings of ACM HCI '92 Conference on Human Factors in Computing Systems* (eds P. Bauersfield, J. Bennett and G. Lynch), ACM, Monterey, CA, pp. 397–404.

Kearsley, G. and Heller, R. S. (1995), 'Multimedia in public access settings: evaluation issues', *Journal of Educational Multimedia and Hypermedia*, **4** (1), 3–24.

Lewis, J. S. (1995), 'IBM computer usability satisfaction questionnaires: psychometric evaluation and instructions for use', *International Journal of Human–Computer Interaction*, **7** (1), 57–78.

Macaulay, L. (1995), *Human–Computer Interaction for Software Designers*, International Thomson Computer Press, London.

Mack, R. and Nielsen, J. (1993), 'Usability inspection methods: report on a workshop held at CHI '92', Monterey, CA, *SIGCHI Bulletin*, January, 30–33.

Molich, R. and Nielsen, J. (1990), 'Improving a human–computer dialogue', *Communications of the ACM*, **33** (3), 338–48.

Morley, E. T. (1995), 'The SilverPlatter experience', *CD-ROM Professional*, March, 111–18.

Nielsen, J. (1989), 'Usability engineering at a discount', in *Designing and Using Human–Computer Interfaces and Knowledge Based Systems* (eds G. Salvendry and M. Smith), Elsevier, Amsterdam, pp. 394–401.

Nielsen, J. (1992), 'Finding usability problems through heuristic evaluation', in *Proceedings of ACM HCI '92 Conference on Human Factors in Computing Systems* (eds P. Bauersfield, J. Bennett and G. Lynch), ACM, Monterey, CA, pp. 373–80.

Nielsen, J. (1993), 'Usability evaluation and inspection methods', in *Bridges between Worlds*, INTERCHI '93 Tutorial Notes: 22 (eds S. Ashlund, K. Mullet, A. Henderson, E. Hollnagel and T. White), Addison-Wesley, Reading, MA.

Parasuraman, A., Zeithaml, V. and Berry, L. (1988), 'SERVQUAL: a multiple-item scale for measuring consumer perception of service quality', *Journal of Retailing*, **64**, 12–40.

Potosnak, K. (1990), 'Big paybacks from discount usability engineering', *IEEE Software*, pp. 107–9.

Preece, J. et al. (1994), *Human–Computer Interaction*, Addison-Wesley, Wokingham.

Rowley, J. E. (1996), 'Customer compatibility management: an alternative perspective on student-to-student support in higher education', *International Journal of Educational Management*, **10** (4), 15–20.

Shneiderman, B., Brethauer, D., Plaisant, C. and Potter, R. (1989), 'Evaluating three museum installations of a hypertext system', *Journal of the American Society for Information Science*, **40** (3), 172–82.

Shneiderman, B. (1992), *Designing the User Interface: Strategies for Effective Human–Computer Interaction*, 2nd edn, Addison-Wesley, Reading, MA.

Slack, F. E. (1996), 'End user searches and search path maps: a discussion', *Library Review*, **45** (2), 41–51.

Smith, S. L. and Mosier, J. N. (1986), *Guidelines for Designing User Interface Software*, ESD-TR-86–278, Bedford, MA, Mitre Corporation.

Spencer, R. H. (1985), *Computer Usability Testing and Evaluation*, Prentice-Hall, Englewood Cliffs, NJ.

Teas, R. K. (1993), 'Expectations, performance evaluation, and consumers' perceptions of quality', *Journal of Marketing*, **57**, 18–34.

Tyldesley, D. A. (1988), 'Employing usability engineering in the development of office products', *Computer Journal*, **31** (5), 431–6.

Walsham, G. (1993), *Interpreting Information Systems in Organisations*, Wiley, Chichester.

Wharton, C., Bradford, J., Franzke, M. and Jeffries, J. (1992), 'Applying complex cognitive walkthroughs to more complex user interfaces: experiences, issues and recommendations', in *Proceedings of ACM HCI '92 Conference on Human Factors in Computing Systems* (eds P. Bauersfield, J. Bennett and G. Lynch), ACM, Monterey, CA, pp. 381–8.

Whiteside, J., Bennett, J. and Holtzblatt, K. (1988), 'Usability engineering: our experience and evolution', in *Handbook of Human–Computer Interaction* (ed. M. Helander), North Holland, Amsterdam.

Zorn, M. J. and Marshall, L. (1995), 'Graphical user interfaces and library systems: end-user reactions', *Special Libraries*, Winter, 28–35.

Index

adult learning 31–32
analytic evaluation 234
art galleries 42–44
ATM's 44–45, 82
attention 29
attributes 146, 164

banking 44–45
bar code reader 52–53
benefits 5–7
berry picking 78–79
Boolean searching 63–65
browsing 80–81
business applications 45–47
buttons 107

CATWOE 136
CD-ROM 12, 13–14, 40–41
CD-ROM – help 196–197
chaining 77–78
charting techniques 73–75
check boxes 107
child users 22–23
citation growing 77–78
classes 146
client-server architecture 57
cognitive dimensions 173–174
cognitive modelling 72–73
cognitive task analysis 171
cognitive walkthroughs 234
colour 117–118
Command language grammar 170
command languages 89–90
competitive advantage 236–237
conceptual help 194–195
conceptual model 26
content – dialogues 11–12

context – dialogues 11–12
contextual enquiry 226–227
contextual help 187
control systems 126
controlled vocabulary 62–63
controls 106
cooperative design 137–138
cooperative evaluation 228–229
cooperative prototyping 229–230
cursor keys 51–52
cursors 106
customer perspective 235–236

data dictionaries 162–163
data flow diagrams 159–160
data logging 210
data modelling 159–164
dialogue boxes 105
dialogues – definition 9–10
direct manipulation 101–112
direct observation 208
discount usability evaluation 233
displaying information 113–114
documentation 188–189

encapsulation 147
entering information 113–114
entity relationship diagrams 163–164
environments 35–59
ethics 139–141
ethnography 227–228
evaluation 203–240
experiments 222–225
expert review 230–231
expert users 21–22
explicit help 185–186

Author index

Alty, J. L. 214
Anderson, J. R. 172
Ashford, J. 112

Baddeley, A. D. 30
Bailey, P. 116
Barnard, P. J. 11
Bastien, J. M. C. 232
Bates, M. J. 72, 78–79, 81, 82
Batterbee, C. 197
Beaulieu, M. 72, 76–77, 197
Beheshti, J. 80–81
Belkin, N. J. 73
Bennett, J. L. 7
Beyer, H. 227
Bias, R. 234
Bills, L. G. 63, 68
Bitner, M. J. 212
Bodker, S. 4
Boehm, B. 128
Booth, P. 5–7, 10, 24, 26, 49, 51, 240
Bosch, V. M. 196
Bowen, C. D. 239
Briggs, P. 25, 27
Byrne, J. 108

Cakir, A. 115–116
Callahan, D. 115
Card, S. K. 171
Carroll, J. M. 78, 107, 190, 192, 210
Catterall, B. J. 166
Cawkell, A. 36, 42, 51, 55
Checkland, P. 136
Cleverdon, C. W. 71
Craik, K. J. W. 25
Crawford, W. 68, 188, 191, 192, 194, 201
Cronin, J. J. 212

Cuff, E. C. 27
Cuomo, D. L. 239

Danilowicz, C. 70
Diaper, D. 208
Dix, A. 244
Dohar, J. 189
Drabenstott, K. M. 69
Dwyer, C. M. 69

Eason, K. 141
Ellis, D. 71, 72, 77
Ellman, J. 83
Ensor, P. 63, 66
Ericsson, K. A. 210

Feinberg, S. 196
Felix, D. 223
Fidel, R. 76
Fischer, G. 190
Flynn, L. 46
Ford, N. 82
Fox, B. 237
Fox, E. A. 112
Furner, J. 82

Galitz, W. O. 116
Garzotto, F. 116
Good, M. 224
Gould, J. D. 229
Graf, W. 223
Green, T. R. G. 173, 174
Grice, R. A. 83
Grissom, S. B. 239
Gronroos, C. 212

Hammond, N. V. 11